The Effects of Leadership

HANAN C. SELVIN

The

Effects

of

Leadership

The Free Press of Glencoe, Illinois

LITHOGRAPHED FOR THE PUBLISHERS BY
NOBLE OFFSET PRINTERS, ING., NEW YORK

DEDICATION

To —

Arthur M. Arkin, M. D.

and

Thomas M. Gellert, M. D.

PREFACE

This is a study of the effects of leadership—how the actions of leaders affect the behavior of their followers. The leaders in this study are the commissioned and noncommissioned officers of several Army training companies, and the followers are the men who received their basic training in these companies at Fort Dix, New Jersey in the Spring of 1952. Although each company was confronted with the same tasks under comparable physical and social conditions, the actions of the leaders varied considerably. In the pages to follow it will be shown that these variations in leadership had pronounced and consistent effects on the behavior of the trainees.

Many characteristics of this study result from the fact that the design and the analysis were carried out by different persons. The questionnaires on which it is based were constructed and administered by Arthur M. Arkin, M. D. and Thomas M. Gellert, M. D. when they were in military service at Fort Dix, Dr. Arkin as Chief of the Mental Health Consultation Service and Dr. Gellert as a psychiatric social worker. Dr. Arkin and Dr. Gellert were seeking to investigate some psychoanalytic hopotheses about the nature of responses to leadership, but their military service ended before they were able to process and analyze their data. Since neither had the necessary time in civilian life (Dr. Arkin established a private practice, and Dr. Gellert entered

medical school), they brought their data to the Columbia University
Bureau of Applied Social Research, where I was able to complete the
work they had begun. In addition to providing the data, they also helped
the Bureau to obtain financial support from the Medical Research and
Development Board, Office of the Surgeon General, Department of the
Army (Contract No. DA-49-007-MD490). The dedication of this volume
is a partial expression of my gratitude to them.

The work done at the Bureau by E. David Nasatir and me followed
a different direction than Arkin and Gellert originally had in mind.
Since our interests were sociological rather than psychoanalytic, we had
to devise methods and to examine relationships that they had not considered in their planning. This is why the emphasis of this study is both
substantive and methodological: it is intended to explore certain sociological and social-psychological aspects of the relationships between
leaders and followers in several Army training companies and to set
forth some new methods and techniques of general applicability in the
analysis of such relationships. As the reader will notice, the findings
and the methods have a reciprocal influence on each other. The relationships between leaders and followers are complex, and this complexity made it necessary to devise new methods of analysis. In turn,
some of the methods made it possible to deal effectively with involved
theoretical relationships that have not heretofore been studied systematically. One result of this reciprocal influence is that the development
of methods and the analysis of data are interwoven throughout the book;
technical details are reserved for the appendices, but the logic of the
analysis and the analysis itself proceed together.

Many of my friends, teachers, and former colleagues at Columbia
University have contributed to this study. E. David Nasatir worked
closely with me in developing the procedures of Chapter II and Appendices A, B, and I; he also supervised the processing of the data and

helped in writing the report to the Office of the Surgeon General. The then Director of the Bureau of Applied Social Research, Dr. Charles Y. Glock (now Professor of Sociology and Social Institutions and Director of the Survey Research Center at the University of California, Berkeley), was an invaluable source of support and constructive criticism, even when the lengthy methodological explorations seemed least promising. Professor Robert K. Merton of the Department of Sociology was particularly helpful during the early months of the study and during the writing of the final report to the Surgeon General. Professors Paul F. Lazarsfeld and Herbert H. Hyman of the Department of Sociology and Professor Theodore W. Anderson, Jr. of the Department of Mathematical Statistics made important criticisms of this report, as did Miss Marjorie Fiske, formerly Research Executive of the Bureau of Applied Social Research and now Research Medical Sociologist at the Langley Porter Clinic of the University of California.

Others at Columbia who gave generously of their time and knowledge were Professor Irving Lorge of Teachers College and Arnold G. Simmel of the Bureau (now with the New York State Department of Health). Professor Harold L. Wilensky of the University of Michigan made several helpful suggestions. James A. Jones (now at the New York School of Social Work) did the greater part of the computations. And my wife Rhoda helped me in many ways in the preparation of the previous report and this book.

Berkeley, California
August, 1959

TABLE OF CONTENTS

The Effects of Leadership

Chapter I

LEADERS' ACTIONS AND FOLLOWERS' BEHAVIOR:
A THEORETICAL INTRODUCTION

Theoretically and practically, the effects of leaders on their followers are central to the study of leadership. The theoretical importance of these effects is obvious: the idea of leadership is not meaningful without considering the followers, at least implicitly. Practically, the effects of the leader's actions are no less important. How, for example can leaders be efficiently selected and trained without some knowledge of the ways in which the followers react to different kinds of leadership? Although this study deals with the actions of officers and noncommissioned officers in several Army training companies, the questions considered here turn up in other kinds of situations as well. Supervisors and workers in industry, and teachers and students in classrooms are the most familiar examples, but the same problem of determining the effects of leadership is found wherever a formally-designated leader is in charge of a group of followers.

Important as this problem appears to be, it has received relatively little attention. An extensive survey of the literature to 1954[1] includes a bare half-dozen studies, and few have appeared since that time. But even this handful of studies displays an impressive cumulation of results. Certain kinds of effects are manifested over and over again, despite differences in theories, procedures, and situations. The present study will be shown to confirm many of these results and to extend them in

1

new directions. In order to demonstrate this convergence and to show how this study builds on and extends the previous research on leadership effects, this chapter is divided into two major sections: (1) a summary of selected results from the major studies of leadership effects, and (2) a theoretical discussion of the principal variables and relationships in the analysis of these effects. These two parts complement each other: the theoretical discussion, or conceptual scheme, is derived from the various studies that have been done, including the present one; in turn, it provides a systematic set of categories for comparing the results of these studies and for indicating problems of theory and methodology that deserve more attention than they have yet received.

FIVE MAJOR STUDIES OF THE EFFECTS OF LEADERSHIP

Autocratic, Democratic, and Laissez-Faire Leadership: the Iowa Studies.[2] Probably the most widely known investigations of leadership, the work of Kurt Lewin and his colleagues at the University of Iowa during the 1930's may be said to have launched the empirical study of leadership. Unlike many pioneer studies, their procedures and analyses can still serve as models of scientific research. In the most elaborate of their researches, four hobby clubs were organized among selected ten-year-old boys, who were as similar as possible in relevant physical, social, and intellectual characteristics. The adult leader of each group, a collaborator of the experimenters, was instructed to behave in an autocratic, a democratic, or a laissez-faire manner, and the behavior of the boys was carefully observed and recorded.

Ingenious and precise experimental controls made it possible to attribute the differences in the boys' behavior to the prescribed actions of

the leaders rather than to such factors as the personalities of the
leaders or events external to the experimental groups. Typical of the
differences noted were a greater amount of aggressiveness in the autocratic groups, both in reacting to the leader and in interacting with the
other boys, and greater attention to "group-minded" suggestions and
"work-minded" conversations in the laissez-faire and democratic
groups. Laissez-faire and democratic leadership also turned out to
differ significantly: a lower level of psychological involvement in the
laissez-faire groups resulted in less work and poorer work than in the
democratic groups.

"Dominative" and "Integrative" Teachers: The Anderson Studies.[3]
These studies may be considered a replication of the Lewin experiments
in a real-life situation, with naturally-occurring variations in leadership rather than experimentally-manipulated group atmospheres. Carefully trained observers characterized the behavior of teachers and their
pupils in several classroom as either "dominative" or "socially integrative." From the descriptions given, dominative behavior by the
teacher seems to be similar to the autocratic leadership of the Iowa investigations, and integrative behavior to resemble democratic leadership. The principal finding was that integrative behavior by the teacher
leads to integrative and productive behavior by the pupils and that dominative teachers correspondingly have a high proportion of dominative
and unproductive behavior in their classrooms.

As in the Lewin experiments, Anderson and his colleagues took
pains to show that these effects were not peculiar to the particular
teachers and students who were studied. Since the actions of the
teachers could not be experimentally manipulated, the researchers un-
dertook an elaborate series of replications: the initial results were confirmed in different grades of the same school, in different types of
schools (departmental and nondepartmental), and for the same pupils

when they changed from one teacher to another. The extent to which
these researches complement those of Lewin is all the more noteworthy
in view of the apparent lack of familiarity with the Iowa studies in
Anderson's group; at least, there is no mention of the Iowa experiments
in Anderson's three monographs. [4]

Participatory and Supervisory Leadership: Preston and Heintz. [5]
Following the Lewin tradition of experimental groups, Preston and
Heintz adopted two important innovations. (1) Instead of an adult leader
chosen by the experimenters, the leaders were elected by the members
of each group and were subsequently instructed in the appropriate experimental behavior. (2) The dependent variable was the group's ability
to achieve consensus on the ranking of twelve potential Presidential can-
didates, rather than the individual activities of the boys in the Iowa investigations. Only two kinds of leadership were considered. "Participatory" leaders took an active part in the process of group decision,
making sure that all topics were discussed with as little prejudice as
possible and encouraging contributions from all members of their
groups. The responsibility of "supervisory" leaders was limited to
"seeing that the work was done with reasonable expedition." They were
instructed to bring the group back to its task if necessary, but otherwise
not to guide the discussion or to stimulate activity among the members.

Participatory leadership resembles the democratic group atmosphere of the Iowa studies, and supervisory leadership the laissez-faire
atmosphere. Many replications of the original experiment confirmed
the principal findings: members of groups with participatory leadership
were more likely to change their opinions to agree with the consensus of
the group, and they were also more satisfied with the consensus than
were the members of supervisory groups. [6]

Supervision and Productivity: the Michigan Studies. [7] The Survey
Research Center of the University of Michigan had studied the relation-

ships between the actions of first-line supervisors and the behavior of the workers under them in a variety of settings—the home office of an insurance company, section gangs of a railroad, agencies of the federal government, and different kinds of factories. The general procedure was to classify each work group as "high productivity" or "low productivity" and to relate these differences to the behavior of the supervisors.

High-production supervisors differed from low-production supervisors in three principal ways: (1) They spent more time in planning, supervision, and other kinds of leader behavior and less time in working alongside their subordinates at the same tasks. (2) Although they behaved more like leaders than did the low-production supervisors, the greater freedom they accorded to their subordinates resulted in higher morale in the work groups, as well as higher productivity—although high morale and high productivity did not go together consistently. (3) High-production supervisors were more likely to be "employee-oriented" and less likely to be "production-oriented." They tried to create a "supportive personal relationship" between themselves and the members of their work groups; they took a greater interest in their subordinates and were more understanding and less punitive.

These findings confirm and extend the Lewin conclusions. Productive and satisfying work conditions are most likely to result from leader behavior that combines effective coordination, a large measure of individual freedom in routine decisions, and respect for the dignity of the individual—all characteristic of "democratic" leadership rather than "laissez-faire" or "autocratic" leadership.[8]

Multidimensional Descriptions of Leader Behavior: The Ohio State Studies.[9] In 1945 the Personnel Research Board of the Ohio State University began a ten-year program of research on leadership. Among the major tasks of the program was the identification of basic dimensions for describing the behavior of leaders in business, educational, and military organizations. Several sets of dimensions were identified at one time or another in this series of studies; here the most relevant dimensions are those identified by Halpin and Winer in a study of aircraft commanders, as rated by the members of their crews.[10] In all, four dimensions were found, but only two of these, "Consideration" and "Initiating Structure," are empirically important. Consideration is associated with "behavior indicative of friendship, mutual trust, respect, and warmth in the relationship between the aircraft commander and his crew." It is negatively associated with "authoritarian and impersonal" behavior by the commander. Initiating Structure measures the extent to which the aircraft commander "organizes and defines the relationship between himself and the members of his crew."[11] Most succinctly expressed, scores on these two composite variables represent the "human relations" and the "get the work out" dimensions.[12]

Dimensions of leader behavior similar to Consideration and Initiating Structure have been found in each of the other studies discussed in this chapter. There is one important difference, however. The Ohio State researchers did not set forth these dimensions a priori. They began with nine tentative dimensions of leadership, for each of which ten to twenty specific indicators were developed. For example, one of the nine dimensions was "Membership," which is measured by "the frequency with which a leader mixes with the group, stresses informal interaction between himself and members, or interchanges personal services with members."[13] It turned out, however, that these nine dimensions were not statistically independent, but could be represented rather well by the two major dimensions of Consideration and Initiating Structure defined above.

Another significant departure of the Ohio State studies was the recognition that these two dimensions do not refer to types of leaders, but rather to types of behavior. Any one leader may have a high score on

Consideration and a high score on Initiating Structure, a low score on both dimensions, or any other combination of scores. This typology of leader behavior turns out to be significantly associated with the behavior of the followers. In Halpin's study of air crews,[14] high performance and high morale among members of the crew were more likely when the commander had high scores on both Consideration and Initiating Structure than for any other pattern of scores, a result theoretically similar to those found in the other studies discussed above, but based on a more careful analysis of the nature of leadership behavior.

The empirical and theoretical convergence of these studies is impressive, especially in the types of leader behavior and in the relationships between these types and the behavior of the followers. The importance for the present study of these similarities—and of the differences, which have not been emphasized thus far—will be made clearer by locating them in a theoretical framework.

Even the most rudimentary theory deals with relationships between concepts. The more developed the theory, the more precisely these relationships are specified. In the present state of leadership theory the most that can be expected is a qualitative statement of the kinds of variables and relationships that should be considered. Such a conceptual scheme is the "paradigm for the study of leadership" devised by Morris and Seeman[15] as part of the Ohio State research program. This excellent paradigm is too broad for the present study: it includes the determinants as well as the consequences of the leaders' behavior. The conceptual scheme to be presented here was suggested by the work of Morris and Seeman, but it concentrates on explaining the effects of leadership, taking the behavior of the leaders as given.

A CONCEPTUAL SCHEME FOR STUDYING
THE EFFECTS OF LEADERSHIP

A conceptual scheme is simply a set of "pigeon-holes" for classify-
ing variables and relationships. This conceptual scheme includes five
types of variables and eight types of relationships between these variables. To make these abstractions more vivid, they are presented
graphically in Figure I-1. The symbols in Figure I-1 will be explained
in the course of the following discussion, but the general nature of this
conceptual scheme should be apparent. For example, the line labelled
"1" indicates that the actions of the leaders are assumed to affect the
ways in which the followers perceive the leaders. Dotted lines indicate
that the category or relationship, although warranting consideration in a
complete theory of leadership effects, is not included in the empirical
analyses of this study. The detailed description of this conceptual
scheme will be organized around the numbered relationships in Figure
I-1. Before turning to this description, however, it is necessary to
clarify the ambiguous terms "leader" and "leadership."

Definitions of Leadership. Few scientific terms have been defined
in so many ways as "leader" and "leadership." In his detailed summary
of the literature, Gibb lists five different definitions of "the leader":
(1) an individual in a given office; (2) the central person of a group,
whose personality is incorporated in the "ego ideals" of his followers;
(3) the person considered most influential by the members of a group;
(4) the person who does most to advance the group toward its goals; and
(5) the person who is most effective in creating a "structure" or consistency in the interaction of the group members.[16] In some groups one
person may satisfy all five definitions; in other groups the status of
"leader" may be attributed to as many as five different persons according to these definitions.

FIGURE I-1.

Categories and Relationships in the Study of Leadership Effects

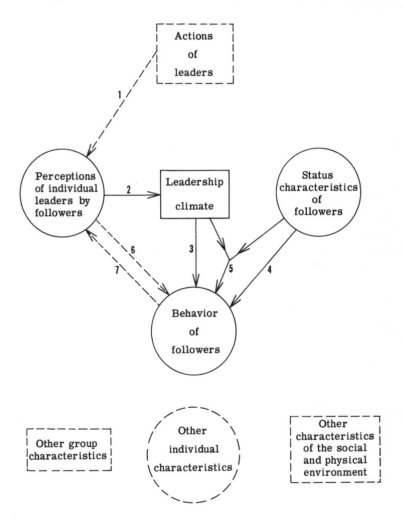

Why are there so many definitions? One reason seems to be that they were framed with different types of situations in mind. Thus the first definition—the leader as an individual in a given office—was obviously intended to apply to formal organizations. It makes sense, and it is useful, to consider the person who occupies the office of President of a corporation as "the leader" of the corporation; and the Commanding Officer of an infantry company should certainly be called a leader of the company (if not the leader). That is, the norms of formal organizations usually attach the status of leader to one or more positions. In informal groups—cliques of friends, sets of co-workers, or several students brought together for a laboratory experiment—there are few formally designated positions; leadership must therefore be defined in such groups on some other basis than occupancy of a position. In other words, definition (1) and the other definitions obviously refer to two different types of leadership, which might be called "formal leadership" and "informal leadership," corresponding to formal and informal groups. [17]

Once it has existed for some time, every formal organization is honeycombed with informal organizations, since no organizational chart can encompass all of the patterns of social interaction that arise when many people must work together. But the speed with which an informal organization arises and its influence on the activities of the group vary considerably from one type of group to another. Where interdependence and interaction are high, as is often the case in industry, then the informal organization may sometimes exercise more control than the official management. But where the members of the group are engaged in similar individual tasks rather than a single group task, and where the formal organization is operating efficiently before the members of the group take their places, then whatever informal organizations emerge will be relatively impotent for a long time. This is the case in Army training companies: the skills taught in basic training require relatively little interdependence among the trainees, and the commissioned and noncommissioned officers who are in charge of a training company have usually been operating as a team for weeks or months before a new trainee enters the company.

This suggests that an important characteristic of a group is the degree to which the informal organization and its informal leaders exercise control. Army training companies are at one extreme, with relatively powerless informal organizations. Assembly-line workers seem to be in a better position for developing informal organizations, since they work together for long periods of time, but the assembly line usually restricts interaction to those who work close to each other. Informal organizations develop still more easily in work situations that require group performance, such as a railroad section gang, or an Army company in combat. Where there is no formal organization at all, as in friendship groups, informal leaders obviously exercise maximum control.

The relative impotence of the informal leadership is one reason why the present study is able to restrict its attention to the formal leaders of each company. Another reason is that whatever informal organization does finally emerge among the trainees can be considered, in large part, as a response to the formal leadership. Since the focus of this study is the relationship between formal leadership and individual behavior, the informal organization may therefore be treated as an "intervening variable": it helps to explain the observed relationship, to show how the actions of the formal leaders are linked to the behavior of the trainees. This is not to minimize the theoretical importance of such intervening variables, but only to point out that data on informal leadership in this situation seem to be less valuable for purposes of predicting or controlling the behavior of the trainees than knowledge about the formal leaders.

Finally, it is a historical fact that studies of leadership effects seldom consider the impact of informal leadership:[18] the studies summarized above all limit themselves to the effects of formal leadership.

This study, then, treats formally-designated leaders only. Its principal emphasis is on the ways in which the actions of these leaders affect the behavior of their followers—that is, the men who are formally subordinate to them. As Figure I-1 indicates, this central relationship is part of a larger network of theoretically important relationships. In the following discussion these relationships are numbered to correspond with Figure I-1.

1. The Leaders' Actions Affect the Followers' Perceptions of the Leaders. The study of leadership effects properly begins with the actions of the leaders and with the ways in which these actions are perceived by the followers. In Tagiuri's words, "Behavior . . . does not consist of the response to the properties of the stimulus field objectively or consensually specified but, rather, of the reactions to what is perceived by the subject."[19] This is why Figure I-1 does not include a direct link between the actions of the leaders and the behavior of the followers; whatever the nature of this relationship empirically, the perceptions of the leaders by the followers are, in principle, intervening variables. In this study, however, these perceptions must be taken as independent variables, for the data on the actions of the leaders come from questionnaires completed by the trainees. Independent evidence of the actions of the leaders—say, from the records of observers other than the followers—would be an important supplement to the perceptual data used in this study (although observers' records also involve perception).

2. Inferring Leadership Climate from Perceptions of Individual Leaders. Most theorists of leadership assume that there is only one leader in a group. This assumption is seldom stated explicitly,[20] but it

is clear in the language they use. Gibb, for example, prefaces each of the five definitions of leadership with the phrase "The leader as one who . . ." And Homans' two chapters on leadership in The Human Group[21] are entitled "The position of the leader" and "The job of the leader." From a theoretical standpoint Gouldner was the first to call attention to the need for studying the "leadership corps" of an organization. [22] An empirical demonstration of the fact that informal leadership behavior is usually shared by two or more persons is found in the work of Bales and Slater on role differentiation in laboratory groups. In the sociometric ratings that the members of these groups gave to each other, there typically appeared a "Task Specialist," whose ideas were considered to contribute most to the solution of the group's problem, and a "Social-Emotional Specialist," who was most liked by the other members. [23] And Berkowitz's study of real-life conference groups showed that under certain conditions there may be two or more "behavioral leaders" in a group in addition to the chairman. [24]

Multiple leadership of this kind is common in formal organizations of moderate size, such as Army companies. Although there is a hierarchy of positions, with ultimate authority vested in a Commanding Officer, the other officers and noncoms also exercise leadership from time to time. Indeed, one or another of these formally subordinate leaders occasionally has more influence on the men in his company than does the C.O. This means that in seeking to explain how the actions of leaders affect the behavior of their followers it is not sufficient to look only at the highest-ranking position in the group. The impacts of the various leaders on their followers must somehow be aggregated into an overall "leadership climate."

One of the major efforts of this study has been to develop a method for measuring the leadership climate of an Army company or a similar group in which there is more than one formally designated position of leadership. This procedure will be presented in detail in Chapter II. For the present it suffices to note the logical difference between these indices of leadership climate and the data from which they are inferred. Each of the eighty-two leaders in the twelve companies was rated on fifteen questions by all of the men in his company—a total of almost 200,000 ratings. These are individual data: every one of the ratings is colored by the idiosyncrasies of the trainee who filled out the questionnaire. But the indices of leadership climate are group data: they characterize an entire company, not the individual trainees in it. (Individual data in Figure I-1 are enclosed in circles, group data in rectangles.) This is similar to what is done in describing a community in terms of the characteristics of the individual residents. For example, the social stratification of a community may be measured by the distribution of individual incomes. "Amount of income" is an individual characteristic; the skewness of its distribution in some community is a group property that cannot be located in any individual member of the group.

Since leadership climate is an artificial construct—a distillation of the data by means of an elaborate statistical analysis—it may be helpful to give it an intuitive meaning. In a sense that will be made clearer in Chapter II, the leadership climate of a company is the way in which its leaders would be described by the "average trainee." This sounds like that favorite fantasy of opinion-pollers: if one could only find an "average county," the outcome of a presidential election could be predicted simply and precisely from the behavior of this average county. The difference is, however, that we did not have to look for twelve average trainees; in effect, they—or at least their ratings—are created by the statistical analysis.

It is instructive to contrast these leadership climates with the "social climates" of Lewin, Lippitt, and White. The Lewin investigators experimentally manipulated the actions of leaders in artificial groups;

we were able to observe different leadership climates in real-life groups. These two differences—observation vs. experimental manipulation and natural vs. laboratory groups—will be seen to have important implications for the theory and empirical analysis of leadership effects.

At least in one sense, our leadership climates are closer to the ways in which the followers experienced these situations. The Iowa experimenters created what they assumed were autocratic, democratic, and laissez-faire atmosphere, and everything that one can learn from their published reports bears out these assumptions. Nevertheless, they are assumptions: there are no direct data on the ways in which the leaders' behavior was actually seen by the followers. That is, each type of leadership was a complex of many characteristics. The leaders were instructed to do certain things, and the observers' reports indicate that the leaders obeyed these instructions. Yet there is no way of knowing which of the different facets of a leader's actions was most important to the boys. Did they, for example, see the autocratic leader as justly strict or as unjustly harsh? And to what extent was there consensus on the nature of the leader's behavior? Questions like this are impossible to answer without knowing the followers' perceptions of their leaders.

In the present study the descriptions of the leaders' behavior are inferred from the perceptions of the trainees in such a way that the idiosyncrasies of individual responses are eliminated. The result is a set of leadership climates that essentially represent the way in which the leaders of each company are perceived by the "average trainee" in that company. In other words, the group as a whole, and not the individual members, describes its own leadership climate.

3. The Effects of Leadership Climate on Behavior. Because they had deliberately selected boys with the same social and psychological characteristics, the Iowa experimenters were able to measure the

effects of leadership on behavior without considering the possible influences of such other factors as differences in social status among the
boys. The situation is quite different for Army trainees. Compared
with the civilian population, Army trainees are a remarkably homogeneous group of men—all in good physical condition, of approximately
the same age, mostly unmarried, and so on. But as Chapters V to VIII
will show, even relatively small differences in such variables as age
and education have important consequences for the behavior of the trainees. And, as the studies of Stouffer and his collaborators have demonstrated, there are marked differences in the ways in which single and
married men adjust to Army life. [25] In assessing the influence of leadership climate on the trainees' behavior it is therefore necessary to remove the effects of differences in the characteristics of the trainees.
This is particularly necessary in view of the variations of these characteristics among the leadership climates: for example, the proportion
of single men ranged from 62 per cent in one climate to 69 per cent in
another. The logic of the procedures by which these differences are
taken into account is presented in Chapter III.

The effects of leadership on behavior vary according to the kinds of
behavior studied. Laboratory studies often treat the effects of leadership on what Cattell has called "syntal" characteristics. [26] These are
qualities of the group's performance as a whole, rather than of the individual members taken separately; an example would be the time required for the group to arrive at a common solution to a problem. In
this study, however, the dependent variables all refer explicitly to individual behavior. They are the rates with which the trainees engaged
in nineteen kinds of leisure-time and off-duty activity, ranging from
reading to fighting and from going on sick call to engaging in sexual intercourse.

Another significant aspect of these activities is that they do not involve the formal tasks of the Army. Such variables as the efficiency of individual trainees or the effectiveness with which the training companies accomplished their assigned tasks are not included. Clearly, the relationships between nonduty behavior and official behavior on both the individual and group levels are important in unraveling the effects of leadership. For example, how much does a high rate of drunkenness during off-duty hours affect the quality and quantity of a company's performance? In further studies of leadership effects it would be desirable to include questions on individual efficiency and group effectiveness, along with the kinds of behavior considered here.

4. The Effects of Status Characteristics on Behavior. There is probably no theoretical relationship that has been more thoroughly investigated than that between status characteristics—such as education, religion, and sex—and expressions of values, attitudes, and other forms of individual behavior. In the field of social stratification alone, there are hundreds of studies on differences in behavior between the various social classes. These status-behavior relationships are so important that they are usually among the first to be considered in applied survey research. Thus Stouffer and his collaborators began the empirical analysis in The American Soldier with an account of the ways in which age, education, and marital condition affected adjustment to Army life.

One reason for this emphasis on status characteristics, and in particular on those related to social class, is the long history of theory devoted to the relationship between class and behavior. Much of the contribution of Karl Marx and his disciples to sociological theory lies in their explanation of differential class behavior. The empirical emphasis of contemporary sociology suggests another reason: the ease with which status characteristics can be studied in the usual types of field investigations. By way of contrast, the recent revival of interest in primary-group relationships and in the study of interaction patterns in large organizations undoubtedly developed more slowly because of the technical problems involved in measuring these variables.

In the study of leadership, however, these emphases are reversed: relatively little attention has been paid to the relationship between status and behavior, while the internal processes of the group have been explored in detail. In part this results from the concentration of leadership research in laboratory settings, where the use of homogeneous groups of subjects means that status differences are removed by the design of the experiment. If the subjects of an experiment are college sophomores, then education, at least, no longer differentiates them from each other. Although some laboratory researchers have dealt with emerging differences of prestige and sociometric rankings, the richness and significance of status differences that originate outside the laboratory cannot be fully captured in an experiment. Indeed, this inability to work meaningfully with the slowly acquired and emotionally significant status characteristics of real life is one reason for a skeptical attitude toward laboratory research on leadership, despite its experimental ingenuity, analytic insight, and sophisticated theory.

In analyzing the relationship between leadership climate and behavior, it is necessary, as noted above, to remove the possibly disturbing influences of the status characteristics on which we have data—age, education, and marital condition. Here, however, the roles of the independent variable and the extraneous disturbances are reversed. It is necessary to take leadership climate into account when assessing the effects of status characteristics on behavior—to ensure, for example, that the observed relationship between marital status and behavior does not result from the fact that the married men are unequally represented in the different leadership climates. The logic of the procedures for doing this will be explained in Chapter III.

5. <u>The Joint Effects of Leadership and Status on Behavior</u>. Once having measured the separate effects of leadership climate and status characteristics on behavior, it might seem that the combined effects of these two independent variables would simply be the sum of the separate effects. This is one of those situations, however, in which statistical concepts are more than tools for the empirical investigation of theoretical problems; here the theoretical relationships are illuminated and enriched by a knowledge of statistical principles. The statistical concept of "interaction of variables" suggests that the joint effects of leadership and status may not simply be the sum of the separate effects: the effects of leadership climate on behavior may depend on the status characteristics of the trainees, and the effects of status on behavior may vary from one leadership climate to another. [27] This is exactly what happens in the empirical analysis of Chapter VII; in fact, not only the size of the relationship between leadership and behavior, but even the direction of this relationship, will often be found to depend on the characteristics of the trainees; and similarly for the relationship between status and behavior in the various leadership climates. For example, in one leadership climate the single trainees have a higher rate of AWOL than the married trainees, but in another climate the direction of the relationship is reversed, with the married men having a higher rate than the single.

The importance of these joint effects in this study calls attention to the lack of a systematic treatment of the interaction of variables in sociological theory and research. A study of voting behavior, for example, may consider the effects of religion in one chapter and the role of opinion leadership in another, but seldom is attention paid to the ways in which the effects of opinion leadership depend on religion. And none of the effects studies presented above even considers the problem of statistical interaction.

One reason for the neglect of joint effects is that reliable conclusions about such effects require larger samples than when only one independent variable is analyzed at a time. Another reason may be the greater complexity of these joint effects: it is much more difficult to make meaningful statements about the interaction of two independent variables in their effects on a dependent variable than to discuss the association between one independent and one dependent variable. In this respect the methodological contributions of Chapter VII may overshadow the substantive results, for a prerequisite of this analysis was the development of a systematic approach to the description of these joint effects in the case where one independent variable is a group characteristic (leadership climate) and the other is an individual characteristic (status). The procedures and the results of Chapter VII thus exemplify Merton's claim that methodological innovations and empirical findings both exert pressure for the reformulation and extension of theory. [28]

6 & 7. Individual Perceptions and Individual Behavior. The relationships between the actions of leaders and the behavior of followers, as considered up to this point, are indirect. The actions of the leaders affect the followers' perceptions; these individual perceptions are combined into leadership climates by means of an elaborate statistical analysis; and these group climates are then related to rates of individual behavior. It is also possible, however, to examine a more direct relationship between individual perceptions of leadership and individual behavior, one that omits the intermediate step of constructing indices of leadership climate. Thus one trainee who perceives his leaders as competent and considerate may not behave the same as another who sees the same leaders as inefficient and harsh. These individual perceptions could have been treated analytically in exactly the same way as the status characteristics; for example, the relationship between perceptions

and behavior could have been examined within each leadership climate, and the relationship between leadership climate and behavior might be considered for trainees with different individual perceptions of leadership.

But this cannot be done where there is more than one leader in a group. Each trainee was exposed to an average of seven company-level leaders during the sixteen-week training cycle. (He had four leaders at any one time—Commanding Officer, Executive Officer, First Sergeant, and Field First Sergeant—and there was considerable turnover of leaders in all companies.) To measure the effects on his behavior of the ways in which he saw any one leader would have required taking into account his perceptions of all the other leaders in his company—an impossibly complicated task.

Matters are simpler where there is only one leader in a group. In his study of the effects of teachers' behavior on their pupils, Cogan[29] was able to use the pupils' perceptions as individual data and as group data. In the former, Cogan related each pupil's individual perceptions of his teacher to his behavior in the classroom; one typical finding was a moderate correlation between a student's perceiving that a teacher acted in a "child-centered" manner and his doing a large amount of required work. More impressive results were obtained by using group data. Cogan averaged the perceptions of all pupils in a class and took these average perceptions as the group's description of the teacher, much as was done in constructing our indices of leadership climate from the perceptions of individual trainees.

Cogan's work suggests another reason for subordinating the relationship between individual perceptions and individual behavior. Within each group in our study there is a great deal of consensus in the perceptions of each leader by the trainees. The procedure used in constructing indices of leadership climate exploits this consensus, for it replaces the different individual perceptions by a single value—the mean perception of all trainees.   The analysis of individual perceptions, however, ignores the consensus and focuses on the dispersion of perceptions for each leader.   To a considerable extent this dispersion does not result from "real" differences in perception, but rather from the operation of such unwanted factors as inadvertent response errors and deliberate distortion as explained in Chapter II.   The association between individual perceptions of leadership and individual behavior is extremely sensitive to such erratic perceptions.   However, since the indices of leadership climate are computed from the mean perceptions of one hundred or more trainees, the association between leadership climate and individual behavior is virtually unaffected by errors in perception, as long as there is substantial consensus.   Finally, even if one were interested in the relationship between individual perceptions of leadership and individual behavior, it would be necessary to take into account the actual behavior of the leaders.   The leadership climates appear to be the best available description of how the leaders behave; in effect, they are the distillation of the ratings of one hundred or more observers.   For all of these reasons, therefore, the effect of individual perceptions on behavior has not been considered in this study.

PLAN OF THE STUDY

The problems of measuring leadership climate, and one set of solutions to these problems, are set forth in Chapter II, and four distinct types of leadership climate are described.   Chapter III presents analytic procedures for studying the effects of these leadership climates on behavior.   Chapter IV draws on previous research studies, both theoretical and empirical, to indicate the kinds of behavior that might be expected to occur more frequently in each of the leadership climates.   The extent to which these predictions are borne out is investigated in Chapter V. Chapter VI presents a parallel discussion of the ways in which age, education, and marital status predispose trainees toward one or another kind of behavior. These two strands of analysis are woven together in the "contextual analysis" of Chapter VII, based on the joint effects of leadership climate and individual characteristics. Chapter VIII examines the reported differences between leisure-time behavior in civilian life and the corresponding behavior in the Army, corroborating and enlarging upon the analyses in the preceding chapters. Finally, Chapter IX singles out those methodological and theoretical aspects of the present study that can be generalized beyond the particular situation of basic training.

Wherever possible, technical details and digressions have been placed in Appendices. These Appendices also include copies of the questionnaires and additional data supporting the conclusions in the text.

24

NOTES TO CHAPTER ONE

1. Cecil A. Gibb, "Leadership" in Gardner Lindzey (ed.), Handbook of Social Psychology (Cambridge, Mass.: Addison-Wesley Publishing Company, Inc., 1954), 877-920.

2. The most recent of the several reports of this study is Ralph White and Ronald Lippitt, "Leader behavior and member reaction in three 'social climates,'" in Dorwin Cartwright and Alvin Zander (eds.), Group Dynamics (Evanston, Ill.: Row, Peterson and Company, 1953), 585-611.

3. Harold H. Anderson and Helen M. Brewer, Studies of Teachers' Classroom Personalities, I; Dominative and Socially Integrative Behavior of Kindergarten Teachers, Applied Psychology Monograph, No. 6 (Stanford: Stanford University Press, 1945); Harold H. Anderson and Joseph Brewer, Studies of Teachers' Classroom Personalities, II; Effects of Teachers' Dominative and Integrative Contacts on Children's Classroom Behavior, Applied Psychology Monographs, No. 8 (Stanford: Stanford University Press, 1946); Harold H. Anderson, Joseph E. Brewer, and Mary Frances Reed, Studies of Teachers' Classroom Personalities, III; Follow-Up Studies of the Effects of Dominative and Integrative Contacts on Children's Behavior, Applied Psychology Monographs, No. 11 (Stanford: Stanford University Press, 1946).

4. Another study of the effects of teachers' behavior on their pupils found results comparable to those of Anderson. Morris L. Cogan, "Theory and design of a study of teacher-pupil interaction," Harvard Educational Review, 26, 1956, 315-342. Cogan's methods, however, differ significantly from Anderson's; they will be discussed briefly later in this chapter.

5. Malcolm G. Preston and Roy K. Heintz, "Effects of participatory vs. supervisory leadership on group judgment," Journal of Abnormal and Social Psychology, XLIV, 1949, 345-355, reprinted in Cartwright and Zander, op. cit., 573-584.

6. Another replication with a different type of group is reported in A. Paul Hare, "Small group discussions with participatory and supervisory leadership," Journal of Abnormal and Social Psychology, XLVIII, 1953, 273-275, reprinted in A. Paul Hare, Edgar F. Borgatta, and Robert F. Bales, Small Groups (New York: Alfred A. Knopf, 1955), 556-560.

7. Robert L. Kahn and Daniel Katz, "Leadership practices in relation to productivity and morale," in Cartwright and Zander, op. cit., 612-628.

8. Argyle and his collaborators have summarized the literature on social factors affecting productivity and have carried out a study that replicates the Michigan investigations with somewhat more elaborate controls but with essentially the same conclusions about supervision and productivity. Michael Argyle, Godfrey Gardner, and Frank Cioffi, "The measurement of supervisory methods," Human Relations, X, 1957, 295-313, and "Supervisory methods related to productivity, absenteeism, and labor turnover," Human Relations, XI, 1958, 23-40.

9. Ralph M. Stogdill and Alvin E. Coons (eds.), Leader Behavior: Its Description and Measurement (Columbus: Bureau of Business Research, The Ohio State University, 1957); Appendix C contains a brief description of other publications in the Ohio State Leadership Series.

10. Andrew W. Halpin and B. James Winer, "A factorial study of the leader behavior descriptions," in Stogdill and Coons, op. cit., 39-51.

11. Ibid., p. 42.

12. Carroll L. Shartle, Executive Performance and Leadership (Englewood Cliffs, N. J.: Prentice-Hall, Inc., 1956), p. 120.

13. John K. Hemphill and Alvin E. Coons, "Development of the leader behavior description questionnaire," in Stogdill and Coons, op. cit., 6-38, at p. 11.

14. Andrew W. Halpin, "The leader behavior and effectiveness of aircraft commanders," in Stogdill and Coons, op. cit., 52-64.

15. Richard T. Morris and Melvin Seeman, "The problem of leadership: an interdisciplinary approach," American Journal of Sociology, LVI, 1950, 149-155. A revised version of this paradigm appears in Carroll L. Shartle's "Introduction" to Stogdill and Coons, op. cit., 1-5.

16. Op. cit., 880-884.

17. An Army company is the lowest operating unit of a vast formal organization, on each level of which there are leaders and followers. It is not very useful, however, to include under the same rubric of "leader" the occupants of such disparate positions as a company commander and the President, as commander-in-chief. The former has "clearly defined operating responsibilities, limited discretion, set communication channels, and a sure position in the command structure." The latter has diffuse responsibilities, great discretion, and access to many channels of communications; he is concerned with large questions of policy and institutional goals, matters that are outside the province of the company commander. For a sociological analysis of leadership at the upper levels of large organizations, see Philip Selznick, Leadership in Administration (Evanston, Ill. : Row, Peterson and Company, 1957); the above quotation is from p. 3.

18. An important exception is the study of "opinion leadership" in research on mass communications. See Joseph T. Klapper, "What we know about the effects of mass communication": the brink of hope," Public Opinion Quarterly, XXI, Winter 1957-58, 453-475.

19. Renato Tagiuri, "Relational analysis: an extension of sociometric method with emphasis upon social perception," Sociometry, 15, 1952, 91-104, partially reprinted in Hare, Borgatta, and Bales, op. cit., 246-252.

20. One exception is the work of the Ohio State studies. "Our concept of leader behavior sidesteps a few important issues. It limits us, for instance, to dealing with formal organizations, and focuses attention exclusively upon the 'head men' within these organizations. The whole question of the distribution of leadership acts among members of the group is avoided." Andrew W. Halpin, The Leadership Behavior of School Superintendents, (Columbus: College of Education, The Ohio State University, 1956), p. 15.

21. George C. Homans, The Human Group (New York: Harcourt, Brace and Company, 1950).

22. Alvin W. Gouldner (ed.), Studies in Leadership (New York: Harper and Brothers, 1950), 44-45.

23. Robert F. Bales and Philip E. Slater, "Role differentiation in small decision-making groups," in Talcott Parsons and Robert F. Bales, Family, Socialization, and Interaction Process (Glencoe, Ill. : The Free Press, 1955), 259-306. See, however, the critical remarks by D. K. Wheeler and the reply by Bales and Slater in Sociometry, 20, 1957, 145-155.

24. Leonard Berkowitz, "Sharing leadership in small, decision-making groups," Journal of Abnormal and Social Psychology, XLVIII, 1953, 231-238, reprinted in Hare, Borgatta, and Bales, op. cit., 543-555.

25. Samuel A. Stouffer et al., The American Soldier, Vol. I, Adjustment During Army Life (Princeton: Princeton University Press, 1949), Ch. IV.

26. Raymond B. Cattell, "Concepts and methods in the measurement of group syntality," Psychological Review, LV, 1948, 48-63.

27. The idea of interaction has, of course, occurred to researchers, who were not familiar with the statistical principle.

28. Robert K. Merton, Social Theory and Social Structure, revised and enlarged ed. (Glencoe, Ill.: The Free Press, 1957), 111-114.

29. Cogan, op. cit.

Chapter II

THE MEASUREMENT OF LEADERSHIP CLIMATE

The development of the technique for measuring leadership climate was a long and complicated process. A good part of that process is described in this chapter, not for its historical value, but because several important theoretical and methodological problems are thereby illuminated. In addition, a clear understanding of these climates will be essential in the following chapters, and this understanding may best be gained by retracing their derivation.

Although the derivation as a whole is complicated, it can be divided into four relatively simple steps:

1. In Chapter I leadership climate was described as the way in which an "average trainee" sees the leaders of his company. This is not altogether a figure of speech: the first step in deriving these quantitative indices is to condense the varied ratings of a given leader on a particular question* into the average of the ratings given to this leader by all the trainees under him. This averaging will be explained more clearly later in this chapter, but the reader may get some idea of what is involved by keeping track of the amount of data that is dealt with in the four steps. Initially, there are almost 200,000 ratings—in each

_____
*The leadership questionnaire is reproduced in Appendix J.

of 12 companies an average of 7 leaders is rated on 15 questions by an average of 150 trainees. The averaging process reduces the data to 1230 ratings—the means of the ratings received by each of the 82 leaders on each of the 15 questions.

2. The responses to the fifteen questions do not represent fifteen theoretically independent aspects of leader behavior. In fact, they turn out to be manifestations of only three basic dimensions. The 1230 ratings are thus reduced to 246—three ratings on these new dimensions for each of the 82 leaders.

3. Leadership climate is the way in which the average trainee sees the leaders of his company as a group, not as separate persons. In each company, therefore, the ratings for the individual leaders are combined into indices characterizing the "leadership corps" of the company as a whole. There are thirty-six of these indices, three for each of the twelve companies.

4. Each company can be further classified into one or another leadership climate according to its position on the three indices —high on all three, high on one and low on the other two, and so on. Of the eight possible climates, four can be identified in the data of this study.

The procedure outlined here is aggregative: in effect, the leadership climates are constructed by aggregating the responses of the individual trainees into perceived characteristics of the leaders and, in turn, combining these characteristics of leaders into indices of leadership for each company. This is not, however, the only conceivable way to measure leadership climate. If one can assume that the leadership climate of a company is adequately expressed in the behavior of the

Commanding Officer, then the measurement of leadership climate would be greatly simplified; one would only have to examine the behavior of a single leader in each company. Indeed, this assumption is implicit in most research on military leadership, such as that of the Ohio State group. On this ground alone, this assumption is worth investigating: in addition, it will yield important information about the nature of leadership for the analysis of Chapter IV.

The assumption that the leadership climate of a company can be reduced to the behavior of a single top leader, such as the commanding officer (the "C.O."), might be justified on either of two grounds: (1) that the influence of the subordinate leaders is negligible, as compared with that of the C.O., or (2) that the C.O. somehow "sets the tone" for the subordinate leaders, so that the leadership behavior they exhibit in dealing with the men is more or less a reflection of the leadership they receive from the C.O. Each of these possibilities will be explored in turn.

The first question on the leadership questionnaire asked for a rating of each officer according to his influence on the trainee's daily life. The ratings ranged from "1" for the leader who had most influence to "3" for the leader with least influence. If it is true that the influence of subordinate leaders is negligible compared to the influence of the C.O., then the average rating received by the C.O.'s of the twelve companies should be much lower than the average ratings received by other positions (since low numerical ratings correspond to high influence). But, as Table II-1 shows, this is not the case.

The average C.O. is thought to have had more influence than the Executive Officer or the First Sergeant, but his influence score is equal to that of the Field First Sergeant. These questionnaire scores thus agree with the reality experienced by many former soldiers: while leaders who are in direct command of troops (the C.O. and the Field First Sergeant) have more influence than leaders whose jobs are largely

Table II-1

AVERAGE INFLUENCE SCORES OF
FOUR COMPANY-LEVEL POSITIONS

	Average score	Number of leaders*
Commanding Officers	1. 67	(17)
Executive Officers	2. 28	(20)
First Sergeants	2. 17	(23)
Field First Sergeants	1. 66	(22)

*The high turnover of leaders accounts for the fact that the twelve companies have more than twelve occupants of each position. This further complicates the problem of multiple leadership over what it would have been with only one leader per position in each company.

administrative, actual influence among the former group is not necessarily proportional to formal authority. One cannot, therefore, assume that the C.O. exercises such a disproportionate influence on the trainees that the other leaders can be neglected.

Now what of the other possibility: does the Commanding Officer "set the tone" for his subordinate leaders, so that the measurement of leadership climate might be based on the leadership behavior of the C.O. alone? By looking ahead to a later part of this chapter it can be shown that this is not so. One of the steps in deriving measures of leadership climate is to compute for each leader a "positive-leadership score." For the moment it will suffice to say that this score measures the extent to which a leader inspires confidence in his men and enjoys their respect. If the C.O. sets the tone of a company, then where he has a high positive-leadership score, his subordinates should also have high scores, and where he is low, they should be low. But in Table II-2 there is virtually no association between the scores of C.O.'s and their subordinates: the positive leadership exerted by the C.O. has no effect on the positive leadership of the Executive Officer and the noncoms. [1] Since the

C.O. neither sets the tone for his subordinate leaders nor exercises a disproportionate influence in all companies, the measurement of leadership climate must take into account the behavior of all leaders, rather than that of the C.O. alone.

Table II-2

THE PERCENTAGE OF C.O.'S WITH SUBORDINATE
OFFICERS OF LIKE AND UNLIKE POSITIVE
LEADERSHIP SCORES

	High Scoring C.O.	Low Scoring C.O.
High Scoring Subordinates	61	63
Low Scoring Subordinates	39	37
	(100)	(100)
Number of Cases*	(23)	(24)

*These totals are smaller than those in Table I-1 for two reasons: (1) the C.O.'s are not counted because the table is based on the number of other leaders whose scores agree or disagree with their C.O.'s score; (2) it was necessary to exclude three companies in which there had been two C.O.'s with markedly different scores.

Leadership climate as the perceptions of an average trainee

When observers are called upon to make judgments, the usual result is a distribution of values, most of them clustered around some central value and a smaller number more or less extreme in either direction. If there had been only one observer, he might have given one of the values in the central cluster, but there is obviously a good chance of selecting a single observer who would have made an extreme judgment. For this reason, where one has to rely on perceived ratings, the usual practice is to take the consensus of the set of judges. In this study the judges are the trainees in each company, and their consensus about a particular leader on some question is expressed as the arithmetic mean of their ratings. Each leader is therefore described by the average ratings of the men under him—or, more vividly, by the "average trainee" in his company.

It will be easier to understand this concept of an average trainee by looking at a portion of the leadership questionnaire filled out by one trainee, Pvt. John Doe of Company X of the __th Infantry.[2]

	C. O.	Exec. Off.	1st Sgt.	Field 1/Sgt.
15. If you were ordered into combat and you could choose the men who would be your leaders, use the No. 1 for those men in your unit you would like MOST to lead you; No. 2 for those men whom you would like LESS to lead you; and the No. 3 for those men you would like LEAST to lead you if at all.	1 3	2	2 1	3 3

During his sixteen weeks of training, Doe had seven company-level leaders—two C.O.'s, one Executive Officer, two First Sergeants and two Field First Sergeants—which is roughly the number that most trainees had.[3] The numbers in the body of the table are Doe's ratings of each officer and noncom as a combat leader. Doe apparently thought that the first C.O. would have made a good combat leader, since he gave him the highest rating, "1." His unwillingness to follow the second C.O. into combat is indicated by the low rating of "3."

Every trainee in Doe's company rated the same company-level officers on this question. For the sake of illustration, assume that there were 100 trainees in this company and that their ratings of the first C.O. as a combat leader were:

Rating	Number of trainees
1	50
2	30
3	20
	100

The average of these ratings is 1.70. This is the rating that the first C. O. would have received from a hypothetical "average trainee." This useful procedure effects a 100:1 reduction in the data. Instead of 100 sets of ratings to analyze in each company, there is only one set. More important, however, is the fact that the average reveals the common elements in the trainees' perceptions of their leaders; the ratings of a trainee with deviant perceptions, from whatever cause, have an insignificant effect on the averages.[4]

One can now disregard the trainees altogether and take each average rating as a perceived characteristic of the leader being rated. Thus the first C. O. in the illustrative example would be said to have a rating of 1.70 as a combat leader. In other words, the average ratings received by a leader may be considered, for purposes of analysis, as his perceived attributes.[5]

Dimensions of perceived leadership

In the leadership questionnaire each leader was rated, as in the foregoing illustrative example, on the extent to which he:

(1) influenced the lives of the trainees. (In the following tables this is referred to simply as "influence.")

(2) commanded the respect of the trainees (respect)

(3) was a "sucker for sob stories."

(4) was a "good Joe" one minute and "mean as Hell" the next (inconsistent)

(5) could create a real fighting spirit against the enemy

(6) acted in such a way that the trainees were afraid of him (induces fear)

(7) could not be depended on to keep his promises (breaks promises)

(8) created a feeling of confidence in the trainees

(9) told the trainees when he thought that an order from higher headquarters was unfair or silly (comments on "silly" orders)

(10) displayed a real interest in the trainees without babying them (interested in men)

(11) treated the trainees "like dirt"

(12) gave more breaks to his favorite trainees than to others (plays favorites)

(13) seized every opportunity to punish his men

(14) tried to have his men excused from "dirty details" ordered by higher authorities ("goes to bat" for men)

(15) would be preferred as a leader in combat

These perceived attributes are not independent of each other. For example, a leader who can instill a fighting spirit in his men also commands their respect; in Appendix Table A-1 the correlation between these two characteristics is 0.82. Similarly, a leader who punishes at every opportunity quite naturally inspires fear; the correlation in this case is 0.84. The size of these correlations is striking: of the 105 correlations in the leadership data, forty-nine are greater than 0.50, and thirteen are greater than 0.80.[6] This is, of course, the result of correlating averages rather than individual responses. All the idiosyncratic variability and virtually all the random errors of response and processing are eliminated; only the average perceptions remain.[7]

The fifteen characteristics about which the trainees were questioned do not, therefore, reflect fifteen distinct traits of leaders. It seems

reasonable to assume that they stem from a smaller and more fundamental set of underlying factors. Before describing how the leadership
factors were identified, a more fundamental question is in order: why
bother with factors anyway? Is it not equally satisfactory to deal only
with the average ratings and perhaps group them according to some
"logical" system, rather than to go through the complicated procedures
of "factoring"? The answer is that factor analysis actually simplifies
the total picture of leadership; it shows that there are patterns of consistency underneath the varied perceptions, and it provides a rational,
systematic process for identifying these patterns.

The situation is analogous to that faced by a psychiatrist whose
patients display a wide variety of physical and emotional signs and
symptoms—phobias, anxieties, compulsions, skin disorders, stomach
ailments, and so on. Alone or in combination, each of these does not
represent a distinct disease entity; rather, they are taken as different
manifestations of one or two underlying emotional conflicts. Any one
emotional conflict or mental disorder may have many seemingly uncon-
nected manifestations; but, when the conflict or disorder is uncovered,
it becomes clear that all the signs and symptoms reflect the same psychological condition and, often, serve the same psychological function.

The techniques of factor analysis make it possible to discern groups
of leadership characteristics that have some underlying uniformity.
Factor analysis is not the only method for doing this, but it is one of
the most useful for mapping unknown areas in an exploratory investigation.[8] The starting point for a factor analysis is a set of correlation
coefficients of each variable with every other variable—in this case the
105 coefficients measuring the extent to which high average ratings on
one question are associated with high average ratings on another question (Table A-1 in Appendix A). Some understanding of the patterns of
association among the different ratings can be gained by a careful ex-

amination of this table, but the full implications of these correlations will become visible only after a long series of computations.

What the factor analyst hopes will result from these computations is a small number of factors that sum up the information contained in his original variables. This hope is well realized in the present study: the ratings of the leaders on fifteen questions can be replaced by their scores on only three factors with very little error.[9] This fact not only makes possible an economical description of the leaders' behavior; it also demonstrates the existence of a meaningful structure in the trainees' ratings. Had there been no such structure, but simply haphazard guesses about the various leaders, then there might have been as many as ten factors instead of three.[10] And these ten factors would not have the obvious cogency that our factors will be seen to display.

It is important to recognize that the isolation of factors depends only on the correlations between the original variables and not on the contents of the variables. Most factor analyses are carried out, as this one was, with the specific variables identified only by number; whatever factors emerge reflect, then, the characteristics of the data, rather than the preconceptions of the researcher. The researcher's theoretical preconceptions and his empirical knowledge do enter, however, in the interpretation of the factors.

The interpretation of factors

The label by which a factor is identified depends on the characteristics that enter into it and their relative importance. These relationships between the three factors and the fifteen perceived characteristics of this study are presented in Table II-3. Across the top of the table are listed the three factors in the order of their power as explanatory concepts (technically, according to the variance in leadership character-

istics accounted for by each factor). The entries in the body of the
table measure the relative importance of each characteristic to the factor at the top of the column. For example, in the first column, the figures of 0.52 for "creates confidence" and 0.11 for "creates fighting
spirit" indicate that the former is more than four times as important as
the latter in determining a leader's score on this factor. [11]

Table II-3

STRUCTURE OF PERCEIVED LEADERSHIP FACTORS*

QUESTION	FACTORS		
	I Positive	II Tyrannical	III Vacillating
8. Creates confidence	.52		-.13
5. Creates fighting spirit	.11		
10. Interested in men	.08		
15. Would prefer as combat leader	.08		
2. Respect	.05		
1. Influence	.05		
14. "Goes to bat" for men	.04	-.06	.04
13. Punishes at every opportunity		.30	.18
6. Induces fear		.28	-.06
11. Treats like dirt		.24	.09
4. Inconsistent		.06	.15
12. Plays favorites			.30
7. Breaks promises			.14
3. Sucker for sob stories			
9. Comments on "silly" orders			

*The figures in each column indicate relative importance of each item. All entries of 0.03 or
less have been dropped for clarity. The question numbers refer to the leadership questionnaire in Appendix J.

I Positive Leadership. The entries in the first column suggest the
name of "positive leadership." A leader with a high score on this factor enjoys the confidence and respect of his men; he is able to inspire

them with a will to fight; and they in turn would like to have him as a
leader in combat. The interest he takes in his men is manifested in his
willingness to "go to bat" for them when his superiors impose unpleasant
duties on the company. The higher a leader's score on this dimension,
the more he has escaped the "dilemma of leadership": he is able to
carry out the requirements of his role and still maintain good relations
with his subordinates. It is also significant that this factor is quantitatively the most important, accounting for more of the variation in
leaders' ratings than either of the other two factors.

These statistically-derived scores are a long way from the raw data,
the trainees' ratings of their leaders. That they make sense is indicated by some of the unsolicited comments on the questionnaires.

One trainee wrote of an officer who turned out to have a particularly
high positive-leadership score:

> I think that our commanding officer, Capt. __ was a great leader,
> he held the respect of all the men and was just about everyone's
> choice to lead them in combat if we ever saw action.

And a First Sergeant who happened to receive a conspicuously low score
on this dimension elicited the remark that:

> . . . . he is the most unsympathetic character that I have ever
> encountered in my life also sneaky. . . . I don't see how   he
> ever earned his stripes for he has the mental capabilities of a
> mongoloid.

II Tyrannical Leadership. A high score on this factor signifies
harsh and oppressive leadership. The trainees report that they are
punished for every minor infraction of the rules, that the leader treats
them "like dirt," and that they are afraid of him. One officer with a
very high score on this factor drew this comment:

> The C. O. beat men until they ran to the I. G. Very few of us
> got passes during basic. We never got breaks on our marches

because the C. O. was either trying to set a record or win some money.

It might be thought that scores on this factor would vary inversely with "positive leadership," that a leader who treats his men "like dirt" would not be respected. But the correlation between these two factors in Table II-4 is only moderately negative, -0. 17. Paradoxical though it may seem, the same leader can have moderately high scores on both factors. [12]

Table II-4
CORRELATIONS BETWEEN FACTORS

		I	II	III
I	Positive	--		
II	Tyrannical	-. 17	--	
III	Vacillating	-. 41	. 45	--

On closer examination of the two sets of traits, however, the paradox disappears. The leader who inspires respect as a soldier and whose men would be willing to follow him in combat is not necessarily liked; he may, in fact, be feared. This bears out Machiavelli's principle that a ruler can secure the obedience of his subjects through making himself loved or making himself feared. A military leader may be tough, or he may be gentle; as long as he knows his business, his followers will re-spect him. Thus the First Sergeant who received the highest tyranny score in this study and an above-average positive-leadership score was described by one trainee as a "tough but good cadreman. "

III Vacillating Leadership. The third factor of leadership meas-ures the extent to which leaders depart from consistency and impartiality in their treatment of the trainees. A high score on vacillating leadership denotes a leader who breaks promises, plays favorites, and is "mean as Hell one minute and a 'good Joe' the next." On the negative side, he does not inspire confidence among the trainees. One might even infer from the factorial structure in Table II-3 that his men do not take him altogether seriously; although he punishes them "at every opportunity," they are not afraid of him. Of the leader who received the highest computed score on this factor, one man wrote:

> If that Captain___ of ___ Co., ___th Inf., wouldn't lie to the
> men so much and stop trying to make major . . . this soldier
> hates his guts for the way he treated me and the rest in basic
> training.

From the standpoint of the followers, a "good" leader is predictable and impersonal, as well as competent. This is corroborated by the negative correlation of -0.41 between positive leadership and vacillating leadership. Note that positive leadership is more closely related to vacillating leadership (more exactly, to lack of vacillation) than to tyrannical leadership.

Two of the fifteen leadership attributes do not contribute to any of these factors—the extent to which a leader is a "sucker for sob stories" and his willingness to tell the men when he thinks an order from higher headquarters is "silly."[13] These are apparently unimportant traits which, like right-handedness or eye color, have no bearing on the factors of leadership.

Of course, no label for a factor is necessarily "correct"; intangibles of judgment always affect the factor analyst's decisions. But this arbitrariness need not lessen the precision of the subsequent analysis provided that one avoids "misplacing concreteness." Naming the factor does not thereby confer on it all that the name connotes, or make it an independently measurable entity. Exploratory factor analyses like this one, particularly when based on data gathered with other ends in mind, yield factors that may best be interpreted as empirical constructs—i.e., as useful indices to summarize a group of related characteristics. The analysis to this point has dealt with individual leaders. The ratings of a given leader by the individual trainees were combined into the ratings of an "average trainee." In turn, these average ratings can be considered as manifestations of three more fundamental aspects of leadership, the factors of positive, tyrannical, and vacillating leadership. Now it is time to combine the ratings of all the leaders in each company to get a single set of leadership characteristics.

Indices of leadership climate

The task here is to describe the leadership of each company as a whole, rather than the individual leaders. Just as there are three factor scores for each leader, so there will be three indices of leadership climate for each company. The simplest procedure would be to average the scores of all the leaders in a company on each factor. For example, the "index of positive leadership" for a company might be computed by simply averaging the positive-leadership scores of all the officers and noncoms. However, this procedure would be open to two serious objections. First, all leaders do not affect the trainees' behavior to the same extent. In one company the C.O. may be the dominant figure, while in another the first sergeant may "run" the company with little interference from the officers. What is needed here is some measure of each leader's relative impact on the trainees. This is supplied by the question on influence (Question 1 on the leadership questionnaire). The mean influence rating accorded to a leader can be used to weight his scores on the three factors in computing the leadership indices for each company.

The second objection to averaging the leadership scores is that many leaders did not serve the full sixteen weeks of the training cycle. The eighty-two officers and noncoms on whom the leadership factor analysis was based occupied only forty-eight positions, an average of almost two occupants per position. Obviously, it will not do to give the same weight to the scores of a first sergeant who served four weeks and his successor who was with the company for twelve weeks. The solution to this problem is to weight the scores of each leader by his relative length of service with the company during the training cycle.

In other words, the indices of leadership climate are based on weighted means of the factor scores of each leader, the weights taking into account his relative influence on the trainees and the proportion of the total training cycle during which he was with the company. The resulting three indices of company leadership climate are presented in Table II-5. The companies are listed in the order of their ranking on the index of positive leadership.

Types of leadership climate

The ultimate aim in developing these indices is to relate leadership climate to the behavior of the trainees. It might seem that this task could be accomplished by studying the association of each index with some form of behavior—for example, comparing the rates of drinking in companies with high and low indices of positive leadership. But closer inspection of Table II-5 reveals that one index of leadership cannot be considered apart from the others. Some companies have high indices of positive leadership and low indices of tyrannical leadership; some display the reverse combination; and others are low on both indices or high on both. [14] To describe the leadership climate of a company adequately, one must use both the positive and the tyrannical indices; if

Table II-5

INDICES OF PERCEIVED LEADERSHIP CLIMATE

COMPANY	I POSITIVE		II TYRANNICAL		III VACILLATING	
	Score	Rank	Score	Rank	Score	Rank
1	.96	(1)	-.26	(7)	-.54	(8)
2	.82	(2)	-1.35	(12)	-1.16	(11)
3	.62	(3)	-.17	(6)	-.36	(7)
4	.58	(4)	.56	(3)	.14	(4)
5	.53	(5)	-.47	(10)	-.68	(9)
6	.52	(6)	-.37	(8)	-.35	(6)
7	.48	(7)	-1.02	(11)	-1.39	(12)
8	.12	(8)	-.43	(9)	-.78	(10)
9	-.01	(9)	-.12	(5)	.13	(5)
10	-.01	(10)	1.41	(1)	.72	(3)
11	-.10	(11)	.81	(2)	.88	(2)
12	-.72	(12)	.23	(4)	1.06	(1)

each index is divided into "high" and "low," this yields four distinct types of leadership climate.

But should not the vacillating-leadership indices also be included, thus making eight combinations instead of four? Actually, the vacillating and tyrannical indices are so highly correlated that, with only a single exception, companies high on one are high on the other. With the small number of companies in this study, it is impossible to separate tyranny from vacillation. Consequently, only the four combinations of indices in Table II-6 are considered.

Table II-6 contains the results toward which this chapter has been building: a set of leadership climates dervied from ratings of individual leaders by trainees. Since leadership climates will be central to the analyses of Chapters V-VIII, it will be useful to recount their principal characteristics briefly. [16]

Table II-6

TYPES OF LEADERSHIP CLIMATE

INDICES OF LEADERSHIP		LEADERSHIP CLIMATES	NUMBER OF COMPANIES	
Positive	Tyrannical & Vacillating		Total	Analyzed*
High	High	"Paternal"	1	0
High	Low	"Persuasive"	6	3
Low	High	"Arbitrary"	3	2
Low	Low	"Weak"	2	2
			12	7

*The discrepancy between the total number of companies and the number analyzed in the succeeding chapters is explained in Appendix B.

Paternal Climate. This climate is characterized by high values on all three indices of leadership—positive, tyrannical, and vacillating. Its leaders are respected, feared, and in part at least, scorned. On the face of it, these qualities are antithetical, particularly the combination of respect and scorn. However, there is only one company in this climate, and the actual scores of this company on the three indices are not as conflicting as this description might indicate. This company has the fourth highest positive-leadership score, the third highest tyranny score, and the fourth highest vacillation score. That is, it displays a moderate degree of all three types of leadership.

The label of "paternal" is taken from Gibb. [17] On a priori grounds he set up a fourfold classification of leadership based on the two dimensions of love and fear ("in the psychoanalytic sense"). From the child's standpoint, his father is both loved and feared; he may also be seen occasionally as inconsistent. The soldiers in this one company seem to experience their leaders in much the same way. Unfortunately, the other data on this company are so scanty[18] as to preclude any analysis of the relationships between leadership and behavior or between characteristics of the trainees and behavior. Therefore, from this point on, only three leadership climates are considered: persuasive, arbitrary, and weak.

Persuasive Climate. This climate comes closest to what is generally regarded as "ideal" leadership. The trainees have confidence in their leaders and would follow them into combat; and the leaders give their men strong support. The leaders are not coercive or punitive; they do not play favorites; and they keep their promises. Although no military service can be altogether free from frustrations or deprivations, the persuasive climate probably generates a lower level of tension than either of the other two climates.

Arbitrary Climate. This climate is diametrically opposed to the persuasive. The leaders do not evoke the confidence of the trainees; they are perceived as aloof, punitive, inconsistent, and untrustworthy. Of the three climates, the arbitrary probably generates the highest level of anxiety. The trainees live in virtually constant fear of punishment, not so much because of what they have done or not done, but rather because of the essentially capricious, nonrational behavior of the leaders.

Weak Climate. Compared with the persuasive and arbitrary climates, the weak climate, as the name implies, has virtually no effective leadership. These trainees are neither inspired by leaders they like nor driven by leaders they fear; in effect, the leaders do not lead. In Gibb's typology such leaders are merely "organizers":

> The central person with whom member relations are
> characterized by little of any emotion, whether love or
> fear, stands in the position of "organizer." He meets
> the criterion of leadership to the extent that he moves
> the group in the direction of its goal, but he engenders
> little or no emotion toward himself.[19]

Without the positive motivations produced by identification with the persuasive leaders or the negative feelings generated by the arbitrary leaders, the weak climate may be expected to have a level of tension intermediate between the persuasive and arbitrary climates.

It is important to repeat that the development of these leadership climates did not depend on preconceptions about the nature of leadership. The quantitative relationships in the data were examined at each step; but except for giving tentative labels to the factors and indices, no attempt was made to interpret the findings or to confirm or deny any existing theoretical analysis. It is all the more striking, then, that these three leadership climates isolated on the basis of a statistical analysis so closely resemble the group atmospheres experimentally devised by Lewin and his co-workers. Taking into account the obvious differences between soldiers in Army training companies and boys in after-school hobby clubs, the democratic, autocratic, and laissez-faire group atmospheres resemble the persuasive, arbitrary, and weak climates, respectively. The similarities between the two studies do not end here, however; in the chapters to come, it will be increasingly clear that this study is in many ways a replication of the Iowa researches, although it was not so intended, either in the design or in the early phases of the analysis.

A good replication is more than a repetition of the original study, even in a new context. It requires the systematic inclusion of new and theoretically important variables. As Chapter I has indicated, the Lewin studies deliberately removed the effects of differences in social characteristics among the followers. The present study, dealing with natural groups, was not able to do this. In Chapter VII it will be shown that, far from their presence proving a handicap, the simultaneous examination of status variables and leadership climate leads to new and important conclusions that have not been considered in most previous work on leadership effects. Meanwhile, however, when it comes to assessing the effects of leadership climate alone, the fact that these status characteristics are not equally distributed in the various companies presents a problem. Techniques for coping with this problem are presented in the next chapter; like several other techniques in this study, their application extends beyond the field of leadership effects.

NOTES TO CHAPTER TWO

1. These results appear to conflict with a well-known finding from industrial studies: Kahn and Katz have shown that a foreman tends to offer his men the same kind of leadership that he receives from his superior. This difference between the army and industry may stem from the procedures for selection and promotion in the two situations. That is, in the Army the personnel of a training company are all assigned by higher headquarters; a commanding officer does not choose his subordinates. In industry, on the other hand, the similarity between the leadership exerted by the foreman and that which he receives from his superior may simply indicate that the superior tends to select foremen who behave as he does. See Robert L. Kahn and Daniel Katz, op. cit., p. 618.

2. The leadership questionnaire is reproduced in Appendix J. The actual questionnaires were anonymous.

3. In addition, the questionnaires asked each trainee to rate his platoon officer and platoon sergeant. Because the men were not seated by platoon during the questionnaire sessions and because the questionnaires were anonymous, it was impossible to identify each trainee's platoon in the data. Hence the analysis of leadership is restricted to the company-level leaders, who were rated by every trainee in the company regardless of his platoon. The effect of omitting platoon officers is, of course, to lessen the precision with which leadership climate is measured and therefore to reduce the associations between leadership climate and the behavior of the trainees. This shortcoming could easily be rectified in future studies, since the method developed for measuring leadership climate can be extended to include the platoon leaders and even the squad leaders without difficulty. In general, it is applicable to the measurement of formal leadership climate in any type of organization.

4. An average is meaningful only where the distribution is unimodal (single-peaked). Evidence that bimodality is not a serious problem in the leadership data is contained in Appendix A. This is, in effect, another way of saying that there is substantial consensus among the trainees in each company.

5. For a systematic use of followers' perceptions to describe the behavior of leaders, see: Morris L. Cogan, "The behavior of teachers and the productive behavior of their pupils: I, Perception analysis; II, Trait analysis," forthcoming in the Journal of Experimental Education. Cogan's study is unique in considering both the relationship between individual perceptions and individual behavior and the relationship between the average perception by a group and individual behavior (relationships 3 and 6 in Figure I-1). An even more extensive investigation of average perceptions is described in two studies by Andrew W. Halpin, The Leadership Behavior of School Superintendents (Columbus: College of Education, The Ohio State University, 1956) and "The leader behavior and effectiveness of aircraft commanders," in Stogdill and Coons, op. cit., 52-68. The successful use of followers' perceptions in these studies and the present one contradicts the assertion of Argyle, Gardner, and Cioffi, op. cit., that followers' ratings are not a good way to describe the behavior of leaders. It is likely, however, that these authors were thinking of individual perceptions, rather than average perceptions for a group. On the problem of "halo effects" raised by Argyle et al., see Appendix A.

6. By way of contrast, see the table of correlations between the various nonduty activities in Appendix I.

7. Two technical questions are raised by this correlation of averages for all company-level officers. One is whether or not we have confused individual and group data and thereby committed the "ecological fallacy"—i. e., taken the correlations between group rates or averages as a substitute for correlations of individual values. The second question is why we have correlated the average ratings of all officers, regardless of company, instead of computing the correlations separately for each company. Both of these questions are considered in Appendix A.

8. For a thorough, if somewhat partisan discussion of the relative advantages of factor analysis and other widely used techniques (cluster analysis, partial and multiple correlation, discriminant-function analysis, etc.), see Raymond B. Cattell, Factor Analysis (New York: Harper & Brothers, 1952), 14-18, 32-33, 357-366. Certain aspects of factor analysis are criticized in Louis Guttman, "A new approach to factor analysis: the Radex," in Mathematical Thinking in the Social Sciences, ed. by Paul F. Lazarsfeld (Glencoe, Ill.: The Free Press, 1954), 261-268, and in Paul F. Lazarsfeld, "The interpretation and computation of some latent structures," in Samuel A. Stouffer, et al., Measurement and Prediction (Princeton: Princeton University Press, 1950), 469-471. Especially clear accounts of the logic and procedures of factor analyses are Godfrey Thompson, The Factorial Analysis of Human Ability (5th ed., London: University of London Press, 1951) and Benjamin Fruchter, Introduction to Factor Analysis (New York: D. Van Nostrand Co. , 1954).

9. Few factor analyses of real data explain so much of the variation in the original data with so few factors. These three factors account for over 80 per cent of the variation between leaders in ten of the fifteen questions. Only for one question does the proportion of explained variation fall below 50 per cent. The reason is that our correlations are high when they should be high: they are not "attenuated" by random errors of response and perception as is inevitably the case when one correlates individual data instead of means and proportions, as we have done. By way of contrast, the Ohio State researchers correlated combinations of items for individuals, rather than combinations of independent individual responses. That is, they did not make use of the fact that several individuals in each of their groups were rating the same leader in order to derive more accurate average perceptions of the leaders. The result is that, although they had much more carefully tested items to work with, their factors do not sum up their data quite as economically as ours do. (Halpin, op. cit., did use average perceptions to describe his leaders, but this came after the factor analyses, not before; both procedures are followed in this chapter.) For details on these factor analyses, see Appendix A of this study; John K. Hemphill and Alvin E. Coons, "Development of the leader behavior description questionnaire," op. cit., 23-27; and Andrew W. Halpin, "A factorial study of the leader behavior descriptions," op. cit., 40-44.

10. The number of factors that can be identified is a function of the number of experimentally independent variables. L. L. Thurstone, Multiple-Factor Analysis (Chicago: The University of Chicago Press, 1947), 291-294.

11. The concepts of the "explanatory power" of a factor and the "importance" of an item to a factor are more fully explained in Appendix A.

12. It is important to remember that the factors of perceived leadership refer to attributes of leaders and not to types of leaders. Every leader receives a score on all three factors. It would therefore be misleading to speak of a "tyrannical leader" unless by this is meant a leader who scores high on this factor and low on the other two.

13. These two traits have the lowest "communalities" in Appendix Table A-2—i. e., relatively little of their variance is accounted for by the three common factors.

14. The points of division into high and low are of course arbitrary. However, when pairs of indices are plotted on a graph, there are more or less "natural" divisions at 0.30 on the positive dimension and 0.10 on the tyrannical and vacillating dimensions.

15. A similar procedure was followed in Andrew W. Halpin, "The leader behavior and effectiveness of aircraft commanders," Ch. IV in Stogdill and Coons, op. cit., 62-64.

16. Not the least interesting aspect of these climates is the extent to which the original questionnaire data have been condensed: almost 200,000 separate ratings went into the derivation of the four climates.

17. Op. cit., p. 907. Gibb's typology is a simplification of the more elaborate treatment by Fritz Redl, "Group emotion and leadership," Psychiatry, V, 1942, 573-596.

18. See Appendix B.

19. Op. cit., p. 907.

Chapter III

THE PROCEDURES OF ANALYSIS

The main task of this study is to examine the relationships between leadership climate and nonduty behavior. If all trainees were alike, other than in being assigned to different companies, the analysis would be simple: one would only have to compare the rates of each kind of behavior in the three climates. But the men are not alike. Some are younger, some older; some single and some married; some have more education and some less. They differ in other ways, too, that are not represented in our data. But these three variables do affect their behavior; it is particularly significant that the effects of these variables vary from one climate to another. These status characteristics must therefore be taken into account in assessing the effects of leadership, just as the influences of the leadership climates must be considered in studying the association between status characteristics and behavior.

In principle, the procedures by which these analyses are carried out are familiar, consisting essentially of detailed cross-tabulations or "survey analysis." There are two reasons for including this chapter here. One is that much of the research on leadership had been done in laboratory settings, where the extraneous variables are controlled experimentally. Under these conditions certain kinds of statistical procedures—notably, tests of statistical significance—are possible and valuable. In natural groups, however, these procedures are not generally applicable; although many researchers have tried to adapt the statistical analyses of the controlled experiment to "observational" or "field"

studies, it will be argued here that these procedures are inherently inapplicable in this kind of survey research. The second purpose of this
chapter is to show how the idea of replications can be integrated into the
survey approach to serve the functions that the usual tests of statistical
significance serve for experimentalists. [1]

LABORATORY EXPERIMENTS AND FIELD OBSERVATIONS

The controlled or laboratory experiment often serves as a model
with which other techniques can be compared and as a goal toward which
development of these techniques should strive. Although it would be difficult to contrive an experiment relating leadership climate to the nonduty
behavior of soldiers in an army training camp, the logic of the analysis
in this study may be clarified by comparing it with such an "ideal" experiment. [2]

Suppose that the experiment is intended to study the relationship between leadership climate and the frequency with which trainees get drunk.
The first step is to list those variables, in addition to leadership, that
might be expected to affect the rates of drunkenness—among others,
age, education and marital status, as in the present study. The researcher would then create or select the required number of experimental training companies, each with a predetermined type of leadership, and assign the appropriate types of trainees to each company.
Thus, if there are, say, six kinds of trainees, he would so design his
experiment that the rates of drunkenness could be measured for each
combination of trainees and leadership. This procedure would take care
of the important "disturbing" variables that could be experimentally
controlled.

In every experiment, however, there are other variables that for
one reason or another cannot be controlled in this way. The information

may be too difficult to gather—for example, personality characteristics. Or custom and law might make it impossible to record characteristics like religion that are known to affect drunkenness. Variables that cannot be directly manipulated to make the experimental groups comparable can be handled by the procedure of randomization. In randomization the aggregate of younger, single, high-school-educated men (assuming that only these three variables are experimentally controlled) would be divided into as many equal parts as there are experimental groups (leadership climates) by a chance procedure: the group to which each trainee is assigned would be determined by some operation like flipping a coin or drawing a random number from a table.

Note that this does not ensure equality of the groups (it would be unusual for instance, if the proportion of Methodists were exactly the same in each group). What randomization does is to ensure comparability. If the assignment of trainees has been randomized, there are statistical tests for measuring the probability that the observed differences in drunkenness could have been produced by the accidental assignment to one climate of trainees with characteristics predisposing them to drunkenness, even if leadership had no effect.

Neither of these conditions, equality or comparability, holds in the present study. The proportions of single men, college-educated men, and younger men differ widely among the companies.[3] Nor were the assignments to the different companies random, which would have made it possible to use the techniques of experimental statistical inference.

Does this mean that one cannot study the relationships between behavior on the one hand and leadership climate and individual attributes on the other? No—as long as some technique is employed to take care of the unwanted disturbances. To measure the effect of leadership climate on behavior one must "hold constant" the social background factors; and, conversely, in assessing the effect of one of the three individual characteristics, the influence of leadership and the other two individual characteristics must be removed.

STATISTICAL CONTROL OF EXPERIMENTAL VARIABLES

Instead of experimental control, which would be virtually impossible in the setting of this study, approximately equivalent results can be achieved by statistical manipulation of the data after they are gathered. Wherever possible, all variables except the one whose influence is being measured are held constant. For example, the relationship between leadership and behavior is examined for younger, single high-school graduates; for older, single graduates; and so on. Sometimes it is not possible to do so because of the limited number of trainees in certain subgroups; in these cases a slightly different technique is used. [4] Because both procedures are based on comparisons within groups of individuals having several characteristics in common, they are called "Homogeneous Subgroup (HSG) Analysis." Neither of these is a new technique: where this study may be unusual, however, is in the extent to which these techniques are systematically used.

The easiest way to understand the logic of HSG analysis is to follow through one example in detail. Suppose that one is interested in the effect of leadership climate on the incidence of drunkenness—the percentage of men who get drunk one or more times during basic training. To further simplify the explanation, consider only the difference between the persuasive climate and the weak climate. The analysis begins with the overall ("marginal") results for each leadership climate. In the persuasive climate 25 per cent of the trainees got drunk at least once during basic training, as compared with 36 per cent in the weak climate. Does this mean that there is something in the nature of the weak climate that, by itself, produces a higher rate of drunkenness? In order to answer this question one must first be reasonably certain that the observed difference could not have been produced by the operation of other, uncontrolled variables, such as age, education, and marital status.

These variables may affect the rates of drunkenness in two ways— through "recruitment" or through "differential impact." Recruitment refers to the possibility that trainees of varying predispositions toward drunkenness may be unequally represented in the two companies. For example, Chapter VI will show that the men under twenty-two are more likely to get drunk than are the older men. Since the younger trainees comprise 63 per cent of the persuasive climate and 70 per cent of the weak, the observed difference in drunkenness may simply reflect this difference in recruitment. The effect of recruitment can, however, be easily removed. One has only to compare the rate of drunkenness among younger men in the persuasive climate with that among younger men in the weak climate, and similarly for the older men in the two climates. If the original difference between the climates persists in these subgroups, it cannot be attributed to age. [5]

This same comparison also makes it possible to determine whether or not the observed relationship between leadership and drunkenness is the result of differential impact—that is, if the greater drunkenness of the weak climate is manifested only (or largely) among one of the two subgroups, the older or the younger. In other words, does the effect of leadership depend on the kinds of men subjected to it, and, if so, in what ways? The assessment of differential impact is a complicated problem; it is explained more fully in Chapter VII.

Age is not the only characteristic of the trainees that is related to drunkenness. Education and marital status are also important. It is therefore necessary to hold constant all three of these variables at the same time in order to assess the effect of leadership on drunkenness: the relation between leadership and drunkenness is studied in subgroups that are homogeneous with respect to all three of these "disturbing" variables. HSG comparisons for seventeen activities are tabulated in Appendix E. In order to explain how these tables are used in the following chapters, a portion of the HSG table on drunkenness is reproduced here:

CHARACTERISTICS OF TRAINEES			LEADERSHIP CLIMATE			
		Marital	Persuasive		Weak	
Age	Education	Status	Per Cent	(N)	Per Cent	(N)
17-21	Not high school grad	Single	38	(60)	45	(53)
17-21	Not high school grad	Married	27	(22)	38	(13)
17-21	High school grad	Single	32	(82)	30	(43)
17-21	High school grad	Married	00	(12)	--	(8)
22-	Not high school grad	Single	17	(12)	--	(8)
22-	Not high school grad	Married	16	(32)	33	(12)
22-	High school grad	Single	16	(32)	23	(13)
22-	High school grad	Married	7	(29)	24	(17)

In this table the comparisons between the persuasive and weak climates are made within homogeneous subgroups, where all three of the trainees' characteristics are held constant. In the first row, for example, there is a higher incidence of drunkenness in the weak climate, 45 per cent, than in the persuasive climate, 38 per cent. This cannot be the result of differences in age, education or marital status in the two companies, since all these men have the same combinations of these three characteristics.

In all, five of the six possible comparisons show that the persuasive climate has a lower incidence of drunkenness than the weak climate. Only in the third row is the relationship in the opposite direction, but this 2 percentage-point difference is so small that it is taken as a "tie." The results of this HSG analysis thus support the results previously found for the total leadership climates; the difference between persuasive and weak climates does not stem from the fact that age, education, and marital status are also related to the incidence of drunkenness. [6] The relationship holds even when these variables are controlled in nearly all possible combinations.

Differences between other pairs of leadership climates can be studied in exactly the same way when there are enough cases to make a reasonable number of comparisons. [7] And essentially the same procedure is employed to test statements about the relationship between each of the three individual characteristics and the incidence of drunkenness. The only difference is that comparisons are made within leadership climates and within the status categories not being studied. For instance, to explore the effect of high school graduation on predisposing a trainee to drunkenness, one would hold leadership climate, age, and marital status constant. Within the persuasive climate one would compare the incidence of drunkenness among the younger, less-educated, single men with the incidence among the younger, more-educated, single men. Similar comparisons would be made in the weak and arbitrary climates.

To sum up, HSG analysis is a systematic method for the statistical control of variables in field studies. It helps to determine whether or not an observed association reflects a genuine relationship or is essentially the result of correlations with one or more additional variables. It is, in other words, a method for testing hypotheses that are suggested by the "marginal" relationships between leadership climates or social attributes and some form of behavior. HSG analysis will be used in Chapter V to test statements about the relationships between leadership climate and behavior; in Chapter VI to verify hypotheses about individual characteristics and behavior; in Chapter VII to see how leadership and individual characteristics interact to affect behavior; and in Chapter VIII in considering changes in behavior from civilian life.

NOTES TO CHAPTER THREE

1. What follows is in part a simplified account of arguments more fully developed in two papers by the writer: "A critique of tests of significance in survey research," American Sociological Review, XXII, 1957, 519-527, and "Durkheim's Suicide and problems of empirical research," American Journal of Sociology, LXIII, 1958, 607-619. These ideas are further developed in a paper entitled "Statistical significance and sociological theory," read at the annual meeting of the American Sociological Association, Chicago, September 4, 1959.

2. In addition to the references in the papers cited in the preceding footnote, a brief discussion of the relations between field studies and laboratory experiments in social psychology is: Social Science Research Council, Items, VIII, 1954, 37-42. See also the more extended discussion in Ernest Greenwood, Experimental Sociology (New York: King's Crown Press, 1945).

3. The between-climate differences in social characteristics are tabulated in Appendix D.

4. Perhaps the best-known application of this type of analysis is in Stouffer et al., The American Soldier, op. cit., 92-95. In their terminology it is called the "method of matched comparisons."

5. Strictly speaking, dividing the age distribution into a dichotomy of younger and older is not equivalent to "holding a variable constant"; one should instead study the relationship between leadership climate and drunkenness for as many age-groups as possible. The same can be said of the use of dichotomies in education and marital status. Nevertheless, they are useful as a first approximation. And, given the limited number of cases in our data, only by using dichotomies instead of finer gradations is it possible to study leadership and three individual characteristics by means of HSG analysis.

6. Criteria for distinguishing ties and for deciding whether or not HSG analysis confirms or refutes a finding based on total leadership climates or total age groups, etc., are presented in Appendix C.

7. When there are not enough cases, a modified version of HSG analysis is used. See the discussion of "Two-item HSG's" in Appendix C.

Chapter IV

LEADERSHIP, TENSION, AND REDUCTION OF TENSION

This chapter presents some propositions about the effects of leadership. These propositions come from a combination of two sources: the intensive examination of leadership climate in Chapter II and the theoretical explanations of Lewin and his co-workers on the Iowa studies of group atmospheres. The reasoning behind this rudimentary theory will be presented in this chapter, and the propositions will be empirically tested in the following chapter. This order of presentation is not meant to suggest that the actual research followed the same sequence. As is often the case, the theory was constructed to account for the observed facts. This means that the empirical test of the theoretical hypotheses is not as compelling as it would have been had the theory come first. Nevertheless, the theory does help to make sense out of the data, and that alone is enough to justify it. Furthermore, even when the ex post facto nature of the hypothesis is taken into account, the data do provide strong and consistent support for these propositions.

The theoretical analysis in the Iowa studies consists essentially of two parts: (1) a demonstration that more psychological tension is generated among the boys in the autocratic group atmospheres than in the laissez-faire and democratic atmospheres; and (2) an examination of the ways in which the boys in the three atmospheres were able to reduce these tensions. Our discussion follows theirs at first. It begins by

59

showing that the arbitrary climate generates the highest level of tension and the persuasive climate the lowest. It then examines the different channels available to the trainees for avoiding the build-up of tension, or, if that is not possible, for releasing their tension once it has accumulated. Because our real-life leadership climates are more complex than the Lewin group atmospheres and because we have data on how the trainees actually perceive their leaders (as against primarily observational data), this analysis can be carried somewhat farther. Lewin and his associates were content to describe differences in the reactions to the three atmospheres without explaining how these differences came about. In this chapter a more detailed analysis of the three leadership climates makes it possible to predict the relative levels of tension-releasing and tension-avoiding behavior.

Levels of tension

All three leadership climates, like all groups and organizations, generate tension among the followers. This necessarily follows from the disparity between the needs of the organization and the needs of the individual; the Army's goals can be approached only at the cost of frustrating some of the trainees' desires.[1] But over and above this "necessary" level of tension, the arbitrary climate apparently produces a higher level than the weak climate and the weak in turn more than the persuasive.

Unfortunately, we do not have any direct measures of tension. To use the rates of nonduty behavior as indicators of tension would be circular, since the differences in tension have been hypothesized in order to explain the differences in behavior. (That is, tension is here considered as an intervening variable through which differences in leadership climate produce differences in rates of behavior.) Some of the comments that the trainees made on their leadership questionnaire might be interpreted as manifesting high levels of tension, but these comments are so unstructured that they are useful only as illustration.

In the absence of direct measures of tension one has to rely on inference. The literature on leadership supports the assumption that the persuasive and arbitrary climate stand at opposite ends of a continuum of tension-generation. As Gibb says,

> It is axiomatic that in the course of group life frustrations will occur, and it is to be expected that there will, from time to time, be hostile and aggressive outbursts against the leader. Especially is this the case, of course, when the leadership has been of a relatively coercive variety. [2]

White and Lippitt, commenting on their group atmospheres, point out that "autocracy"—which is similar to our arbitrary climate—tends to create more hostility and aggression than does "democracy"—close to, but not identical with, our persuasive climate. [3]

And from the psychiatric standpoint Noyes reports that tension and hostility in combat units are significantly affected by leadership behavior similar to that of our arbitrary climate:

> Loss of morale or an attitude of defeatism within the combat unit greatly increased the psychological strain. Such a loss of morale was particularly prone to exist in case of bad leadership, or during a retreat. . . Frustrations, such as unfair treatment in regard to promotions, citations, or leaves, caused hostility, tension and anxiety. [4]

Assuming, then, that tension is greatest on the average in the arbitrary climate and least in the persuasive, how is this tension handled by the trainees? [5]

Techniques for avoiding or releasing tension

Following White and Lippitt, [6] there are four principal ways in which a trainee can act to avoid or reduce the tensions of basic training:

(1) He can "leave the field"; that is, he can get out of the training situation and thereby escape or minimize its frustrations. The most obvious ways to leave the field permanently are to desert and to feign an incapacitating illness. Neither one of these is common in basic training; combat, of course, is another story.

(2) He can express his discontent verbally—by "griping." The efficacy of griping as a safety valve for excess tension probably explains in part why Army tradition has accepted it as harmless and even why official channels for griping have been provided—the chaplain and the Inspector General.

(3) He can lessen his frustration by psychologically identifying himself with the leaders of his unit, thus making his goals coincide with the organization's goals. This is the classical type of the "good soldier" who pours his energy into the training activities because he wants to make himself like (or be liked by) the leaders he admires. For him, frustration and tension are minimized; his goals and the Army's goals coincide.

(4) Finally, he can indulge in various kinds of "release" behavior, activities that provide for the more or less rapid release of tension. The varying frequencies of these activities in the three leadership climates are the main concern of this and the next chapter.

The preceding section may have suggested that differences between climates in the rates of nonduty activities are simply expressions of different levels of tension, the climate with the highest tension having the highest rates of activity. But this listing of alternative ways to reduce tension indicates that matters are not quite so simple (and this conclusion is supported by the data of Chapter V). If nonduty activities are only one of several means of releasing or avoiding tension, why are they more common in one climate than in another? Why, in other words, do trainees in some companies tend to work off their frustrations in nonduty activities, while those in other companies do something else?

Our answer to these questions lies in an additional hypothesis: The more one channel is blocked, the greater is the use of alternative channels. The interclimate differences in behavior thus are a resultant of the differential pressures and the differential availability of channels of tension release in the three climates. Therefore, to explain the differences in nonduty behavior between the three climates one must examine the accessibility of the other three channels.

The first two channels—leaving the field and griping—are of limited use to a trainee. Going on sick call, for example, is an effective way to leave the field, at least for a short time; but, as we shall show in Chapter V, many leaders exert considerable pressure on the trainees to keep them from going. Although sick call does take a soldier away from the routines of training, even as many as a half-dozen visits to the dispensary in the sixteen-week training cycle would allow him to escape only an insignificant proportion of his duty. Similarly, going AWOL for a few hours is not much help; and a longer absence is almost certain to be noticed and to be punished.

Griping is another matter. At least in his off-duty hours, every trainee can gripe as much as he likes. But it is hard to believe that griping is very effective in siphoning off discontent. Its very accessibility robs it of value; it becomes routine and unsatisfying. Both leaving the field and griping are therefore limited as means of tension reduction. This leaves only two possibilities: identifying with the leaders so as to avoid building up much tension in the first place, and letting off steam through a variety of leisure-time behavior. If identification can be shown to take place more readily in one climate than in another, then according to the alternative-channel hypothesis, the rates of nonduty behavior should vary in the opposite direction: where identification is high, the rates of nonduty activities should be low, and conversely.

Theoretical support for this hypothesis is not hard to find. A central idea in theories of character formation or socialization—those of Freud or G. H. Mead, for example—is the identification of the child with his parents and with other people in his environment. The process of socialization is not, however, restricted to childhood. In a sense which is becoming increasingly common in the study of occupations and professions, "socialization" occurs whenever a person's old ways of thinking and behaving give way systematically to those appropriate to a new role. Adjustment to Army life is therefore a process of socialization, of learning to think and act like a soldier instead of a civilian. Just as the child is socialized into the role of the adult through identification with his parents, so the trainee is in part socialized into the role of the soldier by identifying with his leaders.

This identification occurs because the needs of the followers are satisfied by the leader, much as those of the child are satisfied by his parents. In Sanford's words:

> Any American follower brings his ego-needs with him
> when he comes into any group, whether the group is an
> infantry squad, a bomber crew, a PTA organization, or
> a road construction gang. . . The leader of the group,
> both in terms of the follower's perceptions and in terms
> of objective reality, has a good deal to do with the satis-
> faction of these needs. [7]

Where there are several leaders instead of only one, it is necessary to find in each company the leader or leaders with whom the trainees identify. Again, we have no direct data on identification, but it is possible to suggest the characteristics that leaders who are the objects of identification will have. They must behave in such a way as to satisfy the trainees' ego-needs, [8] and they must be in a position with sufficient influence over the trainees' lives that their behavior has some effect. Indices of both characteristics are available in our data: trainess are most likely to identify with leaders who, in the language of Chapter II, have high scores on "positive leadership" and on "influence."

Identification, influence, and positive leadership

In Chapter II we reported that the leaders in direct command of the trainees, the Commanding Officers and the Field First Sergeants, had more influence than did leaders with primarily administrative duties, the Executive Officers and the First Sergeants. [9] And there was no appreciable difference in influence between the C.O. and the Field First Sergeant. These results apply to all eighty-two leaders taken together; now that the companies have been divided among three leadership climates, the question arises: do these two relationships also hold within each climate?

The first relationship still holds true; in each climate in Table IV-1 the C.O.'s and the Field First Sergeants have more influence (lower scores) than either of the other two leaders. And the Executive Officers and the First Sergeants are almost indistinguishable within each climate: the trainees see these two positions as equally lacking in influence. Note, however, the important difference between the C.O.'s and the Field First Sergeants. In the persuasive climate the C.O. is considered to be much more influential than the Field First Sergeant, while the two positions have about the same influence in the other two climates. If trainees tend to identify with leaders who have influenced them most, then identification can most easily take place with the C.O. (especially in the persuasive climate) or with the Field First Sergeant. The other two positions have too little influence.[10]

Table IV-1

AVERAGE INFLUENCE SCORES IN THREE
LEADERSHIP CLIMATES*

| | LEADERSHIP CLIMATES | | |
	Persuasive	Weak	Arbitrary
Commanding Officers	1.46	1.68	1.85
Executive Officers	2.30	2.28	1.98
First Sergeants	2.24	2.25	2.02
Field First Sergeants	1.75	1.63	1.76

*These scores are based on the seven companies that are studied in succeeding chapters, not on the twelve companies used in Table II-1. The differences between the results for the seven companies and those for the twelve companies are negligible in all cases. As before, low scores indicate high influence.

The other requirement for identification was that the leader's behavior satisfy the trainee's ego-needs. Again, there are no questions on the satisfaction of ego-needs in our data, but it seems reasonable that leaders scoring high on the factor of positive leadership should be most likely to satisfy these needs. (Suggestions to this effect are scattered throughout the Lippitt and White account of the Iowa study.) Table IV-2 presents the average scores on this factor for the C.O.'s and the Field First Sergeants, the two positions with enough influence to serve as objects of identification. In this table a high score[11] denotes a leader who can create "a feeling of great confidence" and "a real fighting spirit against the enemy."

Table IV-2

AVERAGE POSITIVE-LEADERSHIP SCORES*

	LEADERSHIP CLIMATES		
	Persuasive	Weak	Arbitrary
Commanding Officers	1.28	.15	-.75
Field First Sergeants	.39	.68	.13

*Unlike the influence scores, these scores are not limited to the range between 1.00 and 3.00. The reason is that these are averages of computed factor estimates, rather than of a single question.

Thus the two requirements for identification are significantly met only in the persuasive climate. The persuasive-climate C.O.'s manifest the right kind of leadership, and they are in a position in which this leadership can influence the trainees. By contrast, the arbitrary-climate leaders have much less influence and much less positive leadership, and the weak climate is again in an intermediate position. To sum up, identification with the company leadership is most likely in the persuasive climate, much less likely in the weak climate, and least likely in the arbitrary climate.

Leadership climate and nonduty behavior

Earlier in this chapter we proposed the hypothesis that the more one channel of tension-reduction is blocked, the greater will be the utilization of alternative channels. Two of the four available channels, leaving the field and griping, are of little use to the trainees. A third alternative is to identify with the company leadership and thereby avoid building up a high level of tension. However, as has just been shown, only the persuasive-climate trainees can easily identify with their leaders; in the arbitrary climate and, to a lesser extent, in the weak climate the characteristics of the leaders discourage identification. Thus this means of avoiding tension is largely blocked for the arbitrary climate and partly so for the weak climate. Only one channel is left: the hypothesis of alternative channels suggests that the arbitrary-climate trainees are most likely to engage in emotionally-satisfying or tension-reducing nonduty activities and that the persuasive-climate trainees are the least likely to do so.

This conclusion would follow even if the levels of tension in the three climates were the same. But the available evidence is that the arbitrary climate also generates the highest levels of tension and the persuasive climate the lowest. These two conditions, higher tension, and less access to alternative outlets, should make for most tension-reducing and tension-avoiding nonduty behavior in the arbitrary climate, less in the weak climate, and least of all in the persuasive climate. The next chapter will examine the extent to which these predictions are supported by the data.

NOTES TO CHAPTER FOUR

1. Barnard distinguishes between "effectiveness," the extent to which the goals of an organization are met, and "efficiency," the extent to which individual desires are achieved. Chester I. Barnard, The Functions of the Executive (Cambridge, Mass.: Harvard University Press, 1948), p. 19.

2. Op. cit., p. 907.

3. Op. cit., p. 599 ff.

4. Arthur P. Noyes, Modern Clinical Psychiatry (3rd ed., Philadelphia: W. B. Saunders Company, 1948), p. 318.

5. Several writers have noted the inadequacy of the simple formula "tension leads to reduction of tension" as a basic principle of motivation. As Kluckhohn and Murray put it, this formula ". . . takes account of only one side of the metabolic cycle." The "positive need systems" such as hunger and sex go through a continual alternation of tension-generation and tension-reduction because ". . . it is not a tensionless state . . . which is generally most satisfying to a healthy organism, but the process of reducing tension. . . " But this more elaborate formula applies only to the positive needs, those which involve approach to an external goal. "The conservative systems that are directed towards riddances (of pain, anxiety, annoyance, etc.), towards withdrawals, avoidances, defenses, and preventions, are adequately covered by the reduction-of-tension formula." Clyde Kluckhohn and Henry A. Murray (eds.), Personality in Nature, Society, and Culture (New York: Alfred A. Knopf, 1949), 15-16. Since most of our analysis deals with these conservative systems, the simpler reduction-of-tension formula should be adequate.

6. Op. cit., p. 602.

7. Fillmore H. Sanford, "Research in military leadership," in Psychology in the World Crisis (Pittsburgh: University of Pittsburgh Press, 1952), p. 64.

8. Gordon W. Allport, "The historical background of modern social psychology," in Lindzey (ed.), Handbook of Social Psychology, op. cit., p. 28.

9. Table II-1.

10. It is also possible that trainees are more influenced by leaders with whom they identify or that these two variables are mutually reinforcing; the analysis would be the same for all three relationships.

11. In the preceding table greater influence was denoted by lower numbers, following the wording of the question in Appendix J. Here, however, the positive-leadership scores are taken from the factor analysis, in which larger numbers indicate a greater degree of positive leadership.

Chapter V

THE EFFECTS OF LEADERSHIP CLIMATE ON BEHAVIOR

The methodological and theoretical analyses of the preceding chapters have paved the way for examining one of the major questions of this study: how do the three leadership climates affect the nonduty behavior of the trainees? After describing the behavior with which this and the following chapters will deal, the first step will be to measure the overall effect of leadership climate on all kinds of behavior; this will be followed by a detailed investigation of four important activities.

A sample of nonduty activities

The behavior questionnaire in Appendix J asked the trainees for information about the time they had spent in twenty-one activities, [1] seventeen of which were selected for analysis. [2] Each trainee was asked how often he

— attended chapel or church (referred to as "chapel" in the tables)

— visited his chaplain [minister, priest, or rabbi] (chaplain)

— went to the movies, USO shows, or sporting events (mass entertainment)

— engaged in a hobby

— "blew his top"

— had a fight

—went to the PX or other restaurant for food after meal times (eating between meals)

—went out drinking

—was really drunk

—saw his wife or girl friend

—had intercourse

—masturbated

—went AWOL for less than twenty-four hours or broke restriction within the company area (short-term AWOL)

—went on sick call

He was also asked how many hours he had spent in

—sports

—bull sessions

—reading

These seventeen activities clearly do not represent the complete spectrum of nonduty behavior. [3] If one tries to reconstruct the actions of a typical trainee after his working day is over, the activities included in this list will account for only a portion of his free time. Not represented are such time-consuming pursuits as listening to the radio or watching television programs, playing cards, walking about the post, resting on one's bed, writing letters, cleaning equipment, and so on.

Furthermore, comparatively few of the seventeen activities are really "time-consuming," in the sense that they could occupy a significant part of the average trainee's nonduty hours day after day. Only five fit this description closely—eating between meals, attending various forms of mass entertainment, reading, participating in sports, and engaging in bull sessions. The others either occur at specified times only (attending chapel) or at infrequent intervals (seeing one's wife or girl), or else they are activities that by their very nature are completed in a few minutes (blowing one's top). Consequently, the task of this chapter is not to account for all of a trainee's nonduty hours, but rather to explain as much as possible of the variations in these selected non-duty activities among the three climates.

Nonduty behavior in the three leadership climates

The overall relationship between leadership and behavior is shown in Table V-1, which is essentially a "profile" of the seventeen activities for each climate. In the first row, for example, 49 per cent of the persuasive-climate trainees went on sick call at least once in an eight-week period, as compared with 58 per cent in the weak climate and 37 per cent in the arbitrary climate. This summary presentation includes only one level of activity for each kind of behavior; no distinction is made between the men who went on sick call only once or twice and those who went more often. (Such distinctions will be made later in this chapter for several important kinds of behavior.)

The different items of behavior in this table are listed according to the apparent effect of leadership climate on them. Going on sick call appears to be most affected by leadership, [4] as indicated by the fact that the maximum difference between any two climates is 21 percentage points (between the weak and arbitrary climates). At the other extreme, whether or not a soldier goes to the movies, the USO shows or spectator sports is independent of leadership; the figures for "mass entertainment" are identical in the three climates.

A great deal of information is summarized in this table—so much that its implications are not immediately obvious. Since an understanding of this table is basic to the rest of this chapter, it warrants close and careful analysis. Perhaps the most important aspect of this table is that the data are presented in the form of proportions or rates, rather than mean frequencies. Thus the table shows that the proportion of

Table V-1

TRAINEE BEHAVIOR IN THREE LEADERSHIP CLIMATES*

ACTIVITY	LEADERSHIP CLIMATES			MAXIMUM INTER-CLIMATE DIFFERENCE
	Persua-sive Per Cent	Weak Per Cent	Arbi-trary Per Cent	Per Cent
Sick call (1 or more times in 8 weeks)**	49	58	37	21
Seeing one's wife or girl (1 or more times in 8 weeks)	67	71	52	19
Short-term AWOL (1 or more times in 16 weeks)	33	47	51	18
Eating between meals (21 or more times in 8 weeks)	74	64	80	16
Hobby (1 or more times in 16 weeks)	23	11	24	13
Drunkenness (1 or more times in 16 weeks)	25	36	34	11
Bull sessions (8 or more hours a week)	29	40	40	11
Chaplain (1 or more times in 16 weeks)	23	20	31	11
Chapel (8 or more times in 16 weeks)	43	38	48	10
Blowing one's top (8 or more times in 16 weeks)	25	30	35	10
Sports (1 or more hours a month)	40	47	48	8
Intercourse (1 or more times in 8 weeks)	49	55	56	7
Drinking (1 or more times in 8 weeks)	62	68	63	6

Table V-1
(Continued)

ACTIVITY	LEADERSHIP CLIMATES			MAXIMUM INTER- CLIMATE DIFFERENCE
	Persua- sive Per Cent	Weak Per Cent	Arbi- trary Per Cent	Per Cent
Fighting (1 or more times in 16 weeks)	24	19	24	5
Reading (4 or more hours a week)	24	26	28	4
Masturbation (1 or more times in 8 weeks)	15	16	18	3
Mass entertainment (8 or more times in 16 weeks)	52	52	52	0

*All data in this table and others of similar construction in this chapter are from HSG tables in Appendix E. Some of the following analyses will consider trainees who never engaged in certain activities during basic training; these data can easily be derived from the "1 or more times" tables in Appendix E by subtracting each percentage from 100 per cent. All percentages in this and the following chapters are based on the "low-discrepancy" trainees, as explained in Appendix B. Six questions (reading, sports, bull sessions, hobby, intercourse and masturbation were not asked in one of the persuasive-climate companies. This probably reduces somewhat the observed effects of leadership climate on these activities.

**The units of time for several activities in this and other tables differ from those in the behavior questionnaire in Appendix J. The reasons for these changes are reported in Appendix B. Since the analyses are based on differences between groups, this change of units does not materially affect the results.

trainees in the persuasive climate who went on sick call one or more times in eight weeks was 49 per cent, instead of reporting that the mean frequency of going on sick call was, say, 0.27 times per week among men in this climate.[5] The variable, "frequency of going on sick call one or more times in eight weeks" has been replaced by an attribute with two classes—"going on sick call one or more times in eight weeks" and "going on sick call less than once in eight weeks."

This common procedure in research is open to criticism. It obscures important differences in behavior, for the men who went only once in eight weeks are counted the same as the "sick-book riders" who went at every opportunity. But, important as these extreme frequencies of behavior are, they are also the most unreliable. [6] Computing the mean frequency of going on sick call in each climate would require taking these extreme responses at face value; the error thus introduced would outweigh the greater information that the mean provides. On the other hand, little or no error results from assuming that the man who reports going twenty times in eight weeks actually went at least once. Greater accuracy, then, is the principal reason for studying proportions rather than means.

Granted that this substitution of proportions for means is advisable, there is a further question: where should the division between the two classes be made? Should one study the proportion of men in each climate who went on sick call one or more times; would it be preferable to raise the "cutting point" to two or more times; or should some other figure be used? The answer is that, for most of the activities considered here, it makes little difference where the cutting point is located since the association between leadership and behavior is relatively unaffected by shifting the cutting point. [7] In the case of chapel attendance, for example, the weak climate retains the lowest rate and the arbitrary climate the highest, regardless of whether one tabulates the proportion who attended once every four weeks, once every other week, or as often as once a week. [8]

This means that the absolute levels of the figures in Table V-1 are unimportant, for they could have been raised or lowered by shifting the cutting point for each activity. What does matter is the pattern of differences between climates (columns), rather than the level of the figures for each activity (row). These differences stand out much more clearly in Table V-2. This table presents exactly the same data as the preceding one, except that the rate for each climate is expressed as a deviation from the overall rate for all trainees, regardless of climate, as shown in the first column. For example, 64 per cent of all trainees saw their

wives or girl friends at least once in eight weeks. Since the rate for the
persuasive climate in Table V-1 is 67 per cent, the corresponding figure
in this table is 3 per cent, indicating a positive deviation of 3 percentage
points above the average. Similarly, the 52 per cent of the arbitrary-
climate trainees who saw their wives or girls are represented here as a
negative deviation, 12 percentage points below the overall average of 64
per cent.

Table V-2

TRAINEE BEHAVIOR IN THREE LEADERSHIP CLIMATES,
EXPRESSED AS DEVIATIONS FROM
THE AVERAGE OF ALL TRAINEES

| | AVERAGE | DEVIATION FROM AVERAGE | | |
| | | Persuasive | Weak | Arbitrary |
	Per Cent	Per Cent	Per Cent	Per Cent
Sick call	48	1	10	-11
Seeing one's wife or girl	64	3	7	-12
Short-term AWOL	42	-9	5	9
Eating between meals	73	1	-9	7
Hobby	21	2	-10	3
Drunkenness	30	-5	6	4
Bull sessions	35	-6	5	5
Chaplain	24	-1	-4	7
Chapel	43	0	-5	5
Blowing one's top	29	-4	1	6
Sports	44	-4	3	4
Intercourse	53	-4	2	3
Drinking	64	-2	4	-1
Fighting	23	1	-4	1
Reading	26	-2	0	2
Masturbation	17	-2	-1	1
Mass entertainment	52	0	0	0

The interclimate differences, which were partially obscured in Table V-1, now stand out in sharp relief. The arbitrary climate has above-average rates in thirteen activities and below-average rates in only three. At the other extreme, the persuasive climate is below the overall average in ten kinds of behavior; and the weak climate is between the other two, with low rates in six activities. Even at first glance, then, the relationship between leadership and behavior appears to agree with that predicted in Chapter IV. But there are two notable exceptions, going on sick call and seeing one's wife or girl. Both activities have their lowest rates in the arbitrary climate, and the interclimate differences for these forms of behavior are the largest in this study. If these "deviant cases" can be explained away, then the hypothesis that the arbitrary climate generates the highest rates of nonduty activity will be even more strongly substantiated than it is in Table V-2.

This is not too difficult. The rates for these activities do not represent the effects of leadership alone. To go on sick call or to see one's wife or girl requires more than the trainee's own decision and action. Unlike the other fifteen activities, these two usually require the prior permission of the company leaders. Except in an emergency, a soldier must have his name entered in the company sick book before he can get medical attention. As we shall show later in this chapter, this is enough to discourage many soldiers from going on sick call for minor ailments. The low rate of sick call in the arbitrary climate may therefore merely reflect the policies of the leaders rather than their indirect effects on the men's choices. Similarly, the low rate of seeing their wives or girl friends among the arbitrary-climate trainees may simply indicate that the leaders are more reluctant to grant passes and not that the trainees are any less eager to spend time with their women. Thus the data for both of these activities serve in large part as direct indicators of the

leaders' behavior, rather than simply as indications of the trainees' reactions to their leaders. [9]

With these two apparent exceptions explained, the consistency of the
other findings in Table V-2 suggests that there is a real difference in
the effects of the three climates on behavior. But there is still one
more problem to consider before these differences can be taken as valid.
As explained in Chapter III, observed differences between leadership
climates may stem from the varying proportions of older, more-educated,
and married trainees in the three climates. In order to say that leadership climate is responsible for the differences shown in Table V-2, the
possible influence of these individual characteristics must be ruled out.
The technique of HSG analysis was developed for this purpose in Chapter III; applied to these data, it yields the results in Table V-3.

The letters in this table summarize the HSG comparisons. They
indicate which of the differences in Table V-2 may properly be attributed
to leadership climate and not to variations in the assignment of different
types of men (older and younger, graduates and nongraduates, single and
married). Consider, for example, the comparison for short-term
AWOL in the third line. The "A, W" in the "high" column and the "P" in
the "low" column summarize two comparisons in Table V-2. The difference between the arbitrary climate (9 percentage points above average) and the persuasive climate (9 percentage points below average) is
confirmed by HSG analysis, as is the difference between the weak climates (5 percentage points above average) and the persuasive climate.
No letters are shown for the three activities at the bottom of the table
because these interclimate differences are smaller than the 5 per cent
minimum established for HSG comparisons in Appendix C.

It is not easy to keep track of the relationships between seventeen
activities and three leadership climates. Let us therefore pause to take
stock of what has been done thus far in this chapter. Table V-1 gave the

Table V-3

TRAINEE BEHAVIOR IN THREE LEADERSHIP CLIMATES:
INTERCLIMATE COMPARISONS CONFIRMED BY HSG ANALYSIS

	Relatively High	Relatively Low
Sick call	W, P	A
Seeing one's wife or girl	W, P	A
Short-term AWOL	A, W	P
Eating between meals	A	W
Hobby	A, P	W
Drunkenness	W, A	P
Bull sessions	A, W	P
Chaplain	A	W, P
Chapel	A	W
Blowing one's top	A	P
Sports	W	P
Intercourse	A	P
Drinking	W	P
Fighting	P, A	W
Reading		
Masturbation		
Mass entertainment		

actual rates for each kind of behavior in the three climates. To focus attention of the differences between climates, the same data were then presented in Table V-2 as deviations from the average for all trainees, regardless of climate. Finally, to determine which of these differences are really the results of leadership, Table V-3 reported the HSG comparisons for each activity. In essence, this table tells the whole story about leadership and behavior; but its very completeness obscures the principal results because of the many cases in which two climates are essentially tied for low or high position. Table V-4 therefore summarizes these comparisons in a form that more clearly reveals the differences between the climates. [10]

Table V-4

SUMMARY OF COMPARISONS IN TABLE V-3

| | LEADERSHIP CLIMATES | | |
	Persuasive	Weak	Arbitrary
Highest	0	2	5
Tied for high	2	3	5
Tied for low	1	1	0
Lowest	7	4	0

The effects of leadership are unmistakable here. Trainees in the arbitrary climate have the highest rates in five activities, and in five others they are essentially tied with one of the other two climates, both tied climates being consistently higher than the third. In none of these twelve activities is the arbitrary climate lower than the other two. The persuasive climate has lowest rates on most activities, and the weak climate is about midway between the persuasive and the arbitrary. This is exactly the order that was predicted in Chapter IV. With more tension to dispose of and fewer alternative outlets, the arbitrary-climate trainees are virtually forced to seek a variety of nonduty activities. Contrariwise, with the least tension caused by their leaders and with the greatest opportunity to work off this tension in the course of their training, the men in the persuasive climate experience the least pressure toward nonduty activities.

With these overall differences in mind, Table V-3 merits another look in order to see the qualitative variations in behavior for the different activities. The main differences to look for are between the persuasive and the weak climates, since the arbitrary climate has high rates on so many activities. The persuasive-climate trainees are less likely to go AWOL for short periods, drink, get drunk, blow their tops, have intercourse, or engage in bull sessions or sports. In general, these are more or less expressive activities involving a rapid release of tension. Thus "persuasive" leadership makes for less participation in these highly emotional and energetic activities. In contrast, the weak climate trainees have low rates of eating between meals, working at a hobby, seeing the chaplain, attending chapel, and fighting. With the sole exception of fighting (for which the interclimate differences are small) all of these are relatively placid and unemotional. Thus the effect of "weak" leadership is to divert the trainees from these calm, easygoing recreations and to direct them toward higher participation in some of the more aggressive or emotionally-tinged activities.

Four important activities

This overall view has not examined each activity in detail, distinguishing, for example, between those men who went on sick call occasionally and those who went more frequently. It is not always necessary to do this, for the relationships between leadership and behavior are, in general, relatively independent of the particular level of activity studied. But this is not true for four significant activities, which are worth a closer examination.

Getting Away from the Company. As any veteran of military service can testify, the first few weeks of basic training are difficult and unpleasant. The ways in which men can escape from the training situation are therefore important. One route of escape, effective but temporary, is to be sick, or at least to report to sick call. Another, more satisfying procedure is to get away from the training camp altogether. But all absences from military surroundings are not equally satisfying. It is therefore instructive to examine a set of three related activities, two of which involve not only the negative gratification of being away from the post, but the positive appeal of being with a woman: seeing one's wife or girl, short-term AWOL, and sexual intercourse.

Another reason for paying attention to these four routes of escape is that two of them—sick call and seeing one's wife or girl—are the only kinds of behavior in which the arbitrary climate has appreciably lower rates than the persuasive and weak climates. As suggested above, the rates of these two activities may be more fruitfully considered as direct indicators of leadership policy than as measures of the trainee's responses to leadership. This detailed analysis will further examine this interpretation.

Going on Sick Call. This is the easiest way to avoid unpleasant duty. A trainee can simply report to his First Sergeant at the appointed time, state his ailment, have his name entered in the company "sick book," and go to the dispensary. Of course, steps are taken to deal with chronic malingerers, but it seems likely that some soldiers confronted with the prospect of a particularly trying day will yield to the temptation of inventing an imaginary ailment or of magnifying a minor one. Recourse to sick call as a means of escaping temporarily from duty may even be unconsciously motivated, as in certain psychosomatic ailments. One might expect, therefore, that the sick-call rates would be highest in the arbitrary climate where the rigors of training are most severe. But, as was found in connection with Tables V-1 to V-3, this is not the case; the arbitrary climate, with the greatest stress, has the lowest proportion of men who ever go on sick call.

As suggested earlier, closer examination of the process of "going on sick call" resolves this anomaly. Except in an emergency a trainee's name must be entered in the company sick book before he can go to the dispensary or hospital. In theory, a soldier has the right to medical attention whenever he wishes, but in practice this right is often conditional. As one trainee wrote on his leadership questionnaire:

> . . . in order to go on sick call we had to pack up all our
> clothes put them in our duffle bag & foot locker and carry
> them over to the supply room first.

To be sure, this has the manifest function of making it easier to store
his equipment should the trainee subsequently be sent to the hospital, but
it also serves the not-too-latent function of discouraging men from going
on sick call for minor ailments.

The low percentage of arbitrary-climate trainees who ever go on
sick call thus probably reflects the informal, but well-established
norms in such companies against reporting oneself sick for anything
but an obviously serious illness. In the persuasive climate, on the other
hand, the leaders are less likely to prevent a trainee from going on sick
call. Even more important is the fact that trainees in these companies
do not have so great a need to escape duty and may very well not want to
go on sick call as much as their comrades in more punitive companies.
The high rates in the weak climate conform to this reasoning; it generates more tension than the persuasive climate, but does not forbid going
on sick call as does the arbitrary climate.

Because going on sick call is the principal "legitimate" method of
avoiding duty, it is important to distinguish between those trainees who
went occasionally—once or twice in an eight-week period—and those who
went more often. One might think that the latter group (the "sick-book
riders") includes a larger proportion of men whose complaints were
consciously or unconsciously motivated—the malingerers and the psychosomatic cases—and that these two groups would be differentially affected
by leadership climate. But Table V-5 disproves this hypothesis. In
both the second and third rows the arbitrary climate has the lowest rate
of reporting to sick call and the weak climate the highest. Leadership
has approximately the same effect on the sick-book riders as on the men
who attend sick call only once or twice.

Table V-5

GOING ON SICK CALL IN THREE LEADERSHIP CLIMATES*

NUMBER OF TIMES IN 8 WEEKS	LEADERSHIP CLIMATES		
	Persuasive Per Cent	Weak Per Cent	Arbitrary Per Cent
None	51	42	63
1-2	34	37	24
3 or more	16	21	12
	101 (277)	100 (170)	99 (168)

*Percentages do not add to 100 because of rounding errors. Interclimate differences of 5 per cent or more are tested by HSG analysis based on the appropriate tables in Appendix E and using the procedure set forth in Appendix C. The HSG comparisons for this table are:

	P-W	P-A	W-A
None	(2-4-0)	(4-2-0)	(12-0-0; 2)
1-2	(3-3-0)	(10-1-1: 2)	
3 or more	(2-2-2)		(9-3-0; 2)

The interpretation of these figures is as follows: Consider the comparison summarized as (4-2-0); this refers to the comparison between the persuasive and arbitrary climates on "never" going on sick call. The greater proportion never going in the arbitrary climate is confirmed in four comparisons, two are essentially tied, and none is in the opposite direction. The fact that this meets the criteria for confirmation in Appendix C is indicated by underscoring. The comparisons between the weak and arbitrary climates are summarized as (12-0-0; 2); this is interpreted in the same way, except that the figure "2" following the semicolon indicates that these comparisons are based on "two-item" HSG's, as explained in Appendix C. The (2-4-0) and (2-2-2) comparisons between the persuasive and weak climates fail to meet the criteria for confirmation.

Sexual Intercourse, Seeing One's Wife or Girl, and Short-Term AWOL. Common sense suggests that these three activities are directly related to each other. For instance, if a trainee is denied a pass, then going AWOL for a few hours is the most obvious way for him to see his wife or girl. But what unaided common sense may not reveal is the way in which the relationships are shaped and modified by different types of leadership.

Consider the finding that the incidence of intercourse—i. e., the proportion of men who had intercourse one or more times during basic training—is greater in the arbitrary and weak climates than in the persuasive climate. This was reported earlier in the chapter and can be seen in the first line of Table V-6 as the higher proportion in the persuasive climate who <u>never</u> had intercourse. One might expect that the higher overall incidence in the arbitrary and weak climates reflects both a greater number of men having intercourse occasionally and a greater number having intercourse frequently. But in Table V-6 the proportion having intercourse only occasionally is the same in all three climates; the higher incidence in the weak and arbitrary climates is accounted for entirely by the men who have intercourse at least four times in eight weeks. [11]

Table V-6

SEXUAL INTERCOURSE IN THREE LEADERSHIP CLIMATES*

NUMBER OF TIMES IN 8 WEEKS	LEADERSHIP CLIMATES		
	Persuasive Per Cent	Weak Per Cent	Arbitrary Per Cent
None	51	45	44
1-3	26	26	26
4 or more	23	29	30
	100	100	100
	(197)	(75)	(162)

*HSG comparisons (See footnote to Table V-5)

	P-W	P-A
None	(6-5-1; 2)	(8-3-1; 2)
4 or more	(7-3-2; 2)	5-6-1; 2

This table suggests another question: is intercourse more frequent in the arbitrary and weak climates merely because these men might have had more opportunity? Were they able to see their sweethearts or wives more often? The answer is that they were not. Although the rate of seeing one's wife or girl in the weak climate is slightly higher than in the persuasive climate (71 and 67 per cent in Table V-1), this difference is hardly enough to account for the higher rate of intercourse in the weak climate. Even more striking, however, is the rate in the arbitrary climate, where only 52 per cent saw their wives or girl friends as often as once in eight weeks. Thus, as compared with the persuasive climate, a relatively high rate of intercourse prevails in the arbitrary climate even though these men have less frequent opportunities.

As with sick call, the low rate of seeing one's wife or girl among arbitrary-climate trainees apparently stems from the fact that the prior permission of the company leadership is usually required. Only by going AWOL can a trainee leave the post without a pass. One manifestation of the capriciousness of the arbitrary leadership is to deny passes when other companies grant them or to enforce the rules so strictly that the men's off-post time is drastically curtailed. As one arbitrary-climate trainee wrote on his questionnaire:

> The C.O. tells of some regulation that he has to go by,
> but other companies don't pay any attention to these reg-
> ulations . . . A bed check Sunday night at eleven and other
> companies have till revelie Monday morning.

It is of course hardly surprising that men who have undergone severe emotional stress seek every possible chance to relax with women. But it is interesting to note that, even though no direct questions were asked about the women with whom the trainees had intercourse, our statistical data suggest that the men in the arbitrary climate made considerably more use of prostitutes or casual "pick-ups." This is most clearly indicated in the following excerpts from Tables V-1 and V-6.

	Persuasive Per Cent	Weak Per Cent	Arbitrary Per Cent
Intercourse (4 or more times in 8 weeks)	23	29	30
Seeing one's wife or girl (1 or more times in 8 weeks)	67	71	52
Short-term AWOL (1 or more times in 16 weeks)	33	47	51

The men in the arbitrary climate were least likely, by a considerable margin, to see their wives or girl friends during basic training. Yet, as compared to the persuasive climate, they were much more likely to absent themselves from the post for a few hours and to have a high rate of intercourse. The comparison with the weak climate shows the same tendency, though not so strongly; with approximately the same rates of intercourse and of short-term AWOL as the weak climate, the arbitrary-climate men still were less able to spend time with "socially-approved" women. It seems reasonable, therefore, to infer that their higher rates of intercourse were made possible through prostitutes or pick-ups.

SUMMARY

Generating the greatest stress on the trainees and providing them with the fewest outlets for their accumulated tensions, the arbitrary climate, as expected, has relatively high levels of nonduty activity. At the other extreme, with relatively little pressure on the trainees and with more alternative channels of tension release, the persuasive climate has low rates in most activities. The weak climate, as foreshadowed by its intermediate place in the leadership analysis, has rates of nonduty activities that lie more or less between those of the other two climates. Not only the general levels of nonduty activity, but also the particular activities emphasized or avoided are affected by leadership climate. Thus the persuasive-climate trainees tend to avoid highly expressive or emotional recreation, while the men in the weak climate shun the more placid ways to spend their off-duty hours. Finally, several ways in which soldiers can escape completely from the training situation were examined in more detail. The repressiveness of the arbitrary climate was shown in the lower rates of going on sick call for two groups of trainees, the men who went only occasionally and those who went so frequently as to be called "sick-book riders." Another apparent effect of the arbitrary climate was a higher level of sexual intercourse, not necessarily with the men's wives or steady girl friends.

The analysis thus far has focused on differences in behavior among the three climates. This does not mean, however, that behavior is uniform within each climate. On the contrary, the various types of trainees react differently to each kind of leadership, so that the differences within climates are even greater than those between climates. The next chapter is therefore complementary to this one; it will examine the effects of age, education, and marital status in predisposing trainees to one or another pattern of nonduty behavior, while holding constant the effects of leadership climate.

NOTES TO CHAPTER FIVE

1. For simplicity we shall frequently omit the qualifying adjective "nonduty," since none of the activities in the behavior questionnaire was directly related to a soldier's formal training.

2. Two of the four omitted questions concerned activities in which too few trainees had engaged to allow a significant analysis: Seeing the Inspector-General and going to the Red Cross for help in getting a pass. The question on number of cigarettes smoked was not meaningfully related to the other forms of behavior. And asking to go on sick call was so highly correlated with actually going on sick call as not to warrant separate analysis.

3. To explore fully the hypotheses of Chapter IV would require a more representative sample of trainees' daily activities. This disparity between theoretical problems and available data is a common difficulty in "secondary analyses."

4. It is important to note that there is virtually no "circular reasoning" in this statement, as there might have been if individual perceptions of leadership had been related to individual behavior. It would then have been difficult to separate the influence of behavior on perceptions of leadership from the influence of perceptions of leadership on behavior. Since the ratings of any one trainee make a negligible contribution to the determination of leadership climate, it is correct to consider only the effect of leadership on behavior.

5. For a reason to be given shortly, this is a fictitious value.

6. See the discussion of Table B-2 in Appendix B.

7. Some exceptions will be considered in the last section of this chapter.

8. Contingency tables with this property—that the direction of the relationship is unaffected by the choice of cutting point—are called isotropic. G. Udny Yule and Maurice G. Kendall, An Introduction to the Theory of Statistics (14th ed. ; New York: Hafner, 1950), 57-59. It is unfortunate that relatively few sociologists are aware of this important concept, since failure to consider whether or not a table is isotropic may lead to reporting as a finding something that is really an artifact of the choice of cutting point. In a non-isotropic table even the apparent direction of the relationship may be meaningless; one cutting point may yield a positive association, while another produces a negative relationship. A similar discussion, though restricted to the treatment of the independent variable, is found in Herbert H. Hyman, Survey Design and Analysis (Glencoe, Ill. : The Free Press, 1955), 184-189.

9. See the further discussion of these two activities in the last section of this chapter.

10. The comparisons in this summary tabulation are based on twelve of the seventeen activities in Table V-3. Sick call and seeing one's wife or girl are not included because they usually require the prior permission of the company leadership; as we have already mentioned, they are in part direct indicators of company leadership policy and therefore less adequate manifestations of the trainees' reactions to leadership. The remaining three activities were not included in Table V-3 because the differences are either zero (mass entertainment) or too small for HSG analysis (reading and

masturbation). Note, however (in Table V-2), that the direction of the difference for reading and masturbation is highest in the arbitrary climate and lowest in the persuasive.

11. The differences between the frequencies in the persuasive and arbitrary climates barely misses being confirmed by HSG analysis, but the direction of the finding is clear.

Chapter VI

THE EFFECTS OF INDIVIDUAL CHARACTERISTICS ON BEHAVIOR

None of the five studies of leadership summarized in Chapter I pays serious attention to the effects of the followers' characteristics on their behavior. The Iowa investigators did try to limit these effects by selecting boys with similar social and psychological characteristics, but they apparently did not consider the possibility that measurable characteristics not controlled in the design of the experiment might have affected the boys' behavior. All of these studies have assumed, in effect, that leadership is the only sociologically significant independent variable affecting the behavior of the followers. Our data make it possible to test this assumption for three characteristics—age, education, and marital status. Each of these will turn out to have important and consistent effects on one or another of the trainees' nonduty activities. Indeed, these effects are often greater than those produced by the leadership climates. This emphasizes the importance of looking at the characteristics of the followers as well as the actions of the leaders.

Another reason for considering the effects of individual characteristics is that they are central to the analysis of Chapter VII on the "indirect" effects of leadership—that is, the ways in which leadership climate affects the association between status and behavior. [1] In evaluating the direct effects, one wants to know, for example, how leadership affects the rate of drunkenness; in analyzing the indirect effects, one looks at the ways in which the association between, say, education and drunkenness varies from one leadership climate to another. This kind of "contextual analysis" uncovers relationships that are often much greater than the leadership-behavior relationships in Chapter V or the status-behavior relationships in this chapter.

Age and behavior

Studies of soldiers in training during World War II have shown many differences in behavior between younger and older men. [2] This suggests that similar associations might be found among our trainees. But the differences between the two situations are perhaps greater than the similarities. Most important, the ages of the trainees cover a much narrower range than did those of their older brothers in World War II: 67 per cent of the trainees were in the three-year range between 20 and 22, and 95 per cent were between 17 and 24. In contrast, the division between younger and older in The American Soldier comes between 24 and 25 years, so that their "younger" age group includes almost all of our distribution. [3] One might expect, therefore, that the effect of age differences would be relatively small in this study because the spread of ages is so narrow.

The relationships between age and several nonduty activities are shown in Table VI-1. The interpretation of this table is similar to those in the preceding chapter: the HSG summary shows the extent to which each difference between younger and older trainees is confirmed in the various homogeneous subgroups; comparisons that meet the standards for confirmation, as set forth in Chapter III and Appendix C[4], are in italics. For example, the figure of (9-2-1; 2) for mass entertainment

indicates that in nine of the possible HSG comparisons the younger trainees attended the movies, USO shows, or sporting events more frequently
than did the older trainees, in two comparisons there is essentially no
difference, and in one comparison the rate is higher among the older
trainees.

Despite the narrow spread of ages, Table VI-1 reveals a moderate
and seemingly consistent relationship between age and several activities.
In six cases the younger men have higher rates; only in sexual intercourse are the older men higher. What stands out in the leisure hours
of the younger trainees is the large amount of boisterous, aggressive
activity—drunkenness, blowing one's top, fighting, and drinking. One
reason for this more active behavior on the part of the younger trainees
is physiological. Kinsey points out that men reach their maximum level
of sexuality between the ages of 16 and 20, [5] apparently because of some
interaction between the endocrine and nervous systems. [6] It seems reasonable to assume that all sorts of internally-created tensions also
reach a maximum at this time, but this is a question for physiology and
psychology, not sociology.

A more sociological (but equally speculative) explanation is that the
older men have learned how to release their tensions in a wider variety
of ways that do not necessarily appear in our list of activities. They
may, for example, sleep or daydream more in their off-duty hours than
do the younger men; or perhaps certain activities afford them greater
release of tension than the same activities do for the younger men.
These older men might find bull sessions more stimulating and thereby
have less need of the more violent activities.

Education and behavior

By and large, the difference between being an 18-year-old trainee
and being a 23-year-old trainee is a difference in degree rather than in

Table VI-1

AGE AND BEHAVIOR*

	17-21 Per Cent	22+ Per Cent	HSG summary
Mass entertainment (8 or more times in 16 weeks)	57	43	(9-2-1; 2)
Drunkenness (1 or more times in 16 weeks)	34	23	(9-1-2; 2)
Blowing one's top (8 or more times in 16 weeks)	33	23	(8-0-4; 2)
Fighting (1 or more times in 16 weeks)	25	17	(7-3-2; 2)
Drinking (1 or more times in 8 weeks)	66	59	(6-4-2; 2)
Eating between meals (21 or more times in 8 weeks)	75	69	(5-6-1; 2)
Intercourse (1 or more times in 8 weeks)	48	61	(6-4-2; 2)

*The activities are listed in the order of decreasing positive difference between younger and older trainees. The data are from the tables in Appendix E.

kind. The older trainee is biologically and psychologically more mature; but, other than being legally an adult, his social statuses and his self-conceptions—the ways in which others see him and in which he sees himself—are not significantly changed by this brief period of time.

More education, however, produces differences that are qualitative as well as quantitative, particularly when high-school graduates are compared with nongraduates, or men who have attended college with those who have not. Men who have passed one of these "points of transition" tend to differ from those who have not—in income, occupation, style of life, attitudes, and many other characteristics of their personality and social position. [7] It is therefore not surprising that education has a pronounced effect on a trainee's behavior. In Table VI-2 there are eight confirmed differences between high-school graduates and nongraduates. [8]

Table VI-2

EDUCATION AND BEHAVIOR

	NOT high-school graduate Per Cent	High-school graduate Per Cent	HSG summary
Chapel attendance (8 or more times in 16 weeks)	33	51	(7-1-0)
Seeing one's wife or girl (1 or more times in 8 weeks)	55	71	(6-1-1)
Sick call (1 or 2 times in 8 weeks)	27	36	(6-1-1)
Short-term AWOL (1 or more times in 16 weeks)	37	46	(5-2-1)
Seeing the chaplain (1 or more times in 16 weeks)	20	27	(4-3-1)
Hobby (1 or more times in 16 weeks)	18	24	(6-4-2; 2)
Sports (1 or more hours per month)	41	47	(6-1-5; 2)
Drinking (1 or more times in 8 weeks)	67	61	(7-3-1; 2)
Sick call (3 or more times in 8 weeks)	21	13	(4-4-0)
Drunkenness (1 or more times in 16 weeks)	35	26	(6-1-1)

The two parts of this table reveal a marked difference in the behavior patterns of the less-educated and the more-educated trainees. The less-educated are more likely to drink, get drunk, and go on sick-call frequently, all activities that are more or less strongly censured, either in American culture as a whole or in the subculture of the Army. On the other hand, the high-school graduates tend to seek calmer and more acceptable diversions; they have higher rates of chapel attendance, seeing their wives or girls, engaging in a hobby, occasional attendance at sick call, and short absences from the post or company area. Even the two activities for which the HSG comparisons fall short of confirmation—seeing the chaplain and sports—also fit into the pattern of non-violet, generally acceptable nonduty behavior among the graduates.

Because educational differences are produced by, and result from, differences in social status, the explanations of these education-behavior relationships are both more familiar and more detailed than those offered for age. Education means more here than intellectual activity and the acquisition of knowledge. For one thing, it is closely related to social class. High-school graduates are more likely than nongraduates to come from middle-class homes and to become members of the middle class themselves when they leave their parental homes. That is, they are likely to come from families with higher incomes, greater prestige and power in the community, and more elaborate styles of life. And they are more likely to be preoccupied with their chances of "upward mobility," or attaining a higher social status than their parents. This often leads to heightened concern with social conformity, for it is typically the middle class that tries to keep up with the Joneses. These and other concomitants of high-school graduation and college attendance are indispensable in explaining the differences in nonduty behavior between the high-school graduates and the nongraduates.[9]

This is not to say, however, that these social-class considerations are the only important factors. In the case of chapel attendance, for example, religion is undoubtedly more important, even though education has more effect on chapel attendance than on any other activity. Given the uniformity of Catholic devotional practices, and the variety of Protestant denominations, it is obviously easier for a Catholic trainee to find a chapel service to his liking than for a devout Protestant member of a small denomination. Race also may play a part here: Negroes may be less willing to attend a predominantly white chapel service if they have been accustomed to a Negro church in civilian life. But even with our limited data, it is possible to gain some further insight into the forces affecting chapel attendance.

By using a more detailed set of educational categories, as in Table VI-3, the relationship between years of schooling and frequent chapel attendance is shown more precisely.

Table VI-3

FREQUENT CHAPEL ATTENDANCE AND EDUCATION

	Some grammar school Per Cent	Some high school Per Cent	High- school Graduates Per Cent	Some college Per Cent
Chapel attendance (8 or more times in 16 weeks)	28	37	52	46
Number of cases	(96)	(177)	(244)	(101)

Up to the point of high-school graduation, the more education a trainee has, the greater the likelihood of his attending chapel frequently. The high-school graduates are almost twice as likely to be devout chapelgoers as are the men who did not attend high school. There is a slight falling-off among the college-educated trainees, but they are still more devout than the men who did not graduate from high school.

Here the relationship between education and middle-class values is suggestive. Among other things, middle-class boys are expected to finish high school and to go to church regularly; thus continued school attendance and frequent churchgoing may be different manifestations of the same set of values. The falling-off in church attendance among the college-educated trainees may be traced to the fact that the transition from high school to college often involves a partial rejection of the values of one's family and community. [10]

The relationship between education and social class also helps to explain why the high-school graduates see their wives or girl friends more often. By and large, the high-school graduates, and particularly those who have gone to college, come from wealthier families than the nongraduates and, if finished with their education, have higher incomes; they can more easily afford to go home on weekends, and their wives and girl friends likewise find it easier to visit them. This reasoning is supported in Table VI-4. When trainees are divided into those whose homes are relatively near Fort Dix (in the middle-Atlantic states) and those who live further away, the relationship between education and seeing one's wife or girl holds in both groups. But the difference caused by education is somewhat greater among the men who are further from home. There is no obvious reason why education in itself should have more effect on the trainees who live outside the middle-Atlantic states. However, the educated men, having more money on the average, are better able to afford these long trips. Among the men whose families live close to Fort Dix, education (and wealth) naturally make less difference.

Sick call and short-term AWOL are important ways of escaping from the rigors of training, even if only temporarily. Education does not affect the incidence of going on sick call; the proportion of men who

Table VI-4

SEEING ONE'S WIFE OR GIRL BY EDUCATION
AND HOME STATE*

| | PROPORTION SEEING WIFE OR GIRL ONE OR MORE TIMES IN EIGHT WEEKS AMONG TRAINEES FROM: | |
	Middle-Atlantic states	Other states
High-school graduates	80%	63%
Non-graduates	72%	49%

*The bases for percentages are: 157 193
                                         74 177

go at least once is virtually the same at all levels of education in Table VI-5. (In fact, it is not affected by age, education, or marital status, although it is significantly related to leadership climate.)[11] But differences appear when the men who go at least once are divided into those who go only occasionally—once or twice in an eight-week period—and those who go more frequently—three or more times in eight weeks (the "sick-book riders"). The more education a trainee has, the less likely is he to go on sick call frequently. Among the college men who attend sick call, more than four times as many go only once or twice as go three or more times (39 and 9 per cent); among the grammar-school educated these two groups are equal (24 per cent). In other words, half of the grammar-school men who go on sick call are "sick-book riders," as compared with only one-fifth of the college men.

Why do so many of the less-educated men "ride the sick book"? They are apparently no more likely to become ill. If they were, fewer of them would report never having gone on sick call, but as the first row of Table VI-5 indicates, this is not the case. One plausible explanation

Table VI-5

GOING ON SICK CALL BY EDUCATION

Number of times in 8 weeks	Some grammar school Per Cent	Some high school Per Cent	High-school Graduates Per Cent	Some college Per Cent
None	52	51	51	52
1 or 2	24	30	34	39
3 or more	24	19	15	9
	100	100	100	100
Number of cases	(102)	(185)	(250)	(101)

is suggested by Stouffer's World War II data. Among a group of privates who had been in the Army less than six months he found that 44 per cent were high school graduates, but among a group of psychoneurotics with the same length of service only 23 per cent had graduated from high school. Psychoneurotic tendencies were therefore considered to be more common among soldiers who had not graduated from high school.[12]

Now sick-book riders are by no means all psychoneurotic, nor is attendance at sick call the only way to manifest neurotic problems. But it seems plausible that there are more neurotics among the men who attend sick call frequently, just as civilian hypochondriacs are especially likely to visit their doctors frequently. Therefore, one hypothesis to account for the scarcity of sick-book riders among the high-school graduates is the lesser incidence of neurotic tendencies among these men. Although this hypothesis cannot be tested with our data, it is possible to gain additional insight into the sick-call rates by contrasting them with the short-term AWOL rates.

As with sick-call, it is enlightening to consider three frequencies

of AWOL and to relate them to four levels of education, as in Table
VI-6. Note the sharp break between the college-educated men and those

Table VI-6
SHORT-TERM AWOL BY EDUCATION

Number of times in 16 weeks	Some grammar school Per Cent	Some high school Per Cent	High-school graduates Per Cent	Some college Per Cent
None	63	63	57	45
1 or 2	22	14	20	18
3 or more	15	23	23	37
	100	100	100	100
Number of cases	(102)	(184)	(246)	(101)

who did not go beyond high school. Trainees who have been to college
are considerably more likely to go AWOL, as shown in the first row of
the table; among those who do go AWOL one or more times, the college-
educated are most likely to be chronic offenders. In the grammar-
school group the one-time or two-time offenders outnumber the men who
went AWOL more frequently (22 and 15 per cent), but this ratio is reversed among the college men (18 and 37 per cent).

A good reason for going AWOL is to see one's wife or girl. This
suggests that the two explanations offered earlier in this chapter to account for the association between education and seeing one's wife or girl
may also apply here. The graduates tend to come from the middle-
Atlantic states; this makes it easier for them to visit and be visited by
their friends and families. And they are presumably also wealthier, so
that they can better afford the trips to and from their homes. Table VI-7

supports this reasoning. The first line shows that the proportion who never went AWOL is higher among the nongraduates when place of residence is held constant, and higher among those from outside the middle-Atlantic states when education is held constant. And the difference between the graduates and nongraduates is slightly greater among the men who live farther away. Once again, it is not education as such that produces this greater difference, but rather the higher income that is usually associated with education.

Table VI-7

SHORT-TERM AWOL BY EDUCATION AND HOME STATE

NUMBER OF TIMES IN 16 WEEKS	MIDDLE-ATLANTIC STATES		ELSEWHERE	
	High-school graduates Per Cent	NOT high-school graduates Per Cent	High-school graduates Per Cent	NOT high-school graduates Per Cent
None	49	53	58	67
1 or 2	19	17	22	16
3 or more	32	30	20	17
	100	100	100	100
Number of cases	(161)	(74)	(178)	(196)

Income is, of course only one correlate of education. It is not difficult to suggest other correlates to help explain the relationship between education and short-term AWOL; for example, high-school graduates are presumably more sophisticated and may therefore be less intimidated by threats of punishment for going AWOL. But neither this hypothesis nor any other based on the assumed correlates of education can be tested with our limited data. There is, however, one criterion for choosing among the many hypotheses in this area: other things being equal, a hypothesis that accounts for several findings is more valuable than one that explains only a single finding. It will be useful therefore to consider an additional hypothesis that helps to explain both the positive association between education and short-term AWOL and the negative association between education and riding the sick book.

Few areas of social behavior have been so thoroughly explored as the relations between social class on the one hand and values, self-conceptions, and aspirations on the other. Sociologists and social psychologists have repeatedly documented the concern of American middle-class men with "getting ahead," both economically and so - cially. [13] This concern also exists among the lower-class man, but not nearly to the same extent. [14] Closely related to this desire to move up the social ladder is the middle-class preoccupation with how other people, particularly members of the middle and upper classes, evaluate them. In "keeping up with the Joneses" the Smiths usually manage to inform the Joneses of their progress.

These two characteristics of middle-class men help to explain why the more-educated trainees have such different sick-call and AWOL behavior. The more education a trainee has, the greater presumably is his desire to get ahead in the Army, to become a noncom or even an officer. This was certainly the case in World War II, as Suchman found: ". . . the proportion wanting to be officers was highest among college men and diminished steadily as one went down the educational ladder."[15] These aspirations are, of course, realistic in proportion to the trainee's education. High-school graduates are far more likely to become officers or noncoms. [16]

An upwardly-mobile trainee keeps on the good side of the cadre, since his chances of being recommended for further training or for retention in the cadre at the end of basic training depend on how key

officers and noncoms appraise him. The label of "gold brick" would be
fatal, and there is no surer way to earn this status than to ride the sick
book. Furthermore, in proportion as the middle-class trainee is "other-
directed"—i. e., conforms to what he thinks are the expectations of
others—he will avoid behavior contrary to the norms of his peers and
superiors.

The taboo against "gold-bricking" is perhaps stronger among trainees than among veteran soldiers. For one thing, in seeking to gain acceptance as "soldiers," the trainees may overconform to the expectations of the cadre. [17] If "real soldiers" condemn gold-bricking, then
the upwardly-mobile trainee may be even more vehement in his dislike
of the sick-book riders. Aspirations aside, there is a rational basis
for this dislike. The man on sick call not only escapes training; he also
frequently avoids such duties as picking up cigarette butts in the company area, so that the burden falls more heavily on his conforming
comrades. By going on sick call frequently, a trainee thus invites the
displeasure of both the cadre and his fellow trainees. Concerned with
advancement and the regard of his comrades, the more-educated
trainees tend to go on sick call only when they are manifestly ill; they
do not ride the sick-book.

Short-term AWOL and breaking restriction, however, are another
matter. Since these activities are carried on after duty hours, they do
not automatically come to the attention of the cadre. In fact, most of the
short-term AWOL reported in the questionnaire apparently went unde-
tected and therefore unpunished. Furthermore, the man who goes AWOL
or leaves the company area after duty hours is not thereby adding to the
duties of his comrades. On both counts, then, short-term AWOL differs from sick call: it is not detected by the cadre, and it is not censured by the trainees. [18] The combination of money, values, and aspirations thus helps to account for the positive association between education

and short-term AWOL and the negative association between education and riding the sick-book.

A similar line of reasoning may explain, at least in part, why drinking and drunkenness, are more common among the nongraduates than among the graduates. American middle-class families place heavy emphasis on behavior that has been called "deferral of gratification." The high-school graduates, to some extent, and the men who went on to college, to a greater extent, have learned to postpone their gratifications, to control their impulses. This is vividly demonstrated in Kinsey's data on education and sexual outlets; the college-educated man and even the boy who will go to college (and is therefore likely to come from a middle-class family or to aspire to be in the middle class) have higher rates of masturbation and lower rates of premarital intercourse than their less-educated companions.[19] They have learned to practice "self-control" so that they do not get into trouble and possibly jeopardize their preparation for white-collar careers by a too-early marriage.[20] Although we do not have comparable data on the psychological functions of drinking and drunkenness, it is reasonable to assume that this emphasis on "correct" behavior also lowers the rates of these activities among the high-school graduates, as compared with the nongraduates.

*   *   *

This section has gone into considerable detail about ten activities in which the high school graduates and the nongraduates differ consistently. Underlying most of these ten differences is something that might be termed "respectability." With the possible exception of short-term AWOL, all the forms of behavior engaged in more often by the high-school graduates are favorably evaluated in American culture. On the

other hand, the three activities that are more common among the nongraduates are condemned, either by a substantial portion of American
society or in the narrower subculture of the Army. [21]

Marital status and behavior

Being drafted into the Army hits the married man[22] harder than
anyone else. The single, high-school graduate and the single, older
trainee may think they are making greater sacrifices than their less-
educated and younger friends, but their deprivations are, in general,
not comparable to that of the married man taken from his wife. This
was certainly the case during World War II; Stouffer and his colleagues
found that the married men were more tense and frustrated than their
single comrades. [23] One would therefore expect marital status to be
associated with more kinds of nonduty behavior than either age or education. Table VI-8 shows that this is true; eleven activities have confirmed differences between single and married trainees, as compared
with eight confirmed differences for education and five for age.

One might also expect that the married men, because of their pre-
sumed greater frustration, would have higher rates in these activities
by way of compensation. But this is not the case; they do see their
wives more often than the single men see their girl friends, and they do
have higher rates of sexual intercourse. But that is all: in every other
activity in this table the single trainees have higher rates. Nor are
these simply a random collection of nonduty activities; they can be
grouped into two general patterns. On the one hand, there are activities
that involve a more or less violent release of tension, often with some
aggressive connotation—drinking, drunkenness, fighting, and blowing
one's top. [24] On the other hand, the single men are also more likely to
engage in unemotional or even passive leisure-time pursuits—attending

Table VI-8

MARITAL STATUS AND BEHAVIOR

	Single Per Cent	Married Per Cent	HSG Summary Per Cent
Mass entertainment (8 or more times in 16 weeks)	57	42	(9-2-1; 2)
Masturbation (1 or more times in 8 weeks)	22	8	(9-1-0; 2)
Drinking (1 or more times in 8 weeks)	68	55	(9-1-2; 2)
Reading (4 or more hours a week)	30	19	(11-1-0; 2)
Fighting (1 or more times in 16 weeks)	26	16	(8-3-1; 2)
Blowing one's top (8 or more times in 16 weeks)	32	23	(8-3-1; 2)
Drunkenness (1 or more times in 16 weeks)	33	25	(6-4-2; 2)
Hobby (1 or more times in 16 weeks)	24	17	(6-2-2; 2)
Sports (1 or more hours a month)	46	40	(9-2-1; 2)
Seeing one's wife or girl (1 or more times in 8 weeks)	62	67	(8-2-2; 2)
Intercourse (1 or more times in 8 weeks) (4 or more times in 8 weeks)	43 15	72 48	(11-1-0; 2) (10-2-0; 2)

the movies, USO shows, or sporting events; engaging in a hobby; and
reading.

It seems only common sense to assume that the married men see
their wives much more frequently than the single men see their girl

friends. After all, the marital relationship is relatively permanent, while girl friends may come and go. But the data in Table VI-8 belie this assumption too. The single men are nearly as likely to see their sweethearts as the married men to see their wives. The explanation of this result may lie in the ambiguity of the word "girl" in the questionnaire. For some men a "girl" is almost any female with whom they spend time; for others "girl" may mean "fiancee."

Fortunately, the behavior questionnaire asked the single men to state whether they were "going steady," so that the casual acquaintances can be separated from the permanent attachments. Insofar as this "approved" feminine companionship is concerned, the men with steady girl friends are virtually indistinguishable from the married men; the proportions with at least one such meeting during basic training are 68 and 67 per cent, respectively. [25] Among the single men not going steady, the proportion is somewhat lower (59 per cent).

It is hardly surprising that the single men have a higher rate of masturbation (22 per cent), almost three times that of the married men (8 per cent). What is surprising is the low level of the single men, as compared with Kinsey's data, which show a median frequency of more than once in two weeks and an incidence of more than 80 per cent in the age groups covered by this study. [26] The low rate for the single trainees may be a true reflection of the facts. Because of the strenuous physical regimen and the lack of privacy, the true rate of masturbation may be lower than for comparable groups of men in non-military settings. [27] Second, the conditions under which the questionnaires were administered (the men were seated so close together that they could often read each other's responses) probably led to the masturbation data being distorted on the low side and the intercourse data on the high side. In both cases, however, the consistency of the differences between the various subgroups is reassuring.

To sum up, despite their presumably greater deprivations, as compared to the single trainees, the married trainees are less active in
many forms of leisure-time behavior, notably four generally aggressive,
emotion-laden activities and an almost diametrically-opposed set of
placid recreations. Unlike the problem of accounting for the age and
education differences, where in each case one single explanation stood
out—physiological factors for age, and social differences for education—
no one explanation seems to account for these differences between single
and married trainees. One possibility mentioned earlier in this chapter
is that the generally lower rates of the married trainees on the activities in Table VI-8 are balanced by higher rates on other activities that
are not included in this study—sleeping, writing letters, resting, or
walking about the post, for example. Another possibility is that the low
rates of activity among the married men and the fact of their relatively
early marriage may both stem from some common psychological pre-
disposition. Or it may be that intercourse, infrequent though it is, provides sufficient outlet for the accumulated tensions of the married men.
None of these three explanations is very convincing, nor can we test any
of them with our data. All that can be said now is that the differences
between single and married trainees are consistent and substantial; further study is obviously needed to identify the sources of these differences.

Combinations of characteristics

The preceding sections of this chapter have treated the characteristics of the trainees one at a time, using HSG analysis to remove the effects of leadership climate and the other two characteristics. This focus
on a single independent variable is desirable, both for theoretical re-
finement and for clarity of exposition, but it involves more abstraction

from reality than is necessary. A trainee is not merely younger or older; he is also either a high-school graduate or a nongraduate and either married or single. And, of course, he simultaneously has many more attributes and statuses not considered in this study.

To move even a little distance from the abstraction of a single status to the reality of whole persons, it is therefore necessary to see how <u>combinations of characteristics</u> are related to behavior.[28] Actually, the size of our sample makes this analysis possible only for a few activities, but even this limited treatment will illuminate the relationship of individual characteristics to behavior. For example, the incidence of drunkenness is related independently to age and to education, the younger trainees being more likely to get drunk than the older, and the men who did not graduate from high school more likely than the graduates. This raises the question: what is the incidence of drunkenness in trainees who are both younger and less educated, younger and more educated, and so on?

With the separate results for age and education in mind, one might expect the highest incidence among the younger, less-educated trainees and the lowest incidence among the "opposite" group—the older, more-educated. Table VI-9 shows the joint effects of these two variables more precisely. Instead of an even progression from the younger, less-educated to the older, more-educated, the high rates of drunkenness are concentrated in the group of younger nongraduates. In other words, the chances of a trainee's getting drunk at least once during basic training are relatively low unless he has both of these characteristics.

Similar results are found for the combination of age and marital status in Table VI-10. Mass entertainment, such as movies or USO shows, is popular among all but one group of trainees—the older, married men. On the other hand, fights occur with noticeably greater frequency among the younger, single men than among the other three groups.

Table VI-9

DRUNKENNESS BY AGE AND EDUCATION

	17-21		22+	
	NOT High-school Graduates Per Cent	High-school Graduates Per Cent	NOT High-school Graduates Per Cent	High-school Graduates Per Cent
Drunkenness (1 or more times in 16 weeks)	41	27	23	24

Table VI-10

MASS ENTERTAINMENT AND FIGHTING BY AGE
AND MARITAL STATUS

	17-21		22+	
	Single Per Cent	Married Per Cent	Single Per Cent	Married Per Cent
Mass entertainment (8 or more times in 16 weeks)	58	50	53	38
Fighting (1 or more times in 16 weeks)	25	15	19	16

Finally, the combination of education and marital status is related
only to the incidence of drinking and of seeing one's wife or girl. Again,
one of the four groups—the single men who did not graduate from high
school—has a particularly high rate of drinking, the single high-school
graduates have an intermediate rate, and the married men, regardless
of their education, have the lowest rate of all. In other words, education makes a difference in the drinking behavior of the single men, who
as a group drink more than the married men, but it does not apprec-

iably affect the incidence of drinking among the married men.

Table VI-11

DRINKING AND SEEING ONE'S WIFE OR GIRL
BY EDUCATION AND MARITAL STATUS

	NOT High-School Graduate		High-School Graduate	
	Single Per Cent	Married Per Cent	Single Per Cent	Married Per Cent
Drinking (1 or more times in 8 weeks)	75	53	64	56
Seeing one's wife or girl (1 or more times in 8 weeks)	53	60	69	73

The only activity that displays an even progression between opposed pairs of statuses is seeing one's wife or girl. The less-educated, single trainees have the lowest rates and the more-educated, married men the highest, with the other two groups evenly spaced between. This suggests that the frequency of feminine companionship is independently affected by education and marital status, in line with the earlier analyses in this chapter.

Although these three tables cover only a few of the activities, they support an important generalization implicit in the preceding sections. It was previously shown that several rather boisterous activities—drinking, drunkenness, blowing one's top, and fighting are more common among the younger trainees than among the older, among the less-educated than among the more-educated, and among the single than among the married. The simultaneous consideration of pairs of these variables suggests that three of these aggressive forms of behavior—drinking, drunkenness, and fighting—are particularly frequent in one group of trainees, the younger, less-educated, single men.[29] This result could not have been foreseen from the more restricted analysis of the preceding sections.

Both this and the preceding chapter have been largely devoted to the relationship between behavior and one of several variables—leadership climate, age, education, and marital status. In each analysis the influence of the other three variables were held constant. Only in the last section of this chapter, where combinations of two individual characteristics were studied, was there more than one independent variable at a time. But just as a trainee cannot be adequately characterized by his age alone, so it is an abstraction from reality to try to specify the effects of leadership climate without taking into account the kinds of men exposed to each climate. Having examined carefully the separate effects of leadership and of the individual characteristics, the next step is to study the joint effects of these two types of variables on the behavior of the trainees.

NOTES TO CHAPTER SIX

1. See the discussion of Relationship 5 in Figure I-1.

2. Stouffer et al., The American Soldier: Adjustment to Army Life, op. cit., ch. IV.

3. The age distributions of the trainees in each leadership climate are tabulated in Appendix D.

4. For simplicity the tables in this chapter include only those activities for which there is at least a difference of 5 percentage points.

5. Alfred C. Kinsey et al., Sexual Behavior in the Human Male (Philadelphia: W. B. Saunders Company, 1948), p. 219.

6. Alfred C. Kinsey et al., Sexual Behavior in the Human Female (Philadelphia: W. B. Saunders Company, 1953), 759-761.

7. An extensive discussion of some of the effects of a college education is contained in Ernest Havemann and Patricia Salter West, They Went to College (New York: Harcourt, Brace and Co., 1952).

8. The educational distributions in each leadership climate and in the total sample are presented in Appendix D. Because of the limited size of our sample, it is not possible to deal with more than two levels of education while carrying through an HSG analysis. Where appropriate, however, as in some parts of this chapter and the next, the effect of education will be considered on four levels instead of two.

9. For accounts of social-class differences in behavior, see Kurt B. Mayer, Class and Society; Doubleday Short Studies in Sociology (Garden City, N. Y.: Doubleday and Company, Inc., 1955) and Reinhard Bendix and Seymour Martin Lipset (eds.), Class, Status and Power (Glencoe, Ill.: The Free Press, 1953), Part III.

10. Some social-psychological mechanisms underlying such changes of values are analyzed in Theodore M. Newcomb, Social Psychology (New York: Dryden Press, 1950), chs. 6, 7.

11. See Appendix Table E-17a.

12. Strictly speaking, Stouffer's data do not demonstrate that relative lack of education causes more psychoneurotic tendencies nor that psychoneurotic tendencies keep men from getting more education. Both phenomena may be caused by a third factor— e. g., certain kinds of home environment. Stouffer et al., op. cit., p. 116.

13. See Harold W. Pfautz, "The current literature on social stratification: critique and bibliography," American Journal of Sociology, LVIII, 1953, 391-418.

14. Mayer, op. cit., 47-48.

15. Stouffer et al., op. cit., p. 245.

16. Ibid., 245-249.

17. See the discussion by M. Brewster Smith of the replacement soldier in a veteran division. Much of his behavior apparently came from his desire for acceptance by the combat veterans. Toward this end the replacement rapidly accepted the norms of the prestigeful veteran soldiers. Samuel A. Stouffer et al., The American Soldier, Vol. II, Combat and its Aftermath (Princeton: Princeton University Press, 1949), ch. 5.

18. The trainee who goes AWOL for a few hours may even be admired as a man who "can get away with it." Thumbing one's nose at regulations that are not obviously designed to protect life or property is an American folkway; witness the widespread violation of parking laws, even when they are enforced.

19. Kinsey, et al., Sexual Behavior in the Human Male, op. cit., 339-343, 347-351.

20. Eli Ginzberg, "Sex and class behavior," in Donald Porter Geddes and Enid Curie, About the Kinsey Report (New York: The New American Library of World Literature, Inc., 1948).

21. This reliance on the correlates of high-school education points up one of the shortcomings of the study, the necessity for making conjectures about the norms, attitudes, and aspirations of the trainees. Direct questions on these topics would have been extremely valuable.

22. The distribution of marital status is tabulated in Appendix D. Appendix F contains a summary table relating all seventeen forms of behavior studied in Chapters V-VII to four "values" of marital status: "single," "single, going steady," "married, no children," "married, one or more children." In general, the single men who are going steady have rates that lie between the other single men and the married men without children, but closer to the single men. N.B.: The data on married men with children are included merely for incidental interest, since the percentages are based on only twenty-two cases.

23. Stouffer, et al., The American Soldier, Vol. I, Adjustment During Army Life, op. cit., p. 109.

24. The difference in drunkenness narrowly misses being confirmed by HSG analysis.

25. See Appendix F.

26. Kinsey et al., Sexual Behavior in the Human Male, op. cit., 270-272, 693ff.

27. See the analysis of changes in masturbation from civilian life in Chapter VIII.

28. We shall present only these combinations where the separate effect of each variable has been verified by HSG analysis. There are only seven activities that are related to any two of the individual characteristics.

29. Because of the limited number of cases in this study, it is not possible to deal directly with combinations of three variables.

Chapter VII

THE JOINT EFFECTS OF LEADERSHIP AND THE CHARACTERISTICS OF THE FOLLOWERS

Techniques of research are often neglected by sociologists who see themselves as primarily concerned with the advancement of theory. This is unfortunate, for, as Merton has pointed out, new techniques of gathering or analyzing data may lead to the modification of existing theory and to new areas of theoretic interest.[1] This chapter is a small case in point. Substantively, it combines the material of the two preceding chapters: it seeks to discover how the effects of age, education, and marital status on behavior vary from one leadership climate to another and how the effects of leadership depend on the characteristics of the trainees. Formally, these "contextual analyses" are carried out by means of two analytical techniques that are not so much new ideas as new adaptations of existing approaches.[2] The application of these techniques to our data will reveal hitherto neglected aspects of the relationships between leadership and individual behavior and will greatly increase the degree to which this behavior can be explained.

One kind of contextual analysis can be found in Durkheim's Suicide.[3] In seeking to determine why suicide is less frequent among Catholics than among Protestants, Durkheim asked whether this might not result from the Catholics being in a minority in many of the countries that he studied. He thus was led to consider countries and provinces where the Catholics were a minority and those where they were the majority; in each of these contexts he compared the suicide rates of the two religions.

A different use of group contexts is presented in The American Soldier. In comparing soldiers of the same military rank and civilian education, it was found that men in the Air Corps were much less likely to express satisfaction with the promotion opportunities available to them than were men of the same rank in the Military Police. The important difference between these two group contexts is that the Air Corps had the highest rate of promotion in the Army and the Military Police one of the lowest. [4]

These two uses of group contexts are obviously dissimilar. Durkheim contrasts two different statuses (Catholic and Protestant) within each group context. In The American Soldier the same status is examined in varied contexts. But the precise nature of the difference is not altogether clear in these examples. Since most of this chapter is devoted to these contextual analyses, it will be useful to set forth as simply as possible their logical structure and the indices that will be used.

Chart VII-1 locates schematically the two "marginal"[5] types of analysis that have been carried out in the preceding chapters and the two "contextual" comparisons that will be considered in this chapter. For simplicity, this chart contains only one pair of opposed statuses, older and younger trainees, and one pair of leadership contexts, the persuasive and arbitrary climates. At the bottom the letter "L" denotes the marginal comparison between total leadership climates. At the right the letter "S" similarly indicates the marginal comparison between total status groups. These are, of course, the comparisons in the analyses of Chapters V and VI, respectively.

What is new in this chart are the contextual comparisons represented by the letters with subscripts—L_y and L_o, S_p and S_a. The two

118

Chart VII-1

TYPES OF GROUP COMPARISONS*

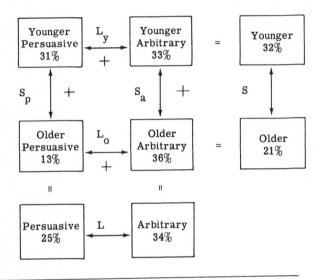

* ———→ connects compared groups. See text for explanation of symbols. The illustrative numbers are the proportions drunk one or more times in sixteen weeks. They differ slightly from the data of Chapter VI and Appendix Table E-11 because the weak climate has been omitted to simplify the illustration.

S-comparisons measure the differences in behavior between <u>opposed statuses within each group context.</u> The S_p-comparison shows that age makes a considerable difference in the persuasive climate: 31 per cent of the younger persuasive-climate trainees were drunk at least once, as compared with only 13 per cent of the older trainees in the same climate. But in the arbitrary climate this difference is much less and is actually reversed in direction: the older, arbitrary-climate men are slightly more likely to get drunk than their younger comrades, 36 to 33 per cent (the S_a-comparison). This examination of the same status-behavior association in different contexts thus adds to our knowledge of the effects of differences in leadership climates: <u>as compared with the persuasive climate, the arbitrary climate sharply reduces the effect of age on drunkenness</u>. This is similar to what Durkheim had in mind when he studied the difference between Protestant and Catholic suicide rates in countries where the Catholics were the majority and in countries where they were in a minority. [6]

The two L-comparisons bring together trainees of the <u>same status in different leadership contexts</u>; this shows how the effects of the several leadership climates are felt by each type of trainee. Thus in the L_y-comparison the younger trainees are affected in virtually identical fashion by the persuasive and arbitrary climates; in the persuasive climate 31 per cent of the younger trainees were drunk at least once, as compared with 33 per cent in the arbitrary climate. On the other hand, the L_o-comparison reveals a marked difference in the reactions of the older trainees to the two climates: the older trainees in the arbitrary climate are nearly three times as likely to get drunk as the older, persuasive-climate men (36 and 13 per cent). Comparing the reactions of the same types of men to different leadership climates provides additional insight into the ways in which such individual characteristics predispose trainees to various patterns of nonduty behavior. Stouffer's analysis of satisfaction with promotion among college-educated men in the Air Force and the Military Police is logically the same; his contextual comparisons reveal how the "same" types of soldiers react to different group contexts. [7]

The differential impact of leadership

This section examines the S-comparisons just described: which leadership climates increase the differences in behavior between groups of trainees, such as the younger and the older, and which tend to reduce these differences? For example, in Chapter VI it developed that the married trainees had lower rates than the single on many activities. But this was an "average" relation; Chapter VI did not raise the question whether this relation holds equally in the three climates or whether it might be stronger in one and weaker in another. As this section will show, however, these indirect effects of leadership climate are at least as important as the direct effects of Chapter V.

As in the preceding chapters, the data come from the detailed tables in Appendix E. Thus the effect of leadership context in modifying the relationships between age and blowing one's top appears in the following excerpt from Appendix Table E-7:

	Persuasive Per Cent	Weak Per Cent	Arbitrary Per Cent
17-21	33	34	31
22	13	20	43

What is important here is not the general level of these figures, but rather the differences between younger and older trainees. As in Chapter VI, it is simpler to look only at these differences, obtained by subtracting the second row above from the first:

	DIFFERENCES BETWEEN YOUNGER AND OLDER		
	Persuasive Per Cent	Weak Per Cent	Arbitrary Per Cent
Blowing one's top	20	14	-12

In the persuasive climate the younger trainees are 20 percentage points more likely than the older to blow their tops frequently during basic training; the weak-climate difference is 14 percentage points; and in the arbitrary climate the younger are 12 percentage points less likely to get drunk, as indicated by the negative sign. All three tables in this section will follow this convention.

Before turning to the contextual analyses, there is one more methodological problem to consider—in fact, the same problem that was explored in Chapter III: to demonstrate that the differences in the age-behavior relationships apparently resulting from variations in leadership do not actually stem from the different proportions of single and married men or of high-school graduates and non-graduates. The solution is essentially the same, a modified version of HSG analysis.[8] In fact, to simplify an otherwise complicated presentation, the tables in this section and the next include only those results that are confirmed by this modified HSG analysis. To have included all the small differences and the unconfirmed larger differences would have obscured the main findings without adding much information.[9]

Turning to the contextual analysis of the associations between age and behavior, Table VII-1 presents the differences in rates between younger and older trainees in the three climates. As reported for the overall comparison of younger and older trainees in Chapter VI, the younger men are in general more active within each climate. In only five of the eighteen differences in this table do the older trainees have higher rates (indicated by negative signs).

What could not have been foreseen, however, from the overall analysis are the different ways in which this greater activity is expressed in each climate. In the persuasive climate the younger trainees lean toward aggressive, emotionally tinged leisure-time behavior—blowing their tops, drunkenness, and fighting. In the arbitrary climate, however, the younger trainees have high rates of relatively passive or at least nonaggressive activities—attending various forms of mass

Table VII-1

DIFFERENTIAL EFFECTS OF AGE IN THREE
LEADERSHIP CLIMATES*

	PERCENTAGE-POINT DIFFERENCE BETWEEN YOUNGER AND OLDER TRAINEES (YOUNGER-OLDER)**		
	Persuasive	Weak	Arbitrary
Mass entertainment		25	15
Blowing one's top	20	14	-12
Drunkenness	18	8	
Intercourse		-14	
Eating between meals		13	
Sports	-5	-8	12
Chaplain	-7		11
Fighting	11		
Hobby			10
Chapel			8
Bull sessions	7		

*Except as noted, in all tables in this chapter the units in which the activities are recorded
are the same as those in Table V-1.

**Younger trainees are ages 17 to 21; older trainees are 22 or more.

entertainment, taking part in sports, seeing the chaplain, going to chapel, and engaging in a hobby; only in blowing their tops do the older, arbitrary climate men have a higher rate than the younger in an "emotional"
activity. Between these two opposed climates the weak climate displays
a mixed pattern; the higher rates of the younger men, as compared to
the older, are manifested in both boisterous and peaceful recreations.

These differences in leisure-time preference among the younger
trainees help to explain why so few activities were found to be correlated
with age in Chapter VI. The effect of a large difference between older
and younger trainees in one climate is reduced when it is combined with
small differences in the other two climates or is cancelled by equally

large differences in the opposite direction. For example, in sports there is only a 1 per cent overall difference between the younger and older men, 45 per cent of the younger and 44 per cent of the older taking part one or more hours a month.[10] Table VII-1 makes clear how this happens: the high rate for the younger trainees in the arbitrary climate is balanced by moderately lower rates for the younger trainees in the weak and persuasive climates.[11]

These "indirect" effects of leadership are even more pronounced when the relation between education and behavior is studied in each climate, as in Table VII-2.

Table VII-2

DIFFERENTIAL EFFECTS OF EDUCATION IN
THREE LEADERSHIP CLIMATES

| | PERCENTAGE-POINT DIFFERENCE BETWEEN NONGRADUATES AND GRADUATES (NONGRADUATES-GRADUATES)* | | |
	Persuasive	Weak	Arbitrary
Seeing one's wife or girl	-23		-26
Chapel	-18	-25	
Sports	-12	-16	
Seeing the chaplain			-16
Short-term AWOL	-15		-9
Drunkenness	8	15	8
Drinking			14
Masturbation		-12	
Sick call**	9	10	
Hobby	-9		
Fighting			8
Blowing one's top			6

*"Graduates" means having graduated from high school.

**The data for sick call refer to those men who went three or more times in eight weeks. See the analysis of the "sick-book riders" in the section on education in Chapter VI.

Again, the important difference is not in the overall levels of activity, for the graduates have higher rates in eight comparisons in this table, and the nongraduates in ten. Rather, the point of this table is the difference in the pattern of activities from one climate to another.

In the persuasive climate the graduates are more likely to compensate for the rigors of training by higher rates of seeing their women, going to chapel, engaging in active sports, or spending time at a hobby. The effect of the weak climate on the education-behavior relationship is not particularly marked. The high-school graduates have higher rates on two activities and lower rates on three others, with no clear pattern emerging. Worthy of note, however, is the markedly higher incidence of chapel attendance among the more-educated men in this climate.

It is in the arbitrary climate that the patterns of behavior are most striking. Under the stress of harsh and capricious leadership, the less-educated and the more-educated trainees react in highly divergent ways. The men who have not graduated from high school move toward the cluster of aggressive activities that has been found before—drinking, drunkenness, fighting, and blowing their tops. The more-educated men seek out three activities that are markedly nonaggressive; they have higher rates of visiting with their wives or girl friends, seeing the chaplain, and short-term AWOL. Thus the arbitrary leadership climate, which apparently produces the greatest stress on the trainees, also most sharply differentiates the behavior of the more- and less-educated men.

An important instance of this differentiation in the arbitrary climate is the much lower frequency of seeing the chaplain on the part of the nongraduates, whose rate is 16 percentage points below that of the graduates. Note, however, that education does not significantly affect chapel attendance in this climate; the graduates are only slightly more likely to attend chapel frequently than are the nongraduates, 50 and 45 per cent, and this difference is not confirmed by HSG analysis. [12] In the other two climates the situation is reversed: the high-school graduates in the persuasive and weak climates have much higher frequencies of chapel attendance than do the nongraduates, but they are no more likely to visit the chaplains.

On a common-sense basis, it might seem that going to chapel and seeing the chaplain would have the same general significance—i. e., the more religious trainees would tend to do both and the less religious neither. But the marked differences between these two activities in Table VII-2 suggest that seeing the chaplain does not necessarily indicate a religious interest; it may simply represent a need for reassurance in a trying situation. Visiting the chaplain is, in part at least, a form of compensation for the deprivations of basic training without actually escaping from them. The chaplain serves as an institutionalized channel of complaint. Every soldier has the right to see the chaplain as often as he wishes without obtaining anyone's permission.

Is it then correct to imply that the religious function of the chaplain, as a representative of the trainee's religious communion, is subordinate to his function of reassurance and social support? Thus far, the only evidence for this assertion is the shifting pattern of relationships between education, chapel attendance, and seeing the chaplain in the three climates. A more compelling reason is found in the overall relationship between attending chapel and seeing the chaplain. If both activities are measures of religious piety, then both should vary together in the entire sample. But the correlation between these two activities is almost zero, 0.05. [13] Whether or not a trainee sees his chaplain during basic training is virtually independent of how often he goes to chapel. This evidence strongly supports the inference that the chaplain's religious functions are subordinate to his psychological functions. [14]

Despite Stouffer's World War II finding that the married men

suffered greater emotional deprivations than the single men, the analysis of Chapter VI showed that in this study the single men actually
have higher rates on almost all nonduty activities. The more detailed
contextual analysis in Table VII-3 confirms this overall conclusion.
Of the twenty-eight comparisons, only eight indicate higher rates among
the married trainees, and three of these are, of course, for sexual
intercourse. But, as was found for age and education, the types of activities on which the single men have higher rates are not the same in
the three climates. Here, too, the social context affects the relationship
between a status characteristic and behavior.

Prominent among the activities on which the single, persuasive
climate trainees have higher rates is the cluster of four "aggressive"
leisure-time pursuits—drinking, drunkenness, blowing one's top, and
fighting. In addition, there is a tendency toward more socially acceptable, or at least less violent, ways to spend off-duty hours; note the
higher frequencies of mass entertainment, chapel attendance, and short-
term AWOL. In the weak climate the emphasis shifts slightly away from
the aggressive to the more peaceable. Drinking and drunkenness no
longer differentiate the single from the married men, but the single
men have added three acceptable diversions to the three found in the
persuasive climate. On balance, therefore, in the weak climate the
single men exceed the married men primarily in more or less "proper"
activities.

In the aggressive climate the single men have moved still further
from the cluster of aggressive activities; only one, drinking, still differentiates them from the married men. On the other hand, they have
gained four relatively nonaggressive activities—masturbation, reading,
engaging in a hobby, and sports. Three of these four activities have a
solitary, almost passive quality about them. Only sports is clearly a
social activity and one that requires a large expenditure of energy. This

is particularly significant in view of the data in Chapter V, which show that the arbitrary-climate trainees have two main types of reactions to the stress imposed by their leaders: aggressiveness and passiveness. This contextual analysis locates the sources of the two different reactions more precisely. Table VII-3 shows that the single men are primarily responsible for the passive reaction to arbitrary leadership; and it will be recalled from Tables VII-1 and VII-2 that the aggressive reaction in this climate is largely attributable to the younger, less-educated men.

Table VII-3

DIFFERENTIAL EFFECTS OF MARITAL STATUS
IN THREE LEADERSHIP CLIMATES

	PERCENTAGE-POINT DIFFERENCE BETWEEN SINGLE AND MARRIED TRAINEES (SINGLE-MARRIED)		
	Persuasive	Weak	Arbitrary
Intercourse	-27	-16	-37
Mass entertainment	20	15	
Drinking	18		10
Blowing one's top	17	15	
Eating between meals		17	-8
Masturbation	9		17
Fighting	12	16	
Drunkenness	16		
Reading		12	14
Hobby			14
Short-term AWOL	12	6	-13
Sports		6	12
Chapel	9		
Seeing one's wife or girl			-9
Bull sessions			-9
Sick call		-7	

The bearing of this finding on the Iowa studies is particularly significant. Lippitt and White report that the autocratic group atmosphere generated two dissimilar reactions—aggressive and submissive. Since they did not consider the implications of status differences among their boys (or, perhaps, of the personality factors that are associated with different statuses in a Midwestern community), this interesting finding is left unexplained.

The discomforts of the arbitrary climate are also evident in the reactions of the married men. They exceed the single men in five activities, as compared with two in the weak climate and one in the persuasive. Note, however, that two of these—short-term AWOL and seeing their wives—are logically related to the high frequency of sexual intercourse. The married men react to this climate principally by escaping as often as they can to the more satisfying company of their wives. The fact that they exceed the rates for the single men in two additional, nonsexual activities, eating between meals and bull sessions, may suggest that the impact of the arbitrary climate on the married men is not altogether compensated by the high frequency of feminine companionship. These men apparently require still other, more or less emotionally satisfying leisure-time activities—in this case, eating between meals and participating in bull sessions.

*   *   *

Because it involves the simultaneous consideration of three levels of variables, this contextual analysis is necessarily complex. Instead of trying to summarize all the findings of this section, it is better to concentrate on a few important results. First of all, the indirect effects of the leadership climates, their influences on the associations between individual characteristics and behavior, are clearest in the two most sharply opposed climates, the persuasive and the arbitrary.

In the persuasive climate there are high rates of

—aggressive behavior among the younger and among the single trainees (drinking, drunkenness, fighting, blowing their tops)[15]

—nonaggressive recreations, often involving escape from the company area or the post, among single trainees (mass entertainment, short-term AWOL, chapel)

In the arbitrary climate there are high rates of

—nonaggressive, socially acceptable leisure-time activities among the younger trainees (mass entertainment, chaplain, hobby, chapel)

—aggressive behavior among the men who did not graduate from high school (drinking, drunkenness, fighting, and blowing their tops)

—relatively passive and solitary behavior among the single men (mass entertainment, reading, hobby).

The obvious next step is to try to explain some of these different patternings. Why is it, for example, that in the arbitrary climate the younger men, the less-educated men, and the single men each exhibit such different forms of behavior? But the very posing of this question foreshadows the difficulty of answering it with our data. These categories of "single," "younger," and "less-educated" are not independent. Fully half of our sample is composed of younger, single men, another quarter of older, married men. To explore further the implications of these findings one might examine the effects of leadership on combinations of individual characteristics: for example, how does the arbitrary climate affect the behavior of younger, less-educated, single trainees, as compared with other kinds of men? With our limited sample this is unfortunately impossible. However, in the second type of contextual

analysis, it will be possible to go somewhat further in this direction.
And at the end of this chapter there is a brief discussion of some social
and cultural factors underlying these contextual relationships.

Differential sensitivity to leadership

This section deals with the "L-comparisons" presented in Chart
VII-1. By comparing the reactions of men with the same characteristics
in different leadership climates, it seeks to measure the differential influence of leadership on each type of trainee. What is the relative sus-
ceptibility of younger and older trainees to differences in leadership?
Are both younger and older equally affected by the three climates, or is
the behavior of one group more or less constant in the three climates
while the other fluctuates sharply?

To see what these comparisons consist of, and to distinguish them
clearly from the differential-impact analysis of the preceding section,
consider once again the illustrative example of blowing one's top.

	Persuasive Per Cent	Weak Per Cent	Arbitrary Per Cent
17-21	33	34	31
22	13	20	43

The preceding section examined the differences between younger and
older trainees in each climate; this one will consider the differences between leadership climates for each age group. As a measure of the sus-
ceptibility of each age group to differences in leadership, we shall use
the maximum difference in rates of behavior between leadership climates. For the younger trainees the maximum difference is 3 percentage points, between the weak climate with 34 per cent and the arbitrary

climate with 31 per cent. Among the older trainees the difference is ten times as great, 30 percentage points, between the 13 per cent of the persuasive climate and the 43 per cent of the arbitrary. The type of climate to which they are assigned makes little difference to the younger men; in all three climates their behavior is about the same. But the behavior of the older men depends to a great degree on the kind of leadership; the older, arbitrary-climate trainees are far more likely to blow their tops frequently than are men of the same age in the persuasive climate. In short, the older men are more sensitive to differences in leadership.

Once again the question arises whether these interclimate differences within each age group are really attributable to the differential effects of age or, instead, result from the fact that other variables such as marital status are associated with age. As in the earlier analysis in this chapter, this possibility is explored by a modified form of HSG analysis.[16]

In Table VII-4 the older trainees are clearly more sensitive to differences in leadership. Their behavior is more variable in nine activities, as compared with only two in which the younger men are more variable (and in only one of the latter is the interclimate difference confirmed). Particularly interesting here are the activities in which the disparities between the older and younger trainees are greatest. Two of these are blowing one's top and drunkenness, both examples of the boisterous, aggressive cluster so often noted. Short-term AWOL, too, involves a deliberate flouting of social norms—if not the informal norms of the trainees, then certainly the formal norms of the Army. Thus the apparent willingness of the older trainees to engage in these "improper" activities is clearly a function of the kind of leadership they are exposed to; they react much more violently to the arbitrary climate than to the persuasive; among the younger trainees, on the other hand, partici-

Table VII-4

VARIABILITY OF BEHAVIOR AMONG YOUNGER AND OLDER
TRAINEES IN THREE LEADERSHIP CLIMATES*

| | Maximum percentage-point difference between leadership climates among trainees who are: | |
	17-21	22 +
Seeing the chaplain	17	3
Chapel	15	2
Blowing one's top	3	30
Drunkenness	7	23
Short-term AWOL	12	28
Eating between meals	12	27
Hobby	11	23
Mass entertainment	4	15
Bull sessions	8	16
Drinking	3	10
Intercourse	6	13

*Differences in italics are confirmed by HSG analysis; see text.

pation in these activities is virtually independent of leadership climate.

The same sharp difference emerges in the comparison between more-educated and less-educated soldiers in Table VII-5. The non-graduates are more sensitive to leadership in eight activities and less sensitive in only two. These activities in which the nongraduates are more affected cover a wide range of behavior; however, only one of the four boisterous leisure-time pursuits, blowing one's top, is included. In general, then, the effect of education in making men more or less sensitive to differences in leadership is confined to activities that do not have a pronounced aggressive or violent cast.

For the last of the three characteristics, marital status, Table VII-6 reveals at a glance the greater sensitivity of the married men. In the

Table VII-5

VARIABILITY OF BEHAVIOR AMONG HIGH-SCHOOL GRADUATES
AND NONGRADUATES IN THREE LEADERSHIP CLIMATES

	MAXIMUM PERCENTAGE-POINT DIFFERENCES BETWEEN LEADERSHIP CLIMATES AMONG: TRAINEES WHO ARE	
	Not high-school graduates	High-school graduates
Seeing one's wife or girl	<u>36</u>	15
Chapel	<u>20</u>	1
Sports	<u>23</u>	11
Blowing one's top	<u>16</u>	6
Short-term AWOL	<u>23</u>	14
Sick call	<u>11</u>	5
Reading	<u>8</u>	2
Masturbation	<u>10</u>	5
Seeing the chaplain	2	<u>16</u>
Bull sessions	8	<u>15</u>

upper part of the table the single trainees display greater variability on four activities, but the differences between the variability of the single and married trainees is confirmed in only two of these four comparisons. In the lower part of the table, however, the married men are more variable in nine activities, and eight of these differences are confirmed. Here, too, the patterning of activities is most apparent. Leadership makes more of a difference to the single men in relatively placid activities, three of which (engaging in a hobby, taking part in sports, or seeing the chaplain) do not usually involve marked emotional gratification. On the other hand, the activities in which the married men are more variable include the "aggressive" cluster repeatedly noted (blowing one's

Table VII-6

VARIABILITY OF BEHAVIOR AMONG SINGLE AND MARRIED
TRAINEES IN THREE LEADERSHIP CLIMATES

	MAXIMUM PERCENTAGE-POINT DIFFERENCES BETWEEN LEADERSHIP CLIMATES AMONG:	
	Single trainees	Married trainees
Hobby	18	8
Sports	11	4
Seeing one's wife or girl	21	15
Seeing the chaplain	14	9
Eating between meals	8	33
Short-term AWOL	11	33
Blowing one's top	3	25
Drunkenness	8	22
Fighting	4	14
Bull sessions	13	21
Intercourse	9	16
Drinking	4	11
Sick call (frequent)	7	12

top, drunkenness, fighting, and drinking), as well as other pursuits of an apparently emotional or sensual nature—eating between meals and sexual intercourse. These differences in sensitivity between the single and married men are among the largest in this section; that is, marital status is more important than either education or age in determining a trainee's differential sensitivity to leadership.

This finding helps to extend the analysis of Chapter V. There it was found that the arbitrary climate generates the highest rates of aggressive behavior and the persuasive climate the lowest. By studying the joint effects of leadership and of the trainees' characteristics, these interclimate differences can be traced to the way in which the behavior of the married men varies from one climate to another. It is their sensitivity to different kinds of leadership that largely accounts for the observed differences in behavior between climates. This result could not have been foreseen from the simple leadership-behavior relationships of Chapter V.

Combinations of characteristics

As remarked earlier, a trainee is not simply married or single; he is also younger or older, a high-school graduate or a nongraduate, and so on. These combinations of characteristics affect his behavior in ways that cannot be predicted from a knowledge of the separate relationships between each status characteristic and behavior. Unfortunately, the differential-impact analysis could not be carried beyond considering one individual characteristic at a time. Even to study two characteristics and three climates requires twelve comparisons for each activity instead of six. With our sample this would have entailed the comparison of percentages based on such small numbers as to be meaningless. It is possible, however, to extend the differential sensitivity analyses which have just been presented—i. e., to determine which of the five groups of trainees in Table VII-7 is most affected by differences in leadership climate.

This table confirms the earlier findings in this chapter. The behavior of the younger, single, high-school graduates is virtually independent of leadership climate; their "average sensitivity" in all activities is only 8. 7 percentage points. And the older, married men who did not graduate from high school are the most strongly affected by differences in leadership, with an "average sensitivity" of 21.2 percentage points. This finding clearly has important implications, both for

Table VII-7

OVERALL SENSITIVITY TO LEADERSHIP DIFFERENCES

Age	Education	Marital status	Average of maximum interclimate differences* Per Cent
Younger	Not High-School Graduate	Single	12.9
Younger	High-School Graduate	Single	8.7
Older	Not High-School Graduate	Married	21.2
Older	High-School Graduate	Single	12.1
Older	High-School Graduate	Married	18.7

*This table is constructed from the detailed HSG tables in Appendix E. The upper section of each of these tables contains the rates of behavior in the three climates for each combination of age, education, and marital status. For example, the first two lines of Appendix Table E-10 on drinking are:

	Persuasive		Weak		Arbitrary	
	Per Cent	N	Per Cent	N	Per Cent	N
17-21 Not High-School Grad Single	76	(59)	75	(48)	74	(39)
17-21 Not High-School Grad Married	48	(21)	50	(14)	--	(5)

As in the preceding section of the text, the sensitivity to leadership of the men represented in the first line of this excerpt can be measured by the maximum interclimate difference of 2 percentage points. The average of such figures over all seventeen activities for this group of trainees is reported in the first line of Table VII-7. In some groups where there were not enough trainees in all three climates the difference used in the tabulations is that between two climates. This is frequently the case for the third and fourth groups in this table, so that the averages for these groups should be interpreted cautiously.

social-psychological theory and for policy decisions as well—for example, the possibility of assigning men to units whose leadership climates will not reinforce their tendencies to "undesirable" leisure-time behavior.

Whether these findings will be borne out in replications of the present study and whether it would be possible or desirable to apply them to the assignment of trainees are questions that cannot be answered here. But these are important questions; indeed, this differential-sensitivity analysis suggests other policy questions of even greater importance. There is every reason to expect that behavior during duty hours will also be affected significantly by this interaction between leadership and the characteristics of the followers. The effectiveness of leadership depends, not only on the leaders' behavior and on the nature of the situation, but also on the kinds of followers. A single set of leaders may have quite different effects on the behavior of the various kinds of men under them.

From the theoretical standpoint, the obvious next step would be to identify the social factors underlying these group differences in sensitivity to leadership. The inquiry must be speculative now, for we do not have the necessary data on the trainees' attitudes, values, and self-conceptions, which would help to illuminate these contextual relationships. As a beginning, we shall try to explain why the older, married nongraduates are most sensitive to leadership and the younger, single, graduates least sensitive.

One type of variable that distinguishes between these groups is the dominant set of expectations and standards. The middle-class culture of the single, high-school graduate stresses conformity to institutional rules (the boys who drop out of high-school before graduation are in large part those who do not find the rules congenial). Furthermore, being younger and single, they are more accustomed to parental restraint than their older, married comrades. The soldier recently removed from his family may find it easier to accustom himself to the varieties of military discipline than the man who has been "on his own" for some time before entering the Army.

Another set of explanations has to do with the social relations between soldiers, the informal social structures of the training companies. Here the trainee learns the "working rules" as distinguished from the "formal rules" of the organization (e. g., which offenses are punished and which ignored); he learns where to go for information and assistance;

and he receives a form of "social support" that helps him to adjust in a more or less effective fashion to the demands of the organization. [17]

Because of his longer education and the shorter time that he has been away from this type of institutional environment, the younger, high-school graduate may well have had more experience with such informal friendship groups in an institutional context. It may not be farfetched, for example, to suggest that in certain respects the situation of the new trainee resembles that of the college freshman. If so, then the same type of informal group that facilitates adjustment to the unfamiliar demands of the college may also operate in the Army to a greater extent among these men. That is to say, the younger, single, high-school graduate, by virtue of his greater experience as a junior member of a large-scale organization may be more likely to develop the same types of informal associations that helped him withstand the pressures of civilian institutions. He may, in short, be more likely to form cohesive groups of friends with other trainees. If this is so, then the lesser sensitivity of these younger, single, high-school graduates may reflect the greater social support they receive from their comrades. On the other hand, if this reasoning is correct, the older, less-educated, married trainee is more isolated; he has less social support to cushion the impact of the different leadership climates.

There are, then, two hypotheses to explain the greater sensitivity to leadership climate among the younger, single, high-school graduates. One is based on the cultural differences carried over from civilian life; the other involves the patterns of friendship developed after entering the Army. It should not be difficult to test or refine both hypotheses in future studies.

SUMMARY

This chapter has presented two types of contextual analysis. The differential-impact analysis compared different types of trainees within each leadership climate. One important result of this analysis was to specify more precisely the situations producing high and low rates of aggressive leisure-time behavior. In the persuasive climate such behavior was conspicuous among the younger and single trainees. However, in the arbitrary climate it was most common among the men who did not graduate from high school. In the differential-sensitivity analysis, men with the same characteristics were compared in the three leadership climates, to determine which types of trainees were most susceptible to differences in leadership. It was found that the older, married men who had not graduated from high school exhibited the most variable behavior, while the group with the opposite characteristics, the younger, single, high-school graduates, had essentially the same rates of behavior in all three climates.

As one examines the tables in this chapter, it is clear that the effects of leadership and individual characteristics do not simply "add up." In most cases the effects of age, education, and marital status are not at all similar in the three leadership climates, and the effects of leadership bear unequally on different kinds of men. The explanation of these patterns of differential impact and differential sensitivity obviously requires a more elaborate theory than has typically been used in research on leadership, for these contextual effects cannot be predicted from propositions about the simple effects of leadership on behavior or from what is known about the patterns of differential class behavior, any more than the joint effects in this chapter can be predicted from the findings of the two preceding chapters. As sociologists turn more and more to the comparative and simultaneous study of groups and statuses, a new theoretical emphasis may emerge to explain such findings.

NOTES TO CHAPTER SEVEN

1. Robert K. Merton, Social Theory and Social Structure (rev. ed., Glencoe, Ill.: The Free Press, 1957), 111-114.

2. Hanan C. Selvin, "Durkheim's Suicide and Problems of Empirical Research," op. cit., 609-610.

3. Ibid.

4. Stouffer et al., Adjustment during Army Life, op. cit., 250-258.

5. "Marginal" refers to the fact that the data of the leadership-behavior analyses and of the status-behavior analyses are located in the margins of the multivariate tables in Appendix E.

6. Selvin, loc. cit.

7. Formally, these contextual analyses are special cases of "statistical interaction". I.e., the association between two variables (marital status and behavior) depends on the value of a third variable (leadership climate). See Selvin, op. cit.

8. For a difference to be entered in one of the next three tables, it must be: (a) at least 5 percentage points, and (b) confirmed by minimum differences of 5 percentage points in three of the four possible HSG comparisons. For example, consider the finding that in the arbitrary climate the older trainees have a higher frequency of blowing their tops than the younger trainees. This can be tested in Appendix Table E-7 by comparing the younger, single trainees with the older, single; the younger, married with the older, married; the younger, less-educated with the older, less-educated; and the younger, more-educated with the older, more-educated. Ideally, one would use the three-item HSG comparisons, but the number of cases is often too small to allow four such comparisons within each leadership climate. For the logic and procedures of HSG analysis, see Chapter III and Appendix C.

9. The omitted data are readily available in the tables of Appendix E.

10. Appendix Table E-5.

11. This points up the necessity of not taking low associations at face value in survey analysis. A low association may stem from mixing two or more subgroups in which there are high associations in opposite directions. Cf. Herbert H. Hyman, Survey Design and Analysis (Glencoe, Ill.: The Free Press, 1955), p. 307. For a further discussion of the meaning of zero associations, see Selvin, op. cit. Of course, not all low correlations need to be explored further; if this were the case, the task of explanation would never end. Such exploration is clearly indicated, however, when there is a theoretical or empirical reason to have expected an association.

12. Appendix Table E-1.

13. Appendix Table I-3.

14. The factor analysis of behavior in Appendix I provides additional support for this hypothesis.

15. The illustrations in parentheses are a sample of the activities with high rates in each group; for complete listings, see the original tables.

16. Differences in italics in the following tables are those in which the direction of the maximum interclimate difference between graduates and nongraduates is confirmed in three of the four possible HSG comparisons by at least 5 percentage points. This and the following two tables include only those activities in which the maximum interclimate differences for the two statuses differ by at least 5 percentage points.

17. George C. Homans, The Human Group (New York: Harcourt, Brace and Company, 1950), chs. 5, 10-12.

Chapter VIII

CHANGES IN BEHAVIOR FROM CIVILIAN LIFE[1]

A soldier's typical ways of behaving do not begin when he enters the Army; what he does in basic training is in part determined by what he did in civilian life. An analysis of the changes in behavior that take place during basic training will therefore help to explain further the patterns presented thus far.

Along with the questions on their behavior during basic training, the trainees were asked whether their rates were greater than, the same as, or less than the rates in "comparable" periods of civilian life. From a practical standpoint, these questions and the trainees' answers are not altogether satisfactory; for example, some questions asked the trainees to compare activities, such as AWOL, for which there is no civilian counterpart. For this and other reasons, which are discussed in Appendix G, only thirteen activities are studied in this chapter. Furthermore, the retrospective nature of the change data imposes certain limitations on the kinds of changes studied; it is impossible, for example, to distinguish between changes which occur immediately on entering the Army and those that take place more slowly. Despite this and other problems considered in Appendix G, the comparative data are a useful supplement to the material already presented.

An overview of changes during basic training

The most striking fact about the changes in behavior during basic training is that they are almost all downward changes. In most forms of nonduty behavior the trainees were less active than they had been in civilian life. For example, 77 per cent reported spending less time on sports in the Army than they had as civilians, and only 4 per cent said that they spent more time. The difference between these two figures, 73 percentage points, is taken as an index of the decline in sports during basic training, as shown in Table VIII-1.

Table VIII-1

NET CHANGES IN BEHAVIOR DURING BASIC TRAINING

	Percentage reporting increase minus percentage reporting decrease Per Cent
Hobby	-73
Sports	-70
Reading	-65
Intercourse	-61
Mass entertainment	-49
Seeing the chaplain	-45
Chapel	-40
Masturbation	-26
Drunkenness	-13
Drinking	-12
Fighting	-10
Bull sessions	-9
Blowing one's top	26

Twelve of the thirteen activities show lower rates in basic training, ranging from the very large decreases in hobbies and sports down to relatively small changes in the aggressive activities of drinking, drunkenness, and fighting. The only activity with a net increase during basic training is blowing one's top. The overall effect of basic training is unmistakable: the quiet and peaceful forms of recreation are reduced to a fraction of their civilian importance, while the aggressive and hostile outlets remain virtually unchanged. The most unambiguous expression of dissatisfaction, blowing one's top, is the only activity that becomes more common during the first few months of Army life.

A partial explanation of these gross shifts lies in a more detailed analysis of the process of change. For every activity in this table there were some men who reported higher frequencies in basic training, others who reported no difference, and a third group who reported lower frequencies. These proportions are presented in Table VIII-2. (Table VIII-1 was derived by subtracting the third column of this table from the first.)

The picture is still much the same as it was in Table VIII-1 for the generally quiet activities in the first eight lines of the table. Comparatively few men report increases in these pursuits during basic training, and, with only one or two exceptions, very few more report that their behavior was unchanged from civilian life. But a much different picture emerges in the "aggressive" activities at the bottom of the table.[2] In all these cases the increases come close to balancing the decreases, so that the small net change reported for these activities in Table VIII-1 really derives from these almost equal cross-currents. In other words, trainees are more likely to increase their "aggressive" activities during basic training than they are to have higher rates of nonaggressive behavior. This raises the question: what kind of men become more aggressive when they enter the Army, and under what conditions of leadership is this aggressiveness manifested? To answer this question it is first necessary to study the overall effects of leadership and individual

Table VIII-2

CHANGES IN BEHAVIOR DURING BASIC TRAINING

	PERCENTAGE STATING THAT THEIR PARTICIPATION IN BASIC TRAINING WAS:		
	MORE than in civilian life Per Cent	SAME as in civilian life Per Cent	LESS than in civilian life Per Cent
Hobby	4	19	77
Sports	6	18	76
Reading	10	15	75
Intercourse	8	23	69
Mass Entertainment	19	13	68
Seeing the chaplain	6	44	50
Chapel	15	30	55
Masturbation	4	66	30
Drunkenness	15	61	24
Drinking	22	44	34
Fighting	14	62	24
Bull sessions	33	25	42
Blowing one's top	50	26	24

characteristics on changes in all thirteen kinds of behavior.

The effects of leadership climate on changes in behavior

It is easier to study the effects of leadership climate if only the "net changes" are considered instead of the more detailed cross-currents of the preceding section. This involves simply dividing the data of Table VIII-1 into three columns, one for each leadership climate, as in Table VIII-3. Except that it deals with changes in behavior rather than with rates of behavior during basic training, this table is similar to Table V-1 in Chapter V.[3] In general, the effect of leadership on changes in behavior is approximately what could have been predicted from the analysis of the training period in Chapter V: The largest net downward changes are usually in climates where the rates during basic training are the lowest. For example, the weak climate has the largest net downward change in chapel attendance, just as it had the smallest proportion attending chapel regularly during the training cycle. Similar results hold in five of the seven activities in which the persuasive climate has confirmed low rates during basic training (Table V-3).

Table VIII-3

LEADERSHIP CLIMATE AND NET CHANGES IN BEHAVIOR
DURING BASIC TRAINING*

| | PERCENTAGE REPORTING INCREASE MINUS PERCENTAGE REPORTING DECREASE IN EACH LEADERSHIP CLIMATE | | | HSG-CONFIRMED COMPARISONS: | |
	Persuasive Per Cent	Weak Per Cent	Arbitrary Per Cent	Largest change	Smallest change
Hobby	-76	-59	-76		
Sports	-74	-67	-66	P	W, A
Reading	-70	-57	-64	P	W
Intercourse	-58	-58	-66	A	P, W
Mass entertain- ment	-54	-43	-46		
Seeing the chap- lain	-45	-43	-46		
Chapel	-36	-54	-37	W	A, P
Masturbation	-23	-32	-25		
Drunkenness	-20	-12	-2	P	W, A
Drinking	-18	-7	-7	P	W, A
Fighting	-4	-23	-6	W	A, P
Bull sessions	-20	8	-4	P	A
Blowing one's top	30	25	21	P	A

*The data of this and the following tables are excerpted from the tables in Appendix H.

The overall relationships between leadership climate and changes in behavior are more clearly displayed in Table VIII-4, which summarizes the confirmed comparisons in Table VIII-3. There are clear differences between the climates. The persuasive

Table VIII-4

SUMMARY OF HSG-CONFIRMED COMPARISONS IN TABLE VIII-3

	LEADERSHIP CLIMATES		
	Persuasive	Weak	Arbitrary
Largest	6	2	1
Tied for larger	0	0	0
Tied for smaller	3	4	5
Smallest	0	1	2

climate has six activities, more than either of the other two climates, in which it has greater proportions of trainees reporting changes; it has more downward changers in five activities, as well as more changers in the one activity that shows a net increase during basic training, blowing one's top. Similarly, the arbitrary climate leads in the number of activities that remain relatively stable (i. e. that have the smallest proportion of changers), and the weak climate is again between the other two. Overall, decreases in activity are most frequent in the persuasive climate, which had, in general, the lowest rates during basic training; and they are least frequent in the arbitrary climate, which most often had the highest rates.

The change data therefore do not add anything materially new to the previous analysis of leadership and behavior. The fact that the two sets of data are roughly complementary provides further support for the more detailed analyses of Chapters IV and V. [4]

The effects of individual characteristics
on changes in behavior

To what extent do age, education, and marital status affect the ways in which trainees change their behavior on entering the Army? The analysis of the effects of leadership climate suggests that here, too, the changes would be complementary, the greatest decreases from civilian life tending to occur among soldiers with the lowest rates during basic training. Detailed study of each characteristic will show, however, that although this is the general rule, there are important exceptions.

Age has little effect on behavior during basic training; the two age groups—those between 17 and 21 years and those 22 or over—had confirmed differences on only five activities, as reported in Chapter VI. And, according to Table VIII-5, age apparently has even less effect on changes from civilian life. There are several moderate differences in this table, but only one, the greater decline in fighting among the younger trainees, is confirmed by HSG analysis. In the sense that negligible changes during basic training are accompanied by negligible changes from civilian life, the two sets of data do complement each other.

But a closer examination reveals that this is not obviously true for some of the most important activities. More of the younger trainees report that they fought less often in basic training than they had before entering the Army, yet the younger also had the higher rate during basic training, 25 per cent to 17 per cent. Similar findings hold for drinking and drunkenness: greater decreases are accompanied by higher rates during basic training. Masturbation, too, declines much more among the 17-21 year group, yet the basic training rates are almost identical. [5]

How does it happen that the men in the age group with the greater decreases also have the higher rate at the end of the period of change? The answer seems to be that they had a considerably higher rate of these activities in civilian life, and that, even though more of the younger trainees reported decreases on entering the Army, their rates during basic training are still higher than those of the older trainees. Kinsey's data on masturbation support this reasoning; both the incidence and the frequency of masturbation decline with increasing age. [6] The greater decline among the younger men in our data thus has the effect of making the two age groups more alike, even though it does not completely remove the differences between them.

Table VIII-5

AGE AND NET CHANGES IN BEHAVIOR DURING BASIC TRAINING

	PERCENTAGE REPORTING INCREASE MINUS PERCENTAGE REPORTING DECREASE		HSG COMPARISONS
	17-21 Per Cent	22+ Per Cent	
Hobby	-72	-76	
Sports	-69	-70	
Reading	-64	-68	(5-0-5)
Intercourse	-57	-69	(5-2-2)
Mass entertainment	-46	-53	(7-1-4)
Seeing the chaplain	-46	-42	
Chapel	-45	-32	(8-1-3)
Masturbation	-34	-14	(6-1-0)
Drunkenness	-17	-5	(6-3-3)
Drinking	-12	-11	
Fighting	-16	1	(8-3-1)*
Bull sessions	-10	-6	
Blowing one's top	25	28	

*Confirmed HSG comparisons are in italics. All comparisons are "two-item" (See Appendix C).

The same reasoning explains the pattern of changes for the two educational levels, as shown in Table VIII-6. It seems plausible to assume that the high-school graduates did more reading as civilians and, because they came from wealthier families on the average, that they were probably able to afford frequent movies and other forms of mass entertainment.[7] These are the only two activities in which the graduates had a greater confirmed decline on entering the Army. And their rates in

Table VIII-6

EDUCATION AND NET CHANGES IN BEHAVIOR DURING
BASIC TRAINING

	PERCENTAGE REPORTING INCREASE MINUS PERCENTAGE REPORTING DECREASE		HSG COMPARISONS*
	Not High-School Graduate Per Cent	High-School Graduate Per Cent	
Hobby	-72	-75	
Sports	-67	-71	
Reading	-60	-69	(6-4-0)
Intercourse	-72	-55	(9-0-1)
Mass entertainment	-42	-54	(8-2-2)
Seeing the chaplain	-57	-37	(10-0-2)
Chapel	-48	-35	(10-1-1)
Masturbation	-31	-23	(5-2-2)
Drinking	-14	-11	
Fighting	-24	0	(10-0-2)
Bull sessions	-15	-5	(6-2-1)
Drunkenness	-17	-10	(6-2-4)
Blowing one's top	10	-37	(10-2-0)

*Confirmed HSG comparisons are in italics. All comparisons are two-item.

basic training, while not markedly different from those of the less-educated men, are still higher in both activities. For these two kinds of

behavior, the Army patterns reflect the civilian patterns, but the differences between groups are smaller. Army life apparently has the effect of making the behavior of the two groups more similar.

This tendency toward similarity is also noticeable in those activities
where the decreases are greater among the nongraduates. Kinsey reports that both premarital and marital intercourse are more frequent
among less-educated men, and it is this group that shows the greater decrease on entering the Army.[8] Complete similarity is not achieved, for
the less-educated do have a higher incidence of intercourse during basic
training; however, the changes are in the direction of similarity between
the two groups.

In fighting and bull sessions the changes on entering the Army do
lead to complete similarity; as was demonstrated in Chapter VI, there is
no difference between the less-educated and the more-educated on these
activities during basic training. Only in the two activities of seeing the
chaplain and going to chapel or church do the groups become less alike.
The downward changes on entering the Army are greater among the less-
educated, but the more-educated trainees have considerably higher rates
while they are in the Army. In general, then, basic training tends to
weaken the relationship between education and behavior.[9]

This tendency toward similar behavior in different status groups is
also found for single and married men, although not to the same degree.
In four of the five activities for which there are confirmed differences
in Table VIII-7, the behavior of the married and the single trainees becomes more alike than it was in civilian life. For example, the married
trainees, who naturally had higher frequencies of intercourse in civilian
life than did the single trainees, are also more likely to report a decline in intercourse during basic training.

To show that the two groups become more alike in masturbation and
bull sessions, one has to assume that the single men had higher fre-

quencies on these activities in civilian life than the married men—hardly unreasonable assumptions. On entering the Army, more of the single men report decreases in these activities, so that here again the two groups tend to become more similar. Chapel attendance follows this pattern also, the greater decline among the single men leading to a virtual equality by the end of basic training.

Table VIII-7

MARITAL STATUS AND NET CHANGES IN BEHAVIOR
DURING BASIC TRAINING

	PERCENTAGE REPORTING INCREASE MINUS PERCENTAGE REPORTING DECREASE		HSG COMPARISONS*
	Single Per Cent	Married Per Cent	
Hobby	-73	-73	
Sports	-69	-70	
Reading	-63	-70	(6-0-4)
Intercourse	-53	-77	(9-0-0)
Mass entertainment	-45	-57	(9-2-1)
Seeing the chaplain	-45	-45	
Chapel	-46	-30	(9-0-3)
Masturbation	-30	-18	(6-1-1)
Drinking	-16	-4	(6-1-5)
Fighting	-12	-5	(6-2-4)
Bull sessions	-13	-1	(6-1-2)
Drunkenness	-18	-1	(8-1-3)
Blowing one's top	-25	28	

*Confirmed HSG comparisons are in italics. All comparisons are two-item.

Only the changes in mass entertainment appear to conflict with this tendency. At the end of basic training the single men have considerably higher frequencies of going to the movies and similar activities, although

the married men are more likely to report a decrease from their civilian levels. Of course, the basic-training frequencies may be closer
together for the married and the single men than their civilian frequencies; this is a plausible assumption, but it cannot be tested with our
data.

* * *

Army life thus reduces the group differentials in many activities; at
least on a hypothetical level, it is not difficult to see why. For one
thing, many of the social and environmental conditions that foster group
differences among civilians are removed in the Army. Everyone lives
under essentially the same conditions. Even more significant, perhaps,
is the diminished importance of group memberships when a man enters
the Army. It is a commonplace in the study of deviant behavior that individual deviations from socially accepted norms are often supported by
membership in a deviant group. [10] The juvenile delinquent may be vio-
lating the norms of the larger society, but, judged by the norms of his
gang, he is conforming. And the college student's interest in Bach often
reflects the interests of his friends as much as the free operation of his
intellect. Like most of us, he acquires the tastes of his friends, and he
chooses his friends because they have tastes similar to his. [11]

When a man enters the Army, this nice balance between friends and
interests is disturbed. He has to choose new friends from among the
trainees with whom he happens to live, and there is only a slim chance
that the interests and values of these new friends will coincide with his.
This will be especially true when a trainee has "deviant" interests of
any kind. More is involved here, however, than simply moving to another social environment: there are at least three reasons why men
are less likely to find support for deviant interests in the Army than in
civilian life.

First, the Army is socially more homogeneous than are comparable civilian age groups; all trainees live under the same conditions, do essentially the same work, wear the same clothes, and so on. Second, friendships are largely restricted to men in the same squad or the same company, at least for the first few weeks of basic training; the trainee inclined toward unusual patterns of behavior is less likely to find others of the same taste to provide social support for him. Third, the behavior of trainees and soldiers in general is more closely supervised, and deviations are more swiftly punished than in civilian life.

In sum, then, the effect of entering the Army is to break many of the group relations that existed in civilian life and to substitute new associations, which are less likely to lead to group differences in behavior. The tendency toward homogeneity of behavior among trainees with different characteristics is thus rooted in the homogeneity of their social environment.

Sources of increased aggressive behavior

Certain kinds of behavior tend to occur together and to be affected by leadership and status characteristics in the same ways. Throughout the preceding chapters this was especially true of drinking, drunkenness, fighting, and blowing one's top; and earlier in this chapter these four activities turned out to have an unusual pattern of change from civilian life. Along with bull sessions, they are the only activities that displayed relatively little net decline during the training cycle: the number of men reporting increases was almost as large as the number reporting decreases. In all the other activities, however, the proportion with lower rates during basic training was at least three times as great as the proportion with higher rates.

This cluster of aggressive activities warrants attention for two reasons. First, they are potentially the most disruptive activities in which a trainee can engage (at least among those included in the questionnaire). It is difficult to imagine how high rates of participating in a hobby or going to the movies or even eating between meals could impair the functioning of individual soldiers or of an entire company, but an excessive rate of drunkenness or of fighting might well have serious consequences for morale and military efficiency. Second, as indicated by its prominence in the preceding chapters, this cluster of four boisterous activities is peculiarly important in the overall picture of nonduty behavior. Among other things, it is the most clearly recognizable cluster, as indicated by the frequency with which all four activities have the same relationship to leadership climate or to the trainees' characteristics. [12] It is therefore important to identify some of the sources of this increased aggressiveness.

The analysis of Chapter VII suggests that the interaction of leadership climate and the three individual characteristics affects the changes in behavior in ways that are not foreshadowed by the preceding, separate analyses in this chapter. And this is indeed true: consider the joint effect of age and leadership climate on this cluster of activities, as shown in Table VIII-8. [13]

The older, arbitrary-climate trainees in the last column are the only group with rates that are all either above average or not consistently different from average (i. e., whose departures from the overall rate for all trainees are not confirmed by HSG analysis). They have above-average increases on drunkenness, drinking, and bull sessions, with essentially average rates on the remaining two activities. This group therefore contains a disproportionate number of men who increased their drinking and drunkenness on entering the Army.

Most of the interesting patterns of change that are produced by the combination of education and leadership take place in the persuasive

Table VIII-8

NET CHANGES IN SELECTED ACTIVITIES DURING BASIC
TRAINING BY LEADERSHIP CLIMATE AND AGE

	OVERALL CHANGE	17-21			22+		
		P %	W %	A %	P %	W %	A %
Drunkenness	-13	-22					22
Drinking	-12		-4	-20	-26		17
Fighting	-10		-26		6		
Bull sessions	-9	-21	18		-17		6
Blowing one's top	26				34	17	

climate, as shown in Table VIII-9. A disproportionately large number of the nongraduates in this climate report decreases in drinking, fighting and bull sessions. The pattern for the graduates is the same for drinking and bull sessions. This is in line with the results of earlier chapters, where the persuasive climate was found to generate the least tension and to provide the most opportunities for the release of tension. What is surprising here is the increase in the incidence of fighting and blowing their tops among the persuasive-climate graduates. These men did not display unusual levels of these activities during basic training, but, compared with their civilian behavior, the Army seems to have made them much more aggressive. And this increased aggressiveness is manifested at the same time that their rates of drinking and drunkenness have been declining sharply. In effect, the persuasive climate directs all the strong emotional reactions of the more-educated trainees into only two channels, fighting and blowing their tops. Unfortunately, this surprising and significant finding cannot be explained with our data.

A more consistent pattern of aggressive and emotional behavior is

Table VIII-9

NET CHANGES IN SELECTED ACTIVITIES DURING BASIC TRAINING BY LEADERSHIP CLIMATE AND EDUCATION

	OVERALL CHANGE	NOT HIGH-SCHOOL GRADUATES			HIGH-SCHOOL GRADUATES		
		P Per Cent	W Per Cent	A Per Cent	P Per Cent	W Per Cent	A Per Cent
Drunkenness	-13				-18		
Drinking	-12	-21			-17		
Fighting	-10	-26	-34		11		-4
Bull sessions	-9	-26			-17	8	1
Blowing one's top	26		18	0	43		

seen in the combination of marital status and leadership. In Table VIII-10 the married, arbitrary-climate trainees have confirmed increases in all four forms of aggressive behavior and in bull sessions. This group, then, is largely responsible for the fact that only in these five activities is the number of trainees reporting increased rates during basic training almost as large as the number reporting decreased rates. These increases are all the more striking when compared with the predominantly negative changes in the other groups. It is important to observe that this increased aggressiveness results only from the combination of arbitrary leadership and married trainees. It does not appear among the married men in the persuasive and weak climates, nor among the single men in the arbitrary climate (with the exception of blowing their tops).

Also noteworthy is the decline in these activities among the single, persuasive-climate trainees. Only in blowing their tops and fighting do they fail to have a greater-than-average decline during basic training.

Table VIII-10

NET CHANGES IN SELECTED ACTIVITIES DURING BASIC
TRAINING BY LEADERSHIP CLIMATE AND MARITAL STATUS

	OVERALL CHANGE	SINGLE			MARRIED		
		P Per Cent	W Per Cent	A Per Cent	P Per Cent	W Per Cent	A Per Cent
Drunkenness	-13	-22					28
Drinking	-12	-22	-2	-23		-18	23
Fighting	-10		-24				8
Bull sessions	-9	-19	5	-14	-21		16
Blowing one's top	26			13			36

This group and the married, arbitrary-climate men are therefore at opposite extremes, one experiencing a marked decrease in aggressiveness and the other an approximately equal increase.

This table also enlarges upon a point made earlier, that basic training makes the behavior of different groups of trainees more similar. If one can assume that in civilian life these aggressive activities were more characteristic of single than of married men, then basic training tends to bring the two groups closer together, but only where each group is assigned to the "right" kind of leadership climate. That is, the decreased aggressiveness of the single men is strongly manifested only in the persuasive climate, and the increased aggressiveness of the married men only in the arbitrary climate.

This analysis of change may help to explain the surprising finding in Chapter VI that the married men, despite their greater "relative deprivation" in military service, apparently develop fewer compensatory mechanisms and means of tension release than do the single men.

Analysis of behavior during basic training may be misleading unless it is seen in relation to the trainees' previous civilian behavior. If the impact of military service on the married men is measured by their behavior during the sixteen weeks of training, then they do not appear to have been greatly disturbed by this experience. But, when the differences between their civilian and military patterns of behavior are examined, it is clear that the Army has made a greater impression on them than on the single men. This is particularly noticeable in the arbitrary climate. The married, arbitrary-climate trainees are the only group which becomes generally more aggressive on entering the Army. This is not contradicted by their somewhat lower rates during basic training, for it is reasonable to assume that in civilian life these aggressive activities are much more common among single men. That is, the married men in the arbitrary climate become much more aggressive in the Army than they had been as civilians, even though they do not reach the level of the single trainees.

SUMMARY

Most leisure-time activities for which comparisons can be made occur much less frequently in basic training than in civilian life. Only a relatively small reduction takes place, however, in bull sessions and three of the four boisterous activities—drinking, drunkenness, and fighting. And the fourth of these highly emotional means of tension reduction, blowing one's top, is the only activity in which there is a higher rate during basic training. Further analysis shows that these five activities are the only ones in which a substantial minority of the trainees actually increase their frequencies. The relationships between leadership climate and changes in behavior complement the associations noted earlier between leadership and behavior in the Army: the greatest de-

creases occur in those climates that have the lowest rates during basic
training. The effect of military life on trainees with different characteristics is to make their behavior more alike. By the end of basic
training the younger men behave more like the older men than they had
as civilians; essentially the same is true for education and marital
status.

A joint analysis of leadership and these three individual characteristics made it possible to locate more precisely the sources of increased
aggressive behavior. High-school graduates in the persuasive climate
have surprising increases in fighting and blowing their tops; at the same
time they drink and get drunk less often than in civilian life. A consistent increase in these four aggressive and emotional activities is
found in only one group, the married trainees in the arbitrary climate.
At the other extreme, the persuasive climate markedly lowers the frequencies of these activities among the single men.

NOTES TO CHAPTER EIGHT

1. I am indebted to Frances Potter Gamble for an incisive critique and reanalysis of part of this chapter.

2. Bull sessions is the only one of the five activities at the bottom of the table that is not basically aggressive. Why it falls among the aggressive activities in this table is not clear.

3. Because the study of change entails both positive and negative differences, it is not feasible to use the simplified presentation of Table V-2, which showed for each activity the positive or negative difference between the frequency in each of the three climates and the overall frequency for all trainees. The double use of positive and negative signs would be confusing. This table also differs from the earlier presentation in including the HSG comparisons instead of presenting them separately.

4. Two principal reasons may be offered to explain why the two sets of data are not more fully complementary than they are. First, the comparative questions asked only for judgments of "more," "less," or "same." Since the trainees were not required to estimate the frequency of each activity in civilian life, large and small downward changes are thereby lumped together. Second, the comparative questions were answered by fewer trainees: these questions were not asked in all companies, and, where they were asked, between 5 and 10 per cent who responded to the questions on basic training did not answer the change questions. For further details on the problems raised by the change data, see Appendix G.

5. See Appendix Table H-15.

6. Sexual Behavior in the Human Male, op. cit., 238-239.

7. See the discussion of education, income and short-term AWOL in Chapter VI.

8. Op. cit., 347-357. Kinsey's data are not exactly comparable to ours, since he includes the high-school graduates with those who have had one to three years of high school.

9. This is an example of a general phenomenon reported in studies of colleges and professional schools. As students move through these institutions, the effects of differences in social backgrounds become progressively less important. See, for example, Robert K. Merton, George G. Reader, and Patricia L. Kendall, The Student-Physician (Cambridge: Harvard University Press, 1957). In less homogeneous environments than a medical school or an Army camp, there are often strong forces acting to differentiate the members at the same time that the attenuation of status factors tends to make them more similar. For evidence of both processes at work among undergraduates, see Hanan C. Selvin and Warren O. Hagstrom, "Determinants of support for civil liberties," forthcoming in the British Journal of Sociology.

10. For a theoretical formulation of this finding and illustrations of it in different types of groups, see Homans, op. cit.

11. The process by which this association between friendship and tastes develops in a new social situation has been explored by Paul F. Lazarsfeld and Robert K. Merton, "Friendship as social process: a substantive and methodological analysis,"

in Morroe Berger, Theodore Abel and Charles H. Page (eds.), Freedom and Control in Modern Society (New York: D. Van Nostrand Company, Inc., 1954), 18-66.

12. A further analysis of the meaning of this and other clusters of activities is contained in Appendix I.

13. This analysis of change is obviously much more complex than the "static" analyses of Chapters V through VII. To superimpose on this complexity with its plusses and minusses the additional plusses and minusses of the contextual analyses in Chapter VII would make the tables virtually incomprehensible. Consequently, the entries in Tables VIII-8 through VII-10 are simply the actual values for the subgroups, as taken from the tables in Appendix H, with the addition of the "overall change" column from Table VIII-1. Since our purpose here is to identify combinations of factors making for exceptionally high or low rates of change, these tables include only those entries that differ from the overall change by at least 5 percentage points. And again, to avoid spurious and chance correlations, the tables present only those differences that are confirmed in at least three of the four possible HSG comparisons.

Chapter IX

CONCLUSIONS AND PROSPECTS

Because the data on leadership and behavior were very detailed and because the analysis had to take into account the interrelated effects of both leadership and individual characteristics, this has been a complicated study. It may therefore be useful to look back over the preceding chapters, not so much to summarize what has been done, as to note the major contributions of this study and to indicate some of their implications for further research.

Several important theoretical aspects of this study (in addition to the design of the two questionnaires) are the work of Arkin and Gellert.[1] One which had far-reaching consequences was their decision to gather data on perceived leadership rather than actual leadership. Knowledge of the actual situation is probably less important here than knowledge of how the trainees define that situation. Had Arkin and Gellert decided to study the "real" leadership climates, it would still have been necessary to know how the trainees perceived this reality, for the trainees' perceptions of leadership act as intervening variables between the leaders' actions and the followers' behavior.

This is not to say, of course, that the relationship between the "actual" leadership climates and the perceived climates is unimportant; by and large, one would expect the two types of climates to be similar, and it would be desirable to identify those situations in which this is not true.

But the two problems—the relation between actual and perceived leadership, and the relation between perceived leadership and behavior—are conceptually distinct. Lacking independent measures of leadership, this study has been limited to the latter problem; the former is perhaps of equal importance for a more complete theory of leadership effects.

Because of the way in which leadership climate was defined (as the perceptions of an "average trainee") it was not necessary to examine individual perceptions, except to remark that in virtually all of the ratings of the leaders there was a high degree of consensus among the trainees. But although consensus prevails for every position and every question, there were many trainees who rated some leaders above or below the modal ratings. It would be a valuable extension of our "aggregative" analysis to consider the relation between these individual perceptions of leadership and the behavior of the same trainees. What, for example, are the dominant behavior patterns of men who have higher opinions of their leaders than the modal opinion embodied in the leadership climates? Note, by the way, that this problem is posed contextually; the foregoing analysis demonstrates the value of studying individual ratings of leadership relative to the leadership climate derived from the ratings of the entire group.

There is no reason why the method developed for inferring measures of perceived leadership from the followers' individual ratings cannot be extended to other characteristics of organizations as well. Systematic comparative studies of bureaucracies and other formal groups are rare; it is difficult to summarize the characteristics of a complex organization or even to select appropriate variables for describing them. One attempt in this direction is the work of the Personnel Research Board of Ohio State University in identifying fifteen dimensions for describing groups.[2] This approach has not been taken over by other students of organizations, perhaps because fifteen dimensions are too many for any one analysis. It seems likely that the procedures we have used will produce a more sharply focused set of dimensions. By using the average perceptions of many group members as the basis for deriving these dimensions—instead of the reports of one or a few members as was done in the Ohio State studies—it may be possible to reduce their fifteen dimensions to a much smaller number.

Fifteen dimensions are obviously too many for meaningful comparative studies, yet it is only in comparative studies that the important characteristics of an organization can be separated from the unique aspects of the particular situation in which it is located. Although our organizational analysis was limited to the measurement of leadership climate, the same methods could readily be extended to include other perceived characteristics—the apparent friendliness of one's comrades, for instance—or even to group characteristics, such as the rates of various illnesses, that are not arrived at through averaging individual perceptions. In other words, the methods developed here provide at least a partial framework for the quantitative comparison of large-scale organizations.

In future research of this type it would be desirable to have more groups or units than the twelve companies on which this study was based, in order to separate the influences of different group characteristics. For example, we were not able to distinguish the effects of tyrannical leadership from those of vacillating leadership, because the two types were almost always found together in our companies.[3] Inspection of the leadership data suggests, however, that a larger sample of companies would have made it possible to find some that displayed a high level of tyrannical leadership along with a low level of vacillating leadership, and vice-versa. This would require a large number of groups—say, one hundred or more—so that group characteristics could be studied like individual characteristics—by cross-tabulation.[4]

Another major methodological emphasis—it can hardly be called an innovation, for its basic principles are familiar—is what we have called Homogeneous Subgroup Analysis. Rather than use the standard principles of statistical inference to generalize our findings to some larger population, real or hypothetical, we have instead tried to demonstrate, insofar as possible, the "pure" effects of each variable that was studied. For example, the finding that the weak climate leads to less frequent eating between meals than does the arbitrary climate is, within the limitations of the data, a "pure" statement about leadership. The HSG comparisons show that this relationship cannot be attributed to the effects of age, education, or marital status. Furthermore, the consistency of the HSGs confirmed findings means that there is little likelihood that they stem from the operation of random factors, such as individual variability of response or errors of processing.

In larger perspective, the importance of this kind of analysis is in its bearing on the logic of empirical verification in the social sciences. Is there any way to assess the applicability of a finding beyond the particular set of circumstances in which it happened to occur? One answer to this question is that confidence in the general validity of hypotheses comes from systematic replications, from repeating a study in different social and cultural contexts, with different individuals, in different physical situations, and so on, continually testing and re-testing the same hypothesis. The more that this hypothesis is not disproved, the greater the confidence in it. Thus verification of hypotheses in the social sciences is essentially an "asymptotic" process: one becomes steadily more confident as the hypothesis under test is not disproved, even though absolute certainty is never reached. It goes almost without saying that the variables used in these replications should be theoretically relevant.[5]

Tests of an hypothesis in varied circumstances might be called external replications; the HSG comparisons would then be internal replications.[6] Both increase confidence in the general validity of an empirical finding. Internal replications help to show that the finding in question did not result from the association of other variables with the dependent variable—i. e., they lead to "pure" relationships within the particular situation being studied. External replications progressively reduce the likelihood that the original finding resulted from the unique character-istics of the situation in which it occurred, rather than from the opera-tion of the variables being analyzed.

All this is not meant to imply that a given relationship, especially one with only a single independent variable, will be confirmed in all con-ceivable replications. There are few, if any, such relationships in sociology. Indeed, actual experience with the analysis of several inde-pendent variables at the same time soon convinces the researcher that all relationships are multivariate and that progress consists in incorp-orating more and better variables in his statements of relationships. Research, in this view, is a process of progressively specifying the con-ditions under which a hypothesis is more nearly true. The value of a particular empirical study is measured by its ability to raise the level of explanation or prediction while keeping the number of independent variables as small as possible.[7] If this argument is valid, then the contextual analyses of Chapter VII represent genuine advances over the previous studies of leadership effects, since the inclusion of one status characteristic sharply refines and increases the associations between leadership climate and behavior.[8]

The chapters relating leadership to behavior have important impli-cations for the theory of organization.[9] They indicate some of the ways in which different organizational characteristics affect the behavior of the members of these organizations. Where the classic Western Elec-tric studies directed attention to the impact of informal organization (within the formal structure of authority in a large factory) on the "of-ficial" behavior of the workers, the present research stresses the relationship between the exercise of formal authority and "unofficial" behavior. This is not to say, of course, that either of these formulations excludes the other; they are different aspects of the same complex interaction between organizational structure and member behavior. On the other hand, these two relationships do not exhaust this interaction between structure and behavior, for there is also an important relationship between "official" and "unofficial" behavior. In the Army situation this question takes the form: to what extent do the nonduty activities of a trainee affect his performance in his official tasks? What, for example, is the effect of frequently seeing his wife or girl friend on the speed with which a trainee becomes proficient in his military tasks? That there are important effects seems quite likely, but the present research gives no clues to the nature and extent of these effects.

Much work needs to be done also on the psychological and social mechanisms underlying the relationship between leadership and behavior. Our theoretical analyses had to rely on inferences about the trainees' attitudes and self-conceptions, but future studies of organizational leadership should supplement the followers' appraisals of their leaders with reports on their own feelings as members of the organization.

Because this was an exploratory study, more concerned with methods and directions of inquiry than with testing a wide variety of specific hypotheses, it included only three characteristics of the trainees—their age, educational level, and marital status. That these variables are among the most important in predisposing the trainees to one or another pattern of nonduty behavior is clear. Nevertheless, it is obvious that at least a half-dozen other variables such as father's occupation, race, rural-urban residence, and so on significantly affect a trainees' adjustment to Army life. In more intensive studies of organizational leadership systematic data on the characteristics of the followers would make it possible to determine whether the associations between group variables and individual behavior are genuine or spurious—that is, may have resulted from accidents of assignment or recruitment by which followers with certain predispositions are more frequently found in one organizational environment than in another.

Even more important than their use in testing for spurious associations between group and individual variables is the function of these status variables in mediating between characteristics of the organization and the behavior of the followers. It has been shown that the impact of any one leadership climate does not fall equally on all types of followers; these results would be enriched by studying other characteristics of the followers in addition to age, education, and marital status. Similarly, it would be theoretically illuminating to learn more about differential sensitivity to leadership. Striking as our own findings are, there are undoubtedly other combinations of status characteristics which display even more variability in behavior from one leadership climate to another. These contextual analyses also have practical applications—for example, in the field of personnel policy. Where the burden of some type of leadership falls largely on one group of followers, it should not be too difficult to devise procedures for assessing these differential effects and, wherever possible, to reassign the followers. In this study, for example, the aggressiveness noted in the arbitrary climate results primarily from the impact of this type of leadership on the married men. If the results presented here are confirmed in more carefully controlled studies, one way to lower the rates of aggressive behavior would be to take into account the characteristics of leaders and followers in assigning men to training companies.

Because of the way in which the data on changes in behavior were gathered—by asking men to compare their military behavior with their civilian behavior—a precise analysis of change was impossible. We were able to identify the men who reported changes and to deal with the direction of these changes, but their magnitude was unknown. Nevertheless, the analysis did show that basic training generally had the effect of reducing the group differences that had obtained in civilian life—i.e., of making the different groups of trainees more similar in their behavior than they had been prior to military service.

Perhaps the most important lesson for future research in these results is the necessity for more systematic collection of data on short-term changes in behavior. Use of the "panel" technique, in which the same persons are interviewed at two or more points in time,[10] would make it possible to measure the changes in behavior more precisely; and, if the interviews or questionnaires are scheduled at intermediate points as well as at the beginning and end of the field study, the rate of change could also be determined. Indeed, it would seem desirable to give the study of change primary emphasis, for group differences at the end of training are merely the outcome of a process of change, which should be examined as it operates, rather than when it has ended.

NOTES TO CHAPTER NINE

1. See above p. vii.

2. John K. Hemphill and Charles M. Westie, "The measurement of group dimensions," Journal of Psychology, 29, 1950, 325-341.

3. Durkheim faced exactly the same problem of "confounded" variables in a small sample of groups (countries). See Selvin, "Durkheim's Suicide and problems of empirical research," op. cit.

4. Eight times as many groups, or more, would seem to require eight times as much data, but this is not necessarily true. Because the study of group characteristics, such as leadership climate, is based on averages of individual characteristics and because relatively small samples yield stable averages, the data on leadership and other group characteristics could be based on a much smaller number of respondents than is used for the dependent variables of individual behavior.

5. The ideas in this paragraph derive from Robert K. Merton's lectures on "Social theory as applied to research."

6. We are indebted to Patricia L. Kendall for this terminology. See also Selvin, "Durkheim's Suicide . . . ," op. cit.

7. More exactly, increasing the number of distinct "levels" of independent variables appears to promise the greatest return. In the present study, for example, significant increments of knowledge would result from including data about the informal structures of the companies, the characteristics of the platoons and squads, and even the distinctive nature of the training regiments of which these companies were part. Combining many variables on the same level into scales or indices is also valuable, but not nearly to the same extent. Variables on different levels increase the theoretical richness of the explanation. A scale produces higher associations, simply because it is more reliable than a single question; it does not enlarge the theoretical structure of the relations being studied.

8. In their summary of the literature on supervision and productivity, Argyle and his collaborators report that social factors ". . . have never been shown to be of very great significance as determinants of productivity differences between otherwise similar departments . . . the effect of supervision and group organization may be expected to lead to differences of the order of 7 per cent to 15 per cent when these factors are changed or when otherwise similar work groups are compared." They remark that the differences between individuals are often greater than the differences between groups, but they do not take the crucial step of considering the joint effects of group and individual variables. Michael Argyle, Godfrey Gardner, and Frank Cioffi, "Supervisory methods related to productivity, absenteeism, and labour turnover," Human Relations, XI, 1958, 23-40, p. 24.

9. A concise and stimulating appraisal of the contributions of sociologists to the study of military organizations is contained in a recent monograph prepared for the American Sociological Association by Morris Janowitz: Sociology and the Military Establishment (New York: Russell Sage Foundation, 1959).

10. Paul F. Lazarsfeld and Morris Rosenberg, The Language of Social Research, (Glencoe, Ill.: The Free Press, 1955), Section III, "The analysis of changes through time."

APPENDICES

Appendix A

THE DERIVATION OF LEADERSHIP CLIMATES: NOTES ON METHODS AND TECHNIQUES

Since the technique of inferring leadership climates where there is more than one leader in a group is apparently an original contribution of this study, the reasoning behind the technique was explained at some length in Chapter II. This appendix presents additional details on the processes by which the leadership climates were derived and takes up some methodological problems.

The "ecological fallacy"

The derivation of the leadership indices in Chapter II began with the ratings of each leader by all the men in his company. These ratings were then averaged, to give one figure for each leader on each question—the "average perception" of this leader by his trainees. The correlations between each pair of average ratings were computed, and these correlations were factored to get the three dimensions of perceived leadership.

The important point here is that the correlations are based on group or aggregate data, the averages of the trainees' ratings, and not on the individual ratings themselves. Instead of computing the group averages and correlating them, we could have correlated the original ratings (and, indeed, we did compute many such correlations in developing the method actually used). For example, we could have computed the correlation between the trainees' ratings of the C.O. in Company X on "influence" and "respect," the first two questions on the leadership questionnaire.

This correlation would have been based on pairs of responses from the questionnaires of each trainee in that company. What we actually did, however, was to compute the correlation between the mean ratings on "influence" and the mean ratings on "respect" of all the eighty-two company-level leaders. This correlation, to repeat, is based on aggregate data, rather than on individual responses.

The "ecological fallacy" refers to the improper use of correlations or other measures of association based on aggregate data as substitutes for correlations based on individual data--for example, using the correlation between the average income and the average number of years of education in several census tracts as a substitute for correlating the income and education of each person in these tracts.[1] As Robinson has shown, the relationship between these two kinds of correlation is so loose that one is hardly ever justified in taking the ecological correlation (which may be more easily obtained) as a substitute for the individual correlation.

Now it might appear that we have committed the ecological fallacy, since our factor analysis is admittedly based on ecological correlations. However, what is fallacious, as Menzel points out,[2] is not the use of ecological corelations per se, but their use as substitutes for individual correlations. Where one is interested in the correlations between characteristics of the groups as such, then the use of ecological correlations is not only justified, but essential. This is the case in the present analysis, which examines the interrelationships between the characteristics of the leaders, as they are preceived by all the trainees in their companies-- i.e., by the "average trainee" in each company. The average ratings are aggregate data, and ecological correlations are the appropriate way to study the relationships between them.

The factor analysis of average ratings[3]

Table A-1 depicts the correlations between the average ratings for

Table A-1

INTERCORRELATIONS OF AVERAGE LEADERSHIP RATINGS*
(82 Company-Level Leaders)

	1	2	3	4	5	6	7	8	9	10	11	12	13	14	15
1 Influence	--														
2 Respect	72	--													
3 Sucker	28	32	--												
4 Inconsistent	-05	-41	-30	--											
5 Fighting spirit	80	82	24	-11	--										
6 Fear	-08	-28	-41	74	-01	--									
7 Breaks promises	-19	-56	-21	69	-35	54	--								
8 Confidence	78	86	23	-20	95	-04	-44	--							
9 Passes buck	56	45	37	12	57	-11	-20	52	--						
10 Interested	66	82	26	-22	85	-10	-54	88	57	--					
11 Like dirt	-32	-66	-37	80	-40	77	80	-45	-22	-52	--				
12 Plays favorites	04	-39	04	68	-24	36	74	-33	13	-41	66	--			
13 Punishes	-11	-45	-30	85	-16	84	74	-24	00	-29	90	67	--		
14 Sticks up for men	67	79	42	-36	74	-40	-53	75	62	76	-64	-28	-47	--	
15 Combat leader	78	86	28	-31	85	-17	-55	91	49	81	-57	-38	-38	74	--

*See questionnaire in Appendix J for complete wording of questions. Decimal points have been omitted.

the eighty-two leaders. The extent to which the use of averages eliminates individual variation and enhances central tendencies in leadership
perception (as is implied in the use of an average) is striking, particularly
when this table is compared with the corresponding table for the behavior
correlations, Appendix Table I-3.

This correlation matrix was factored by Thurstone's "complete centroid
method,"[4] yielding three factors as shown in Table A-2. Then this factor matrix
was rotated by the matrix of Table A-3 to the oblique simple structure shown in
Table A-4.[5] It seemed desirable to carry out the tedious process of oblique rota-
tion, rather than impose the artificiality of an orthogonal structure on the data.

In interpreting the meaning of uncorrelated factors one has only to
consider the relationship between each item and the factor. However, in
dealing with correlated factors, as in this study, each item makes two
contributions to each factor--a "direct contribution" resulting from its
correlation with the factor and an "indirect contribution" resulting from
its correlation with other factors which, in turn, are correlated with the
factor being interpreted. The sum of these two contributions is the "total
contribution" of the item to the factor, as reported in Table II-3 of Chapter II.[6]

The next step was to compute scores for each of the eighty-two leaders on the three factors. The estimating equations for these scores were
derived by means of Holzinger's and Harman's "Shortened Method."[7] It
was possible to simplify the estimation without appreciable loss of accuracy so that none of the estimating equations has more than six items.
Chapter II describes how these factor scores were combined into indices
of leadership climate for each company; the factor scores of each leader
were weighted by his relative influence and the proportion of the total
training cycle that he served.

In retrospect, this procedure was unnecessarily complicated. For
the kinds of analysis that ultimately were undertaken in this study, it

Table A-2

UNROTATED MATRIX OF
CORRELATIONS OF LEADERSHIP ITEMS
WITH REFERENCE VECTORS

		R_1	R_2	R_3	h^2
1	Influence	64	56	19	76
2	Respect	88	26	-09	85
3	Sucker	42	-05	42	36
4	Inconsistent	-61	66	12	82
5	Fighting spirit	77	56	-10	92
6	Fear	-54	63	-41	86
7	Breaks promises	-75	38	25	77
8	Confidence	81	52	-21	97
9	Passes buck	48	45	37	57
10	Interested	82	40	-19	87
11	Like dirt	-85	45	-04	93
12	Plays favorites	-54	43	56	79
13	Punishes	-69	66	-03	91
14	Sticks up for men	85	22	23	83
15	Combat leader	86	36	-12	88

Table A-3

TRANSFORMATION MATRIX*

	R_1'	R_2'	R_3'
R_1	71	-37	-08
R_2	68	53	43
R_3	16	-76	90

*Entries are direction cosines of angles between unrotated reference vector system in Table A-2 and final reference vector system in Table A-4.

Table A-4

FINAL REFERENCE-
VECTOR MATRIX*

		R'_1	R'_2	R'_3
1	Influence	87	-08	36
2	Respect	79	-12	-04
3	Sucker	33	-50	32
4	Inconsistent	03	48	44
5	Fighting spirit	91	09	09
6	Fear	-02	85	-05
7	Breaks promises	-23	29	45
8	Confidence	90	14	-03
9	Passes buck	71	-22	49
10	Interested	84	05	-06
11	Like dirt	-30	58	23
12	Plays favorites	00	00	73
13	Punishes	-05	63	31
14	Sticks up for men	79	-37	23
15	Combat leader	84	-04	-02

*This is the original set of reference vectors in Table A-2 rotated to oblique simple structure.

would have been equally satisfactory to select one or two highly dis-
criminating items from each of the three factors in Table II-3 and combine them into simple indices of leadership. Even the weighting for the
relative influence of the different leaders probably required more work
than was justified by the crude typology that was finally used: had the
various leaders been assumed to be equally influential, the results would

not have been much different. With an average of seven leaders per company, the variations in influence weights would have had to be much greater than they were to have a significant effect on a company's score, as compared with what would have been obtained with equal weights.[8]

This is not to say, of course, that such rough-and-ready methods should have been used in this study. When one is exploring a relatively unknown area, uncertain even as to the kinds of analyses that ultimately will be done, it is best to retain as much precision as possible. However, once an exploratory study like this one has indicated some fruitful directions for analysis, the less technical complexity the analyst has to cope with, the more time he will have for theoretical and substantive questions.

"Pooled" and "separate" factor analyses

The outcome of a factor analysis depends on two sets of variables-- the content of the tests or questions and the population to which the tests are given. In this study three clear factors of leadership have been identified for the population consisting of all eighty-two company-level leaders. Alternatively, the factorial composition of the leadership ratings could have been determined separately in each of the twelve companies by means of twelve separate factor analyses. Should this have been done? Apart from the expense, which would be multiplied at least eight or ten times, there is a good reason for using only one "pooled" factor analysis instead of twelve separate ones.[9] The factors are simply composite variables synthesized from the perceived characteristics of each leader. Using one "pooled" factor analysis ensure that all twelve companies are described with the "same" variables. Had we factored the leadership correlations in each company separately, it would have been impossible to compare the leadership climates of different companies, since dimensions of leadership would have been different in each company.[10]

"Bimodality" of ratings

The problem of bimodality arose in connection with the use of average ratings. Arithmetic means or other measures of central tendency are satisfactory only with distributions that are unimodal (single-peaked). If half of the men in a company gave a leader the rating of "1" on some question and the other half gave him the rating of "3," it would be meaningless to say that the average rating was "2." If such bimodal distributions had occurred frequently, it would mean that there was little consensus on the ratings of the officers; the entire approach to leadership climates would have had to be different.

Each of the 1230 distributions (82 leaders times 15 questions) was examined to see how many exhibited even a slight degree of bimodality. A distribution was judged bimodal if the proportion of "2" ratings was 10 percentage points or more below either of the other two proportions--for example, a leader's ratings on some question would be considered bimodal if 40 per cent of the men gave him a "1" rating; 25 per cent, "2"; and 35 per cent, "3." This occurred for less than 3 per cent of the 1230 distributions. Only four leaders had more than one bimodal distribution out of fifteen, and only one leader had as many as three. Bimodality thus occurs so rarely and is so thinly spread across the total set of leaders that it is not a serious problem.

It is noteworthy that there were no cases of bimodality in the influence ratings. This is important because of the central position of influence in the computation of leadership indices. Question 11 ("treats trainees 'like dirt' ") had the greatest number of bimodal distributions, six out of a possible eighty-two, perhaps indicating some ambiguity in the wording of this question.

"Halo" effect

This problem is basic to the whole technique of measuring leadership climates. We have assumed that the ratings of the different leaders in a company are psychologically independent, that the men were able to discriminate between the leaders on all questions. But it is also possible that some sort of "halo" effect operated, that the personality of the most influential leader in a company so dominated the minds of the trainees that they tended to rate the other leaders in the same way.

To test the hypothesis of a halo effect it is necessary to examine the distribution of responses for an average of seven leaders in twelve companies on either the fifteen original questions or the three factors--a minimum of 246 distributions. Both of these distributions were examined minutely in the course of developing the leadership ratings, and virtually no evidence of a halo effect was found. Within each company the variation between leaders on either the factor scores or the original questions is so large that the halo hypothesis is not substantiated.

NOTES TO APPENDIX A

1. W. S. Robinson, "Ecological correlations and the behavior of individuals," American Sociological Review, 15, 1950, 351-357. The term "ecological" refers to the use of such census-tract correlations by students of "urban ecology." Much of the analysis in Durkheim's Suicide is based on this kind of fallacious reasoning, but Durkheim also used procedures that, on other kinds of data, would have compensated for his ecological associations. See Selvin, "Durkheim's Suicide...," op. cit.

2. Herbert Menzel, "Comment on Robinson's 'Ecological correlations and the behavior of individuals,'" American Sociological Review, 15, 1950, p. 674.

3. For the reader who is not acquainted with factor analysis, Fruchter's text is a simple treatment; Benjamin Fruchter, Introduction to Factor Analysis (New York: D. Van Nostrand Company, Inc., 1954).

4. L. L. Thurstone, Multiple Factor Analysis (Chicago: University of Chicago Press, 1947), p. 161 ff.

5. Raymond B. Cattell, Factor Analysis (New York: Harper and Brothers, 1952), Ch. 13.

6. A more extended treatment of these "contributions" is contained in Karl J. Holzinger and Harry H. Harman, Factor Analysis (Chicago: University of Chicago Press, 1941), p. 271. In a personal letter to the writer Dr. Harman indicated his belief that these "contributions" are the best indices for interpreting the meanings of factors. Nevertheless, it should be recognized that interpretation is essentially an extra-statistical problem; the adequacy of an interpretation cannot be demonstrated on purely statistical grounds, even though it is based on statistically-derived indices.

7. Ibid., p. 278.

8. This point was suggested to the writer by Professor Louis Guttman of the Israel Institute of Applied Social Research.

9. An additional difficulty in "separate" factor analyses is the small number of leaders in each company--slightly less than seven, on the average. But this difficulty is an artifact of the present situation, not a general defect of the method.

10. Doppelt faced exactly this choice in measuring differences in the "general intelligence" factor between five age groups. "The general factor was thus a new variable the influence of which was to be studied at different age levels. This plan presupposed that the general factor would be the same variable for the different age levels. If five general factors were determined, one for each of the five age levels, any comparisons among them would become comparisons among five somewhat different variables. A more satisfactory procedure is to obtain one general factor for all the age levels and to determine what happens to it as age increases. In this way the analysis deals with the same variable throughout the age range, rather than with five different variables which have the same name." Jerome Edward Doppelt, The Organization of Mental Abilities in the Age Range 13 to 17, Ph.d. dissertation (New York: Bureau of Publications, Teachers College, Columbia University, 1950), p. 22.

Appendix B

THE QUALTY OF THE BEHAVIOR DATA

The size of the sample

The leadership analysis is based on 1782 questionnaires from trainees in twelve companies. The behavior analysis, however, uses only about a third of this total, 636 questionnaires. The principal reason for this smaller sample in the behavior analysis is that the original data included two different types of companies, eight with sixteen-week training cycles and four with eight-week cycles. Since many of the questions deal with the frequency of behavior during the total training cycle, it is impossible to compare rates between companies with cycles of different length. Furthermore, one of the sixteen-week companies received a radically abridged behavior questionnaire, so that the behavior analysis uses only seven companies for which comparable data are available. Since the leadership questionnaires were identical for all twelve companies, the leadership analysis was not affected by the differences in length of training.

Unusable answers

Inspection of the questionnaires revealed a high proportion of facetious and incomplete answers, which apparently stemmed from several causes. The physical arrangements under which the questionnaires were filled out often encouraged facetious or deliberately falsified answers. In some companies the men were seated so close together that a trainee could easily read his neighbor's responses. Under these conditions many

185

gave inaccurate answers, especially in such areas as masturbation and intercourse. Then, too, the questionnaires were administered after the end of the training cycle, when the men were finally free from the restraints of basic training; they were chafing at the least delay in getting their post-training furloughs, and many resented the idea of filling out questionnaires. All these conditions undoubtedly made for carelessness, exaggeration and outright lying.

Another factor that led to inadequate responses was the complexity of the questionnaires. On the leadership questionnaire, the instructions were difficult to follow--for example, trainees frequently said that they had had two CO's but rated only one. Errors also were frequent on the behavior questionnaire, where the time interval varied from one question to the next. One question asked trainees to state the number of times during basic training that they had spent at a hobby, the next question dealt with the number of hours per month devoted to sports, and the following question asked for the number of hours per week spent in bull sessions. Many of the inconsistent or apparently facetious answers may have resulted from failing to keep these changing units in mind.

For a meaningful analysis it was necessary to separate the valid responses from the invalid. Some of this was done in the processing of the questionnaires. Manifestly impossible responses were coded as "unusable": no one can engage in a leisure-time activity for 100 hours a week--at least, not an Army trainee. But what should be done with the trainee who says that he spent twenty-five hours a week in bull sessions? This is not physically impossible, but it seems unlikely, judging from the responses of other trainees. On the other hand, if one simply discards extreme responses, there is the corresponding risk of eliminating those trainees whose behavior is actually extreme. It was therefore necessary to devise a procedure, based on some objective criterion, for detecting extremely inaccurate or careless respondents.

The discrepancy-score technique

Although no direct measure of consistency or accuracy was available for the behavior data, it was possible to make internal checks of consistency on the leadership data. On the last page of the leadership questionnaire (Appendix J) each trainee was asked to state how many leaders had occupied each position in his company and platoon during the training cycle--how many commanding officers, executive officers, first sergeants, etc. Comparing these figures for each trainee with the number of persons he actually rated in each position yielded a "discrepancy score," which distinguished between trainees who had filled out the questionnaire accurately and those who had not.

The index was based on the last two leadership questions. Each trainee was asked to rate six positions, four company-level and two platoon-level. If in each of these answers he rated the same number of leaders as he had reported for that position elsewhere in the leadership questionnaire, his discrepancy score is zero. The maximum discrepancy score is 12, indicating that the trainee rated the wrong number of leaders in all twelve spaces. ("Wrong" refers to his own statement of how many leaders there were in each position.) Table B-1 shows how the discrepancy scores were distributed.

It was decided to base the main analyses of this report, those relating behavior to leadership and to the individual characteristics of trainees, on the responses of trainees in the first two lines of this table--that is, trainees with few or no discrepancies. This decision assumes that high discrepancy-scores on the leadership questionnaire also indicate a tendency toward mistakes or lies in the behavior questionnaire. This assumption is borne out in Table B-2, which shows the relationship between the discrepancy-scores and the number of "no answers" or otherwise unusable answers on six behavior questions.

Table B-1

DISTRIBUTION OF DISCREPANCY SCORES ON
LEADERSHIP QUESTIONNAIRES

Discrepancy score	Proportion of all trainees who filled out questionnaires
	%
0	45
1-4	25
5-8	11
9-12	19
	100
Number of cases	(1702)

Table B-2

DEFECTIVE ANSWERS ON SELECTED BEHAVIOR QUESTIONS
BY DISCREPANCY SCORE ON LEADERSHIP QUESTIONNAIRE

Discrepancy score:	Proportion of defective answers* among trainees with indicated discrepancy scores			
	0 %	1-4 %	5-8 %	9-12 %
Drinking	5	5	12	12
Fighting	2	4	9	16
Intercourse	7	9	15	18
Reading	6	4	14	15
Sick call attendance	4	5	5	14
Short-term AWOL	3	5	7	15

*"Defective answers" include "no answers" and "unusable answers" (facetious or obviously impossible answers). The bases for percentages range from 136 to 771.

Among the trainees with zero discrepancy scores, only 5 per cent failed to answer the question on drinking or else made obviously facetious or impossible answers. The same proportion is found among those with low discrepancy scores (one to four disagreements), but among those with moderate or high scores in the third and fourth columns of the table the proportion of defective answers rises to 12 per cent. This same sharp break between the first two columns and the last two is repeated for most of the six questions. That is, the men with moderate or high discrepancy scores on their leadership questionnaires were also more likely to answer the behavior questions in an unsatisfactory manner.

Defective answers among the trainees with high discrepancy scores are undoubtedly more frequent than indicated in the table. As previously remarked, it was often impossible to differentiate between obviously extreme answers and answers that may really have reflected a high rate of activity. In all such cases the trainee was given the benefit of the doubt, so that many extreme responses have been taken at face value. Since these extreme answers are somewhat more frequent among men with high discrepancy scores, the figures in Table B-2 underestimate the proportion of defective answers among these men. This is another reason for excluding them from the analysis.

Discrepancy scores and the factor analyses[1]

The decision to use only the zero-discrepancy and low-discrepancy trainees produces higher correlations between the different kinds of behavior. Unfortunately for the behavior factor-analysis, the decision to use the discrepancy-score in this way was made long after the factor analyses had been completed.

The leadership factorization was based on correlations between averages taken over at least 100 men in each company. Since the aberrant responses of a few trainees have little effect on these averages, the leadership results are not significantly affected by the failure to use the discrepancy-score technique.

This is not true for the behavior factors, which were inferred from correlations of individual responses, not averages. Any dilution of valid responses with defective responses probably has the effect of lowering the correlations between different activities.[2] The low level of the behavior correlations is one of the major reasons why it is impossible to study the behavior factors as single quantitative variables.[3]

Conversion of units

To facilitate computation, a single numerical code for the frequencies of all types of activity is desirable. The limitation of ten numerical punches in each column of an IBM card led to these categories: 0 (times, hours, etc.), 1, 2, 3, 4, 5, 6-7, 8-10, 11-20, and 21 and over. In order to bring the entire range of reported frequencies within this set of categories, it was frequently necessary to change the units: for example, question 12 inquired into the number of times per week that a trainee saw his wife or girl. Many trainees did this only once in two weeks or less often and consequently gave fractional answers. To make all answers whole numbers the coders converted this question to times in eight weeks, multiplying each response by eight.

Thus the data in many of the tables are reported in units that differ from those in the original questionnaires. Since all questionnaires are treated alike, and since the basis of the analysis is the comparison of differences between groups of trainees, this coding procedure does not affect the results. The following were converted from the original frequency to "times in eight weeks": questions 9, 10, 12, 14, 15, and 17.

NOTES TO APPENDIX B

1. The behavior factor-analysis referred to in this section is presented and discussed in the first part of Appendix I.

2. It is not possible to be more precise about the effects of these facetious answers without a full-scale correlation study based on the low-discrepancy score only. Statistical theories of reliability, which show that unreliability of measures attenuates correlations, are inapplicable here because the "errors" of facetiousness and deliberate falsification have unknown distributions. It is unlikely that these distributions are equivalent to those generated by random processes.

3. A more complete discussion of the reasons for low behavior correlations and the inadequacy of the behavior factors is found in Appendix I.

Appendix C

ASSESSING THE CONSISTENCY OF RESULTS: PROCEDURES FOR HOMOGENEOUS SUBGROUP (HSG) ANALYSIS[1]

A common problem in research is to decide which associations or differences are "important" enough to warrant discussion. One approach is to use a test of statistical significance, commenting on the findings that are "significant" and ignoring those that are not. Apart from the fact that these tests are often inapplicable,[2] the validity of tests of statistical significance as indicators of substantive importance is dubious. A finding can be statistically significant but empirically meaningless, or it may fail to meet the criteria of statistical significance, yet have potential implications that cannot be overlooked. Given a sufficiently large sample, a 1 per cent difference between two groups will be statistically significant, but it is difficult to conceive of any theoretical or practical applications in which such a small difference would have meaning. Conversely, with the small samples that are often used in exploratory research, a relatively large difference of 15 or 20 per cent may be statistically insignificant, but of potentially great theoretical or practical importance.[3]

The decision as to whether or not an association is important thus rests ultimately on the researcher's judgment of the uses to which the results may be put: there are no statistical rules in this area. The exploratory character of this research makes it desirable to examine relatively small differences so as not to overlook possible clues to further research in which refined theory and improved techniques may yield higher associations. Accordingly, the rule of thumb adopted for Chapters V-VIII is to consider as important—i. e., as meriting confirmation

192

by HSG analysis--all differences of 5 per cent or more, whether between leadership climates or between groups of trainees with different combinations of individual characteristics. (For convenience, these differences between climates or groups of trainees are referred to as "marginal differences," by virtue of their occurrence at the margins of the HSG tables.)

Working rules of HSG analysis

In the illustrative example of Chapter III, on drunkenness and leadership climates, five of the six possible HSG differences were found to agree with the marginal difference between leadership climates, none was strongly opposed, and one was so small that it could reasonably be considered as a tie: the hypothesis suggested by the marginal distribution was accordingly accepted. Since most of the marginal differences reported in Chapters V-VIII are confirmed by HSG analysis, it is necessary to set forth the working rules of this procedure in detail, so that the reader will be able to verify any of the conclusions in the text by referring to the HSG tables in Appendix E.

In explaining these rules, a bit of symbolism will be helpful. Instead of referring to the number of comparisons that agree with the marginal hypothesis, the number that neither agree nor disagree (ties), and the number that contradict it, we shall simply state the hypothesis and append to it a set of three figures in parentheses. For example, "Trainees in persuasive climates have a lower incidence of drunkenness than do trainees in weak climates (5-1-0)." This means that of the six HSG comparisons for which there were enough cases to make the percentages meaningful (arbitrarily taken as a minimum of ten cases in each cell of the HSG table), five revealed a lower incidence of drunkenness in the persuasive climate than in the weak climate, one difference was so small as to be considered a tie, and in no comparisons did the persuasive climate have a higher proportion of men who got drunk during basic training.[4]

194

Rules for determining ties

Since HSG percentage comparisons are usually based on small numbers (less than 100 in all cases), exact ties in percentages are relatively infrequent. A base of 20 cases, for example, yields percentages that differ by multiples of 5 per cent, and for a base of 14 the percentages differ by about 7 per cent. Only for 10/20 and 7/14, or 50 per cent, do percentages computed for these two bases coincide exactly. But what is one to make of a pair of values like 2/20, or 10 per cent, and 2/14 or 14 per cent? It would be misleading to report this 4 percentage-point difference as anything but a tie, since the percentages based on a total of 14 cases cannot be any closer to 10 per cent than either 7 per cent (1/14) or 14 per cent (2/14). Thus both the 7 per cent and the 14 per cent figures based on 14 cases should be considered as ties when they are compared with a figure of 10 per cent (for any base).

The problem arises from the smaller of the two bases. This makes it easy to formulate a working rule for deciding on ties in HSG comparisons:

Size of smaller base	Score as tie when difference is less than or equal to:
1-9	Do not compute percentages
10-11	5%
12-14	4%
15 or more	3%

This rule is more restrictive than necessary for large bases: differences of 3 per cent or less are scored as ties regardless of the direction of the difference or the size of the bases involved. This prevents us from confirming a series of findings on the basis of HSG analysis where the differences are so small as to be empirically meaningless. In other words, this rule of thumb makes it harder to verify hypotheses suggested by the marginal distributions, rather than easier.

Rule for confirming marginal hypothesis

When all the HSG comparisons are in the same direction, the marginal hypothesis is obviously confirmed. Similarly, the marginal hypothesis is not confirmed where the HSG comparisons split evenly--for example, four in agreement with the marginal hypothesis and four opposed, or two in agreement, two tied, and two opposed. Such HSG findings are easy to interpret: more difficulty is encountered when the results are not as clearcut as the above examples. Here again, there is no a priori criterion; instead we have had to establish rules of thumb to indicate when the HSG comparisons are taken as confirming a marginal hypothesis.[5]

Consider the three figures showing the number of HSG comparisons that agree with the marginal difference (A), are tied with it (T), and disagree (D). These are represented symbolically in the text and in the tables in Appendix E as (A-T-D). The marginal difference is taken as confirmed when the following conditions are satisfied:

(1) $A + T + D \geqq 6$ (for leadership-climate comparisons)

$\geqq 8$ (for age, education, or marital-status comparisons)

(2) If $D \neq 0$: (2') If $D = 0$:

$A > 2D$ $T \leqq A$
and $T \leqq \dfrac{(A + D)}{2}$

Some representative HSG comparisons and the appropriate decisions are:

Leadership: (4-1-0) Hypothesis not confirmed (Rule 1)

(4-1-1) Hypothesis confirmed

(3-3-1) Hypothesis not confirmed (Rule 2)

Age, education or marital status:

(5-5-0) Hypothesis confirmed (Rule 2')

"Two-item" HSG analysis

The maximum number of HSG comparisons between any two leader-ship climates is eight, since there are eight combinations of the three social attributes when each is dichotomized. And the maximum number of HSG comparisons between the two groups of trainees that differ on some individual characteristics--e.g., older and younger trainees--is twelve, with four combinations of the other two social attributes in each of the three leadership climates. (Perhaps the easiest way to verify these numbers is to look at one of the HSG tables in Appendix E.) In any given table, however, the number of comparisons that can actually be made always falls short of these maximums, because the number of train-ees in certain cells of the table is less than the minimum of ten for which percentages are computed.[6]

As long as the actual number of HSG comparisons is close to the maximum, there is no difficulty. When eight comparisons are theoret-ically possible, it seems reasonable to test the marginal hypothesis on the basis of six HSG comparisons. On the other hand, when the number of usable HSG comparisons falls below two-thirds of those theoretically possible, it does not seem reasonable to give as much credence to the HSG test of the marginal hypothesis. Particularly is this true when the "missing" comparisons are concentrated in one leadership climate or among soldiers with one social attribute in common.

There seem to be two ways out of this dilemma--either to accept the reduced number of comparisons as the best that can be done under the circumstances or to cast about for some alternative way of testing the marginal hypothesis. We have already rejected the first alternative as inconclusive. Fortunately, there is another procedure, which approxi-mates HSG analysis as set forth above. This procedure is called " 'two-item' HSG analysis." We shall illustrate this analysis with the same data that were used in Chapter III, where the logic of the HSG analysis was explained.

The basic HSG analysis was performed with subgroups that are homogeneous with respect to three variables: the younger, less-educated single men; the younger, less-educated, married men; and so on. The two-item HSG analysis follows exactly the same procedure, except that it is done with groups that are homogeneous on two items, rather than on three. These two-item HSG's can be seen in the second part of any HSG table in Appendix E (the twelve lines immediately below the three-item HSG's).

When these two-item HSG comparisons are made on data previously analyzed with the three-item comparisons, the results are in general agreement. In the illustrative example of Chapter III, the lower incidence of drunkenness in the persuasive climate, as compared to the weak climate, was confirmed (5-1-0). The two-item comparisons give essentially the same results (10-2-0;2).[7] A marginal hypothesis that is decisively confirmed by the standard three-item HSG analysis is usually decisively confirmed by the two-item analysis, and vice versa.

This practical equivalence between the two techniques does not mean, however, that the choice between them is a matter of indifference. On the contrary, the two-item technique is inferior in principle and occasionally gives misleading results. In the three-item HSG comparisons each of the groups is independent of all others, because each trainee is in one and only one HSG. A trainee counted in the younger, less-educated, single group is not included elsewhere. The two-item HSG's, on the other hand, are not independent: the same trainee appears in three groups. For instance, the younger, less-educated, single trainee of the three-item HSG appears in the younger, less-educated group; the younger, single group; and the less-educated, single group in the two-item comparisons.

198

Since the two-item HSG's are not independent, each comparison contributes less support than does a single comparison among the three-item groups. The criteria for confirming a hypothesis through two-item HSG analysis are simply more rigorous versions of the rules for the three-item comparisons. The marginal hypothesis is confirmed by two-item HSG analysis when, using the (A-T-D) terminology:

(1) $A + T + D \geqq 8$

(2) If $D \neq 0$:   (2') If $D = 0$:
$A \geqq 3D$ $T < A$

and $T \leqq \dfrac{(A + D)}{2}$

NOTES TO APPENDIX C

1. See Chapter III.

2. Selvin, "A critique of tests of significance. . . , op. cit.

3. As Mosteller and Bush put it, "The [statistical] test is used to give some way of deciding whether to believe in the reality of the observed effect. Having established the reality, there is another question--whether the size of the difference is of any material value." Frederick Mosteller and Robert R. Bush, "Selected quantitative techniques" in Lindzey, Handbook of Social Psychology, op. cit., 289-334, at p. 332. Mosteller and Bush do not, however, take up the converse proposition stated above, that a finding may have apparent material value but not be statistically significant, perhaps because of a small sample.

4. The only exception to this usage will be where "two-item" HSG analysis is necessary; see below, p. 196.

5. Such rules of thumb may seem arbitrary, but they are neither more nor less arbitrary than the decision to use the 5 per cent level of significance instead of some other level.

6. Ten cases is a small number; it would be dangerous indeed to make statements about relationships where the only evidence comes from comparing two groups with as few as ten cases in either group. When such small groups appear in HSG comparisons, however, they are not used alone, but always as part of a total configuration involving a minimum of six intergroup comparisons. Furthermore, in these comparisons it is only the direction of the relationship that is important, not its absolute size.

7. The "2" following the semi-colon denotes a two-item HSG comparison.

Appendix D

DISTRIBUTION OF AGE, EDUCATION, AND MARITAL STATUS IN EACH LEADERSHIP CLIMATE

Table D-1

AGE AND LEADERSHIP CLIMATE

	Persuasive (per cent)	Weak (per cent)	Arbitrary (per cent)
17	3	3	2
18	4	6	5
19	6	12	4
20	12	21	13
21	37	28	42
22	18	13	16
23	6	10	9
24	7	4	7
25+	7	3	2
	100	100	100
Number of cases	(305)	(179)	(181)

Table D-2

EDUCATION AND LEADERSHIP CLIMATE

	Persuasive (per cent)	Weak (per cent)	Arbitrary (per cent)
6th grade or less	4	3	3
7 - 8	13	15	11
9	7	9	7
10	12	10	11
11	11	15	7
12	35	36	45
1 year of college	2	2	2
2 years	5	4	6
3 years	1	1	1
4 years	6	3	5
5 or more years	4	2	2
	100	100	100
Number of cases	(307)	(177)	(182)

Table D-3

MARITAL STATUS AND LEADERSHIP CLIMATE

	Persuasive (per cent)	Weak (per cent)	Arbitrary (per cent)
Single	37	45	29
Single, going steady	27	24	33
Married, no children	28	28	33
Married, 1 child	2	1	1
Married, 2 or more children	3	1	1
Other (widowed, divorced, etc.)	3	2	3
	100	101	100
Number of cases	(304)	(175)	(180)

Appendix E

HOMOGENEOUS SUBGROUP (HSG) TABLES OF BEHAVIOR DURING BASIC TRAINING

These tables are numbered to correspond with the activities on the behavior questionnaire in Appendix J. The rationale of these tables is explained in Chapter III, the techniques of interpretation in Appendix C. The symbol (--) indicates that the percentage has not been computed because the base is less than 10. The following abbreviations have been used in the HSG comparisons at the bottom of each table:

P   Persuasive climate
W   Weak climate
A   Arbitrary climate

Y   Trainees between the ages of 17 and 21
O   Trainees 22 and over

L   Trainees who have not graduated from high school
H   Trainees who have graduated from high school

S   Single trainees
M   Trainees who are, or have been married

$>$ "Is greater than"
$<$ "Is less than"

$\not>$ "Is not greater than"
$\not<$ "Is not less than"

Table E-1

CHAPEL
(8 or more times in 16 weeks)

CHARACTERISTICS OF TRAINEES			LEADERSHIP CLIMATES			TOTAL
Age	Education	Marital Status	Persuasive	Weak	Arbitrary	
			% (N)	% (N)	% (N)	% (N)
17-21	Not HS grad.	Single	37 (59)	23 (47)	46 (39)	
17-21	Not HS grad.	Married	33 (21)	36 (11)	-- (6)	
17-21	HS grad.	Single	53 (78)	43 (42)	49 (57)	
17-21	HS grad.	Married	41 (12)	-- (8)	80 (10)	
22+	Not HS grad.	Single	10 (10)	-- (7)	-- (4)	
22+	Not HS grad.	Married	32 (28)	16 (12)	38 (13)	
22+	HS grad.	Single	59 (29)	46 (13)	-- (9)	
22+	HS grad.	Married	42 (31)	59 (17)	47 (30)	
17-21	Not HS grad.		36 (80)	26 (58)	47 (45)	
17-21	HS grad.		52 (90)	48 (50)	54 (67)	
22+	Not HS grad.		26 (38)	21 (19)	41 (17)	
22+	HS grad.		50 (60)	53 (30)	44 (39)	
17-21		Single	46 (137)	35 (89)	48 (96)	
17-21		Married	36 (33)	42 (19)	69 (16)	
22+		Single	46 (39)	40 (20)	38 (13)	
22+		Married	37 (59)	41 (29)	44 (43)	
	Not HS grad.	Single	33 (69)	24 (54)	47 (43)	
	Not HS grad.	Married	33 (49)	26 (23)	42 (19)	
	HS grad.	Single	55 (107)	47 (55)	47 (66)	
	HS grad.	Married	42 (43)	56 (25)	55 (40)	
17-21			44 (170)	36 (108)	51 (112)	44 (290)
22+			41 (98)	41 (49)	43 (56)	41 (203)
	Not HS grad.		33 (118)	25 (77)	45 (62)	33 (257)
	HS grad.		51 (150)	50 (80)	50 (106)	51 (336)
		Single	46 (176)	36 (109)	47 (109)	44 (394)
		Married	37 (92)	42 (48)	51 (59)	42 (199)
Total			43 (268)	38 (157)	48 (168)	43 (593)

HSG Comparisons

P ≯ W (8-1-3;2)   P ≮ A (7-2-3;2)   L < H (7-1-0)
W < A (7-4-1;2)

Table E-2

CHAPLAIN
(1 or more times in 16 weeks)

CHARACTERISTICS OF TRAINEES			LEADERSHIP CLIMATES			TOTAL
Age	Education	Marital Status	Persuasive	Weak	Arbitrary	
			% (N)	% (N)	% (N)	% (N)
17-21	Not HS grad.	Single	22 (59)	13 (52)	21 (39)	
17-21	Not HS grad.	Married	10 (21)	25 (12)	-- (6)	
17-21	HS grad.	Single	22 (81)	20 (44)	41 (58)	
17-21	HS grad.	Married	9 (11)	-- (8)	40 (10)	
22+	Not HS grad.	Single	20 (10)	-- (7)	-- (3)	
22+	Not HS grad.	Married	25 (32)	31 (13)	14 (14)	
22+	HS grad.	Single	32 (31)	25 (12)	-- (9)	
22+	HS grad.	Married	28 (29)	17 (17)	28 (29)	
17-21	Not HS grad.		19 (80)	16 (64)	24 (45)	
17-21	HS grad.		21 (92)	21 (52)	41 (68)	
22+	Not HS grad.		24 (42)	30 (20)	12 (17)	
22+	HS grad.		30 (60)	21 (29)	29 (38)	
17-21		Single	22 (140)	17 (96)	33 (97)	
17-21		Married	9 (32)	25 (20)	44 (16)	
22+		Single	29 (41)	26 (19)	25 (12)	
22+		Married	26 (61)	23 (30)	23 (43)	
	Not HS grad.	Single	22 (69)	15 (59)	19 (42)	
	Not HS grad.	Married	19 (53)	28 (25)	25 (20)	
	HS grad.	Single	25 (112)	21 (56)	40 (67)	
	HS grad.	Married	22 (40)	20 (25)	31 (39)	
17-21			20 (172)	18 (116)	35 (113)	23 (401)
22+			27 (102)	24 (49)	24 (55)	26 (206)
	Not HS grad.		20 (122)	19 (84)	21 (62)	20 (268)
	HS grad.		24 (152)	21 (81)	37 (106)	27 (339)
		Single	24 (181)	18 (115)	32 (109)	24 (405)
		Married	20 (93)	24 (50)	29 (59)	24 (202)
Total			23 (274)	20 (165)	31 (168)	24 (607)

HSG Comparisons

P < A (7-4-1;2)   L ⊄ H (4-3-1)
W < A (8-3-1;2)

Table E-3

MASS ENTERTAINMENT
(8 or more times in 16 weeks)

CHARACTERISTICS OF TRAINEES			LEADERSHIP CLIMATES			TOTAL
Age	Education	Marital Status	Persuasive	Weak	Arbitrary	
			% (N)	% (N)	% (N)	% (N)
17-21	Not HS grad.	Single	66 (56)	61 (49)	62 (39)	
17-21	Not HS grad.	Married	25 (20)	54 (13)	-- (6)	
17-21	HS grad.	Single	54 (76)	56 (43)	53 (58)	
17-21	HS grad.	Married	55 (11)	-- (8)	60 (10)	
22+	Not HS grad.	Single	36 (11)	-- (7)	-- (4)	
22+	Not HS grad.	Married	37 (32)	23 (13)	31 (13)	
22+	HS grad.	Single	68 (31)	62 (13)	-- (9)	
22+	HS grad.	Married	45 (31)	29 (17)	45 (29)	
17-21	Not HS grad.		55 (76)	60 (62)	62 (45)	
17-21	HS grad.		54 (87)	58 (51)	54 (68)	
22+	Not HS grad.		37 (43)	20 (20)	35 (17)	
22+	HS grad.		56 (62)	43 (30)	45 (38)	
17-21		Single	59 (132)	59 (92)	57 (97)	
17-21		Married	35 (31)	62 (21)	62 (16)	
22+		Single	60 (42)	45 (20)	46 (13)	
22+		Married	41 (63)	27 (30)	40 (42)	
	Not HS grad.	Single	61 (67)	55 (56)	60 (43)	
	Not HS grad.	Married	33 (52)	39 (26)	42 (19)	
	HS grad.	Single	58 (107)	57 (56)	52 (67)	
	HS grad.	Married	48 (42)	44 (25)	49 (39)	
17-21			55 (163)	59 (113)	57 (113)	57 (389)
22+			49 (105)	34 (50)	42 (55)	43 (210)
	Not HS grad.		49 (119)	50 (82)	55 (62)	50 (263)
	HS grad.		55 (149)	53 (81)	51 (106)	53 (336)
		Single	59 (174)	56 (112)	55 (110)	57 (396)
		Married	39 (94)	41 (51)	47 (58)	42 (203)
Total			52 (268)	52 (163)	52 (168)	52 (599)

HSG Comparisons
Y> O (9-2-1;2)
S> M (9-2-1;2)

Table E-4

HOBBY
(1 or more times in 16 weeks)

CHARACTERISTICS OF TRAINEES			LEADERSHIP CLIMATES			TOTAL
Age	Education	Marital Status	Persuasive	Weak	Arbitrary	
			% (N)	% (N)	% (N)	% (N)
17-21	Not HS grad.	Single	22 (41)	7 (15)	29 (38)	
17-21	Not HS grad.	Married	00 (13)	-- (6)	-- (5)	
17-21	HS grad.	Single	21 (58)	18 (22)	31 (54)	
17-21	HS grad.	Married	-- (9)	-- (2)	10 (10)	
22+	Not HS grad.	Single	-- (7)	-- (4)	-- (4)	
22+	Not HS grad.	Married	17 (23)	-- (8)	17 (12)	
22+	HS grad.	Single	40 (20)	-- (5)	-- (9)	
22+	HS grad.	Married	25 (20)	00 (10)	18 (27)	
17-21	Not HS grad.		17 (54)	10 (21)	26 (43)	
17-21	HS grad.		24 (67)	21 (24)	28 (64)	
22+	Not HS grad.		20 (30)	8 (12)	19 (16)	
22+	HS grad.		32 (40)	00 (15)	17 (36)	
17-21		Single	21 (99)	14 (37)	30 (92)	
17-21		Married	18 (22)	-- (8)	7 (15)	
22+		Single	37 (27)	-- (9)	15 (13)	
22+		Married	21 (43)	6 (18)	18 (39)	
	Not HS grad.	Single	23 (48)	5 (19)	28 (42)	
	Not HS grad.	Married	11 (36)	14 (14)	12 (17)	
	HS grad.	Single	26 (78)	15 (27)	29 (63)	
	HS grad.	Married	31 (29)	8 (12)	16 (37)	
17-21			21 (121)	16 (45)	27 (107)	22 (273)
22+			27 (70)	4 (27)	17 (52)	19 (149)
	Not HS grad.		18 (84)	9 (33)	24 (59)	18 (176)
	HS grad.		27 (107)	13 (39)	24 (100)	24 (246)
		Single	25 (126)	11 (46)	29 (105)	24 (277)
		Married	20 (65)	12 (26)	15 (54)	17 (145)
Total			23 (191)	11 (72)	24 (159)	21 (422)

HSG Comparisons

P > W (8-2-0;2)   L < H (6-4-2; 2)
W < A (9-1-0;2)   S > M (6-2-2;2)

Table E-5

SPORTS
(1 or more hours per month)

CHARACTERISTICS OF TRAINEES			LEADERSHIP CLIMATES			TOTAL
Age	Education	Marital Status	Persuasive	Weak	Arbitrary	
			% (N)	% (N)	% (N)	% (N)
17-21	Not HS grad.	Single	34 (38)	50 (14)	44 (39)	
17-21	Not HS grad.	Married	20 (15)	-- (7)	-- (5)	
17-21	HS grad.	Single	43 (60)	44 (23)	60 (57)	
17-21	HS grad.	Married	-- (9)	-- (4)	60 (10)	
22+	Not HS grad.	Single	-- (8)	-- (4)	-- (4)	
22+	Not HS grad.	Married	38 (29)	-- (9)	46 (13)	
22+	HS grad.	Single	45 (22)	-- (6)	-- (9)	
22+	HS grad.	Married	50 (22)	40 (10)	34 (29)	
17-21	Not HS grad.		30 (53)	48 (21)	41 (44)	
17-21	HS grad.		43 (69)	41 (27)	60 (67)	
22+	Not HS grad.		38 (37)	69 (13)	47 (17)	
22+	HS grad.		48 (44)	37 (16)	37 (38)	
17-21		Single	40 (98)	46 (37)	53 (96)	
17-21		Married	29 (24)	36 (11)	47 (15)	
22+		Single	43 (30)	60 (10)	46 (13)	
22+		Married	43 (51)	47 (19)	38 (42)	
	Not HS grad.	Single	35 (46)	61 (18)	44 (43)	
	Not HS grad.	Married	32 (44)	50 (16)	39 (18)	
	HS grad.	Single	44 (82)	41 (29)	58 (66)	
	HS grad.	Married	48 (31)	36 (14)	41 (39)	
17-21			38 (122)	44 (48)	52 (111)	45 (281)
22+			43 (81)	52 (29)	40 (55)	44 (165)
	Not HS grad.		33 (90)	56 (34)	43 (61)	41 (185)
	HS grad.		45 (113)	40 (43)	51 (105)	47 (261)
		Single	41 (128)	49 (47)	52 (109)	46 (284)
		Married	39 (75)	43 (30)	40 (57)	40 (162)
Total			40 (203)	47 (77)	48 (166)	44 (446)

HSG Comparisons

P < W (8-2-2;2)   L ⫃ H (6-1-5;2)
P ⫃ A (8-1-3;2)   S > M (9-2-1;2)

Table E-6

BULL SESSIONS
(8 or more hours per week)

CHARACTERISTICS OF TRAINEES			LEADERSHIP CLIMATES			TOTAL
Age	Education	Marital Status	Persuasive	Weak	Arbitrary	
			% (N)	% (N)	% (N)	% (N)
17-21	Not HS grad.	Single	32 (31)	54 (13)	36 (33)	
17-21	Not HS grad.	Married	27 (15)	-- (4)	-- (6)	
17-21	HS grad.	Single	33 (57)	39 (18)	40 (53)	
17-21	HS grad.	Married	-- (9)	-- (3)	60 (10)	
22+	Not HS grad.	Single	20 (10)	-- (3)	-- (3)	
22+	Not HS grad.	Married	36 (25)	-- (8)	58 (12)	
22+	HS grad.	Single	31 (16)	-- (6)	-- (9)	
22+	HS grad.	Married	19 (22)	50 (10)	38 (26)	
17-21	Not HS grad.		30 (46)	41 (17)	36 (39)	
17-21	HS grad.		33 (66)	38 (21)	42 (63)	
22+	Not HS grad.		31 (35)	27 (11)	47 (15)	
22+	HS grad.		18 (38)	50 (16)	37 (35)	
17-21		Single	33 (88)	45 (31)	38 (86)	
17-21		Married	29 (24)	-- (7)	50 (16)	
22+		Single	27 (26)	-- (9)	25 (12)	
22+		Married	23 (47)	39 (18)	45 (38)	
	Not HS grad.	Single	29 (41)	50 (16)	33 (36)	
	Not HS grad.	Married	32 (40)	16 (12)	50 (18)	
	HS grad.	Single	33 (73)	42 (24)	39 (62)	
	HS grad.	Married	16 (31)	46 (13)	44 (36)	
17-21			32 (112)	39 (38)	40 (102)	36 (252)
22+			25 (73)	41 (27)	40 (50)	33 (150)
	Not HS grad.		31 (81)	35 (28)	39 (54)	35 (163)
	HS grad.		28 (104)	43 (37)	41 (98)	36 (239)
		Single	32 (114)	45 (40)	37 (98)	35 (252)
		Married	25 (71)	32 (25)	46 (54)	34 (150)
Total			29 (185)	40 (65)	40 (152)	35 (402)

HSG Comparisons
$P < W$ (8-1-1;2)
$P < A$ (11-1-0;2)

Table E-7

BLOWING ONE'S TOP
(8 or more times in 16 weeks)

CHARACTERISTICS OF TRAINEES		Marital	LEADERSHIP CLIMATES			TOTAL
Age	Education	Status	Persuasive	Weak	Arbitrary	
			% (N)	% (N)	% (N)	% (N)
17-21	Not HS grad.	Single	33 (55)	32 (47)	37 (35)	
17-21	Not HS grad.	Married	26 (19)	18 (11)	-- (5)	
17-21	HS grad.	Single	35 (77)	39 (41)	26 (53)	
17-21	HS grad.	Married	30 (10)	-- (6)	40 (10)	
22+	Not HS grad.	Single	18 (11)	-- (7)	-- (4)	
22+	Not HS grad.	Married	00 (24)	-- (9)	46 (13)	
22+	HS grad.	Single	20 (30)	23 (13)	-- (9)	
22+	HS grad.	Married	13 (30)	12 (17)	41 (27)	
17-21	Not HS grad.		31 (74)	29 (58)	35 (40)	
17-21	HS grad.		34 (87)	40 (47)	29 (63)	
22+	Not HS grad.		6 (35)	25 (16)	47 (17)	
22+	HS grad.		17 (60)	17 (30)	41 (36)	
17-21		Single	34 (132)	35 (88)	31 (88)	
17-21		Married	28 (29)	29 (17)	33 (15)	
22+		Single	20 (41)	30 (20)	46 (13)	
22+		Married	7 (54)	12 (26)	42 (40)	
	Not HS grad.	Single	30 (66)	33 (54)	38 (39)	
	Not HS grad.	Married	12 (43)	15 (20)	39 (18)	
	HS grad.	Single	31 (107)	35 (54)	29 (62)	
	HS grad.	Married	17 (40)	22 (23)	40 (57)	
17-21			33 (161)	34 (105)	31 (103)	33 (369)
22+			13 (95)	20 (46)	43 (53)	23 (194)
	Not HS grad.		23 (109)	28 (74)	39 (57)	28 (240)
	HS grad.		27 (147)	31 (77)	33 (99)	30 (323)
		Single	31 (173)	34 (108)	33 (101)	32 (382)
		Married	14 (83)	19 (43)	39 (55)	23 (181)
Total			25 (256)	30 (151)	35 (156)	29 (563)

HSG Comparisons

P ≮ W (6-6-0;2)   W < A (9-0-3;2)   Y ≯ O (8-0-4;2)
P < A (9-2-1;2)   S > M (8-3-1;2)

Table E-8

FIGHTING
(1 or more times in 16 weeks)

CHARACTERISTICS OF TRAINEES			LEADERSHIP CLIMATES			TOTAL
Age	Education	Marital Status	Persuasive	Weak	Arbitrary	
			% (N)	% (N)	% (N)	% (N)
17-21	Not HS grad.	Single	30 (61)	22 (51)	26 (39)	
17-21	Not HS grad.	Married	9 (23)	7 (14)	-- (6)	
17-21	HS grad.	Single	32 (81)	29 (42)	25 (56)	
17-21	HS grad.	Married	33 (12)	-- (9)	10 (10)	
22+	Not HS grad.	Single	17 (12)	-- (8)	-- (4)	
22+	Not HS grad.	Married	15 (33)	8 (12)	36 (14)	
22+	HS grad.	Single	19 (31)	00 (13)	-- (9)	
22+	HS grad.	Married	17 (30)	12 (17)	13 (30)	
17-21	Not HS grad.		24 (84)	18 (65)	29 (45)	
17-21	HS grad.		32 (93)	24 (51)	23 (66)	
22+	Not HS grad.		16 (45)	25 (20)	28 (18)	
22+	HS grad.		18 (61)	7 (30)	18 (39)	
17-21		Single	31 (142)	25 (93)	25 (95)	
17-21		Married	17 (35)	4 (23)	25 (16)	
22+		Single	19 (43)	19 (21)	23 (13)	
22+		Married	16 (63)	10 (29)	20 (44)	
	Not HS grad.	Single	27 (73)	25 (59)	23 (43)	
	Not HS grad.	Married	12 (56)	8 (26)	40 (20)	
	HS grad.	Single	29 (112)	22 (55)	26 (65)	
	HS grad.	Married	21 (42)	8 (26)	12 (40)	
17-21			28 (177)	21 (116)	25 (111)	25 (404)
22+			17 (106)	14 (50)	21 (57)	17 (213)
	Not HS grad.		21 (129)	20 (85)	29 (63)	22 (277)
	HS grad.		27 (154)	17 (81)	21 (105)	23 (340)
		Single	28 (185)	24 (114)	25 (108)	26 (407)
		Married	16 (98)	8 (52)	22 (60)	16 (210)
Total			24 (283)	19 (166)	24 (168)	23 (617)

HSG Comparisons

P > W (4-2-0) Y > O (7-3-2;2)
W < A (7-5-0;2) S > M (8-3-1;2)

Table E-9

EATING BETWEEN MEALS
(21 or more times in 8 weeks)

CHARACTERISTICS OF TRAINEES			LEADERSHIP CLIMATES			TOTAL
Age	Education	Marital Status	Persuasive	Weak	Arbitrary	
			% (N)	% (N)	% (N)	% (N)
17-21	Not HS grad.	Single	77 (57)	68 (50)	76 (33)	
17-21	Not HS grad.	Married	67 (21)	62 (13)	-- (6)	
17-21	HS grad.	Single	79 (80)	74 (43)	78 (54)	
17-21	HS grad.	Married	75 (12)	-- (8)	80 (10)	
22+	Not HS grad.	Single	70 (10)	-- (7)	-- (4)	
22+	Not HS grad.	Married	74 (31)	33 (12)	86 (14)	
22+	HS grad.	Single	63 (30)	62 (13)	-- (9)	
22+	HS grad.	Married	68 (31)	65 (17)	83 (30)	
17-21	Not HS grad.		74 (78)	67 (63)	80 (39)	
17-21	HS grad.		78 (92)	69 (51)	78 (64)	
22+	Not HS grad.		73 (41)	42 (19)	78 (18)	
22+	HS grad.		66 (61)	63 (30)	85 (39)	
17-21		Single	78 (137)	71 (93)	77 (87)	
17-21		Married	70 (33)	52 (21)	87 (16)	
22+		Single	65 (40)	60 (20)	77 (13)	
22+		Married	71 (62)	52 (29)	84 (44)	
	Not HS grad.	Single	76 (67)	67 (57)	73 (37)	
	Not HS grad.	Married	71 (52)	48 (25)	90 (20)	
	HS grad.	Single	75 (110)	71 (56)	79 (63)	
	HS grad.	Married	70 (43)	56 (25)	82 (40)	
17-21			76 (170)	68 (114)	80 (103)	75 (387)
22+			69 (102)	55 (49)	82 (57)	69 (208)
	Not HS grad.		74 (119)	61 (82)	79 (57)	72 (258)
	HS grad.		73 (153)	67 (81)	81 (103)	74 (337)
		Single	75 (177)	69 (113)	77 (100)	74 (390)
		Married	71 (95)	52 (50)	85 (60)	70 (205)
Total			74 (272)	64 (163)	80 (160)	73 (595)

HSG Comparisons

P > W (4-2-0)   P < A (9-3-0;2)   Y ≯ O (5-6-1;2)

W < A (12-0-0;2)

Table E-10

DRINKING
(1 or more times in 8 weeks)

CHARACTERISTICS OF TRAINEES			LEADERSHIP CLIMATES			TOTAL
Age	Education	Marital Status	Persuasive	Weak	Arbitrary	
			% (N)	% (N)	% (N)	% (N)
17-21	Not HS grad.	Single	76 (59)	75 (48)	74 (39)	
17-21	Not HS grad.	Married	48 (21)	50 (14)	-- (5)	
17-21	HS grad.	Single	64 (78)	68 (40)	59 (56)	
17-21	HS grad.	Married	50 (12)	-- (8)	-- (9)	
22+	Not HS grad.	Single	45 (11)	-- (8)	-- (4)	
22+	Not HS grad.	Married	50 (32)	58 (12)	46 (13)	
22+	HS grad.	Single	71 (31)	50 (10)	-- (9)	
22+	HS grad.	Married	52 (31)	71 (17)	55 (31)	
17-21	Not HS grad.		69 (80)	69 (62)	77 (44)	
17-21	HS grad.		62 (90)	67 (48)	58 (65)	
22+	Not HS grad.		49 (43)	70 (20)	59 (17)	
22+	HS grad.		61 (62)	63 (27)	58 (40)	
17-21		Single	69 (137)	72 (88)	65 (95)	
17-21		Married	48 (33)	55 (22)	71 (14)	
22+		Single	64 (42)	67 (18)	77 (13)	
22+		Married	51 (63)	66 (29)	52 (44)	
	Not HS grad.	Single	71 (70)	77 (56)	77 (43)	
	Not HS grad.	Married	49 (53)	54 (26)	61 (18)	
	HS grad.	Single	66 (109)	64 (50)	60 (65)	
	HS grad.	Married	51 (43)	68 (25)	55 (40)	
17-21			65 (170)	68 (110)	66 (109)	66 (389)
22+			56 (105)	66 (47)	58 (57)	59 (209)
	Not HS grad.		62 (123)	70 (82)	72 (61)	67 (266)
	HS grad.		62 (152)	65 (75)	58 (105)	61 (332)
		Single	68 (179)	71 (106)	67 (108)	68 (393)
		Married	50 (96)	61 (51)	57 (58)	55 (205)
Total			62 (275)	68 (157)	63 (166)	64 (598)

HSG Comparisons

P < W (3-2-1)   S > M (9-1-2;2)   L > H (7-3-2;2)
W ≯ A (7-1-4;2)   Y ≯ O (6-4-2;2)

212

Table E-11

DRUNKENNESS
(1 or more times in 16 weeks)

CHARACTERISTICS OF TRAINEES			LEADERSHIP CLIMATES			TOTAL
Age	Education	Marital Status	Persuasive	Weak	Arbitrary	
			% (N)	% (N)	% (N)	% (N)
17-21	Not HS grad.	Single	38 (60)	45 (53)	42 (38)	
17-21	Not HS grad.	Married	27 (22)	38 (13)	-- (6)	
17-21	HS grad.	Single	32 (82)	30 (43)	27 (56)	
17-21	HS grad.	Married	00 (12)	-- (8)	10 (10)	
22+	Not HS grad.	Single	17 (12)	-- (8)	-- (4)	
22+	Not HS grad.	Married	16 (32)	33 (12)	29 (14)	
22+	HS grad.	Single	16 (32)	23 (13)	-- (9)	
22+	HS grad.	Married	7 (29)	24 (17)	42 (31)	
17-21	Not HS grad.		35 (82)	44 (66)	45 (44)	
17-21	HS grad.		28 (94)	31 (51)	24 (66)	
22+	Not HS grad.		16 (44)	40 (20)	22 (18)	
22+	HS grad.		11 (61)	23 (30)	42 (40)	
17-21		Single	34 (142)	39 (96)	33 (94)	
17-21		Married	17 (34)	38 (21)	31 (16)	
22+		Single	16 (44)	33 (21)	31 (13)	
22+		Married	11 (61)	28 (29)	38 (45)	
	Not HS grad.	Single	35 (72)	46 (61)	38 (42)	
	Not HS grad.	Married	20 (54)	36 (25)	40 (20)	
	HS grad.	Single	27 (114)	29 (56)	29 (65)	
	HS grad.	Married	5 (41)	28 (25)	34 (41)	
17-21			31 (176)	38 (117)	33 (110)	34 (403)
22+			13 (105)	30 (50)	36 (58)	23 (213)
	Not HS grad.		29 (126)	43 (86)	39 (62)	35 (274)
	HS grad.		21 (155)	28 (81)	31 (106)	26 (342)
		Single	30 (186)	38 (117)	33 (107)	33 (410)
		Married	14 (95)	32 (50)	36 (61)	25 (206)
Total			25 (281)	36 (167)	34 (168)	30 (616)

HSG Comparisons

P < W (5-1-0)   S ⊅ M (6-4-2; 2)   Y > O (9-1-2;2)

P < A (8-3-1;2)   L > H (6-1-1)

Table E-12

SEEING ONE'S WIFE OR GIRL
(1 or more times in 8 weeks)

CHARACTERISTICS OF TRAINEES			LEADERSHIP CLIMATES			TOTAL
Age	Education	Marital Status	Persuasive	Weak	Arbitrary	
			% (N)	% (N)	% (N)	% (N)
17-21	Not HS grad.	Single	51 (57)	66 (50)	39 (38)	
17-21	Not HS grad.	Married	77 (22)	71 (14)	-- (5)	
17-21	HS grad.	Single	76 (75)	75 (44)	58 (57)	
17-21	HS grad.	Married	80 (10)	-- (9)	90 (10)	
22+	Not HS grad.	Single	33 (12)	-- (8)	-- (4)	
22+	Not HS grad.	Married	50 (32)	90 (10)	36 (14)	
22+	HS grad.	Single	77 (31)	61 (13)	-- (9)	
22+	HS grad.	Married	80 (30)	60 (15)	64 (31)	
17-21	Not HS grad.		58 (79)	67 (64)	37 (43)	
17-21	HS grad.		76 (85)	75 (53)	63 (67)	
22+	Not HS grad.		45 (44)	89 (18)	33 (18)	
22+	HS grad.		79 (61)	61 (28)	60 (40)	
17-21		Single	65 (132)	70 (94)	51 (95)	
17-21		Married	78 (32)	74 (23)	67 (15)	
22+		Single	65 (43)	71 (21)	38 (13)	
22+		Married	65 (62)	72 (25)	56 (45)	
	Not HS grad.	Single	48 (69)	69 (58)	38 (42)	
	Not HS grad.	Married	61 (54)	79 (24)	32 (19)	
	HS grad.	Single	76 (106)	72 (57)	56 (66)	
	HS grad.	Married	80 (40)	67 (24)	71 (41)	
17-21			67 (164)	71 (117)	53 (110)	65 (391)
22+			65 (105)	72 (46)	52 (58)	63 (209)
	Not HS grad.		54 (123)	72 (82)	36 (61)	55 (266)
	HS grad.		77 (146)	70 (81)	62 (107)	71 (334)
		Single	65 (175)	70 (115)	49 (108)	62 (398)
		Married	69 (94)	73 (48)	58 (60)	67 (202)
Total			67 (269)	71 (163)	52 (168)	64 (600)

HSG Comparisons

P > A (12-0-0;2)   L < H (6-1-1)
W > A (10-1-1;2)   S < M (8-2-2;2)

Table E-13

READING

(4 or more hours per week)

CHARACTERISTICS OF TRAINEES			LEADERSHIP CLIMATES			TOTAL
Age	Education	Marital Status	Persuasive	Weak	Arbitrary	
			% (N)	% (N)	% (N)	% (N)
17-21	Not HS grad.	Single	20 (35)	29 (14)	31 (36)	
17-21	Not HS grad.	Married	13 (15)	-- (7)	-- (5)	
17-21	HS grad.	Single	30 (60)	32 (22)	33 (57)	
17-21	HS grad.	Married	-- (9)	-- (3)	00 (10)	
22+	Not HS grad.	Single	20 (10)	-- (4)	-- (4)	
22+	Not HS grad.	Married	28 (29)	-- (7)	23 (13)	
22+	HS grad.	Single	32 (22)	-- (6)	-- (9)	
22+	HS grad.	Married	18 (22)	27 (11)	23 (31)	
17-21	Not HS grad.		18 (50)	24 (21)	29 (41)	
17-21	HS grad.		28 (69)	28 (25)	28 (67)	
22+	Not HS grad.		26 (39)	18 (11)	29 (17)	
22+	HS grad.		25 (44)	29 (17)	25 (40)	
17-21		Single	26 (95)	31 (36)	32 (93)	
17-21		Married	12 (24)	10 (10)	7 (15)	
22+		Single	28 (32)	30 (10)	38 (13)	
22+		Married	24 (51)	22 (18)	23 (44)	
	Not HS grad.	Single	20 (45)	28 (18)	32 (40)	
	Not HS grad.	Married	23 (44)	14 (14)	22 (18)	
	HS grad.	Single	30 (82)	32 (28)	33 (66)	
	HS grad.	Married	16 (31)	21 (14)	17 (41)	
17-21			24 (119)	26 (46)	29 (108)	26 (273)
22+			25 (83)	25 (28)	26 (57)	26 (168)
	Not HS grad.		21 (89)	22 (32)	29 (58)	24 (179)
	HS grad.		27 (113)	29 (42)	27 (107)	27 (262)
		Single	27 (127)	30 (46)	33 (106)	30 (279)
		Married	20 (75)	18 (28)	19 (59)	19 (162)
Total			24 (202)	26 (74)	28 (165)	26 (441)

HSG Comparisons
S > M (11-1-0;2)

Table E-14a

INTERCOURSE
(1 or more times in 8 weeks)

CHARACTERISTICS OF TRAINEES			LEADERSHIP CLIMATES			TOTAL
Age	Education	Marital Status	Persuasive	Weak	Arbitrary	
			% (N)	% (N)	% (N)	% (N)
17-21	Not HS grad.	Single	44 (39)	56 (16)	55 (38)	
17-21	Not HS grad.	Married	69 (13)	-- (7)	-- (5)	
17-21	HS grad.	Single	38 (58)	44 (23)	36 (55)	
17-21	HS grad.	Married	-- (8)	-- (4)	100 (10)	
22+	Not HS grad.	Single	36 (11)	-- (4)	-- (3)	
22+	Not HS grad.	Married	64 (25)	-- (6)	61 (13)	
22+	HS grad.	Single	44 (23)	-- (6)	-- (9)	
22+	HS grad.	Married	70 (20)	-- (9)	83 (29)	
17-21	Not HS grad.		50 (52)	52 (23)	58 (43)	
17-21	HS grad.		41 (66)	48 (27)	46 (65)	
22+	Not HS grad.		56 (36)	80 (10)	50 (16)	
22+	HS grad.		56 (43)	53 (15)	76 (38)	
17-21		Single	40 (97)	49 (39)	44 (93)	
17-21		Married	67 (21)	55 (11)	93 (15)	
22+		Single	41 (34)	50 (10)	42 (12)	
22+		Married	67 (45)	73 (15)	76 (42)	
	Not HS grad.	Single	42 (50)	60 (20)	51 (41)	
	Not HS grad.	Married	66 (38)	62 (13)	67 (18)	
	HS grad.	Single	40 (81)	41 (29)	39 (64)	
	HS grad.	Married	68 (28)	69 (13)	87 (39)	
17-21			45 (118)	50 (50)	51 (108)	48 (276)
22+			56 (79)	64 (25)	68 (54)	61 (158)
	Not HS grad.		52 (88)	61 (33)	56 (59)	55 (180)
	HS grad.		47 (109)	50 (42)	57 (103)	52 (254)
		Single	40 (131)	49 (49)	44 (105)	43 (285)
		Married	67 (66)	65 (26)	81 (57)	72 (149)
Total			49 (197)	55 (75)	56 (162)	53 (434)

HSG Comparisons

P ≮ W (6-5-1;2) Y ≮ O (6-4-2;2)
P < A (8-3-1;2) S < M (11-1-0;2)

Table E-14b

INTERCOURSE
(1 to 3 times in 8 weeks)

CHARACTERISTICS OF TRAINEES			LEADERSHIP CLIMATES			TOTAL
Age	Education	Marital Status	Persuasive	Weak	Arbitrary	
			% (N)	% (N)	% (N)	% (N)
17-21	Not HS grad.	Single	29 (39)	37 (16)	37 (38)	
17-21	Not HS grad.	Married	31 (13)	-- (7)	-- (5)	
17-21	HS grad.	Single	28 (58)	14 (23)	25 (55)	
17-21	HS grad.	Married	-- (8)	-- (4)	20 (10)	
22+	Not HS grad.	Single	18 (11)	-- (4)	-- (3)	
22+	Not HS grad.	Married	24 (25)	-- (6)	23 (13)	
22+	HS grad.	Single	27 (23)	-- (6)	-- (9)	
22+	HS grad.	Married	30 (20)	-- (9)	17 (29)	
17-21	Not HS grad.		29 (52)	30 (23)	37 (43)	
17-21	HS grad.		26 (66)	18 (27)	24 (65)	
22+	Not HS grad.		23 (36)	40 (10)	19 (16)	
22+	HS grad.		28 (43)	20 (15)	23 (38)	
17-21		Single	28 (97)	23 (39)	30 (93)	
17-21		Married	24 (21)	28 (11)	26 (15)	
22+		Single	23 (34)	30 (10)	34 (12)	
22+		Married	27 (45)	26 (15)	20 (42)	
	Not HS grad.	Single	26 (50)	45 (20)	34 (41)	
	Not HS grad.	Married	27 (38)	16 (13)	28 (18)	
	HS grad.	Single	28 (81)	10 (29)	28 (64)	
	HS grad.	Married	25 (28)	38 (13)	18 (39)	
17-21			27 (118)	24 (50)	30 (108)	27 (276)
22+			26 (79)	28 (25)	22 (54)	24 (158)
	Not HS grad.		26 (88)	34 (33)	32 (59)	29 (180)
	HS grad.		27 (109)	19 (42)	24 (103)	25 (254)
		Single	26 (131)	25 (49)	31 (105)	28 (285)
		Married	26 (66)	27 (26)	21 (57)	24 (149)
Total			26 (197)	26 (75)	26 (162)	26 (434)

HSG Comparisons
L ⊅ H (6-3-3;2)
S ⊅ M (7-2-3;2)

Table E-14c

INTERCOURSE
(4 or more times in 8 weeks)

CHARACTERISTICS OF TRAINEES			LEADERSHIP CLIMATES			TOTAL
Age	Education	Marital Status	Persuasive	Weak	Arbitrary	
			% (N)	% (N)	% (N)	% (N)
17-21	Not HS grad.	Single	15 (39)	19 (16)	18 (38)	
17-21	Not HS grad.	Married	38 (13)	-- (7)	-- (5)	
17-21	HS grad.	Single	10 (58)	30 (23)	11 (55)	
17-21	HS grad.	Married	-- (8)	-- (4)	80 (10)	
22+	Not HS grad.	Single	18 (11)	-- (4)	-- (3)	
22+	Not HS grad.	Married	40 (25)	-- (6)	38 (13)	
22+	HS grad.	Single	17 (23)	-- (6)	-- (9)	
22+	HS grad.	Married	40 (20)	-- (9)	66 (29)	
17-21	Not HS grad.		21 (52)	22 (23)	21 (43)	
17-21	HS grad.		15 (66)	30 (27)	22 (65)	
22+	Not HS grad.		33 (36)	40 (10)	31 (16)	
22+	HS grad.		28 (43)	33 (15)	53 (38)	
17-21		Single	12 (97)	26 (39)	14 (93)	
17-21		Married	43 (21)	27 (11)	67 (15)	
22+		Single	18 (34)	20 (10)	8 (12)	
22+		Married	40 (45)	47 (15)	56 (42)	
	Not HS grad.	Single	16 (50)	15 (20)	17 (41)	
	Not HS grad.	Married	39 (38)	46 (13)	39 (18)	
	HS grad.	Single	12 (81)	31 (29)	11 (64)	
	HS grad.	Married	43 (28)	31 (13)	69 (39)	
17-21			18 (118)	26 (50)	21 (108)	21 (276)
22+			30 (79)	36 (25)	46 (54)	37 (158)
	Not HS grad.		26 (88)	27 (33)	24 (59)	26 (180)
	HS grad.		20 (109)	31 (42)	33 (103)	27 (254)
		Single	14 (131)	24 (49)	13 (105)	15 (285)
		Married	41 (66)	38 (26)	60 (57)	48 (149)
Total			23 (197)	29 (75)	30 (162)	27 (434)

HSG Comparisons
P < W (7-3-2;2)   Y ⊄ O (7-2-3;2)
P ⊄ A (5-6-1;2)   S < M (10-2-0;2)

Table E-15

MASTURBATION
(1 or more times in 8 weeks)

CHARACTERISTICS OF TRAINEES			LEADERSHIP CLIMATES			TOTAL
Age	Education	Marital Status	Persuasive	Weak	Arbitrary	
			% (N)	% (N)	& (N)	% (N)
17-21	Not HS grad.	Single	12 (33)	12 (16)	28 (35)	
17-21	Not HS grad.	Married	15 (13)	-- (5)	-- (5)	
17-21	HS grad.	Single	22 (55)	23 (22)	22 (54)	
17-21	HS grad.	Married	00 (10)	-- (4)	00 (10)	
22+	Not HS grad.	Single	-- (9)	-- (3)	-- (2)	
22+	Not HS grad.	Married	16 (25)	-- (8)	00 (11)	
22+	HS grad.	Single	19 (21)	-- (6)	-- (9)	
22+	HS grad.	Married	5 (20)	10 (10)	14 (28)	
17-21	Not HS grad.		13 (46)	10 (21)	25 (40)	
17-21	HS grad.		18 (65)	19 (26)	19 (64)	
22+	Not HS grad.		18 (34)	9 (11)	00 (13)	
22+	HS grad.		12 (41)	25 (16)	16 (37)	
17-21		Single	18 (88)	18 (38)	25 (89)	
17-21		Married	9 (23)	-- (9)	00 (15)	
22+		Single	20 (30)	-- (9)	18 (11)	
22+		Married	11 (45)	6 (18)	10 (39)	
	Not HS grad.	Single	14 (42)	16 (19)	27 (37)	
	Not HS grad.	Married	16 (38)	00 (13)	00 (16)	
	HS grad.	Single	21 (76)	29 (28)	22 (63)	
	HS grad.	Married	3 (30)	7 (14)	11 (38)	
17-21			16 (111)	15 (47)	21 (104)	18 (262)
22+			15 (75)	18 (27)	12 (50)	14 (152)
	Not HS grad.		15 (80)	9 (32)	19 (53)	15 (165)
	HS grad.		16 (106)	21 (42)	18 (100)	18 (249)
		Single	19 (118)	23 (47)	24 (100)	22 (265)
		Married	10 (68)	4 (27)	7 (54)	8 (149)
Total			15 (186)	16 (74)	18 (154)	17 (414)

HSG Comparisons
S > M (9-1-0;2)

Table E-16a

SHORT-TERM AWOL
(1 or more times in 16 weeks)

CHARACTERISTICS OF TRAINEES			LEADERSHIP CLIMATES			TOTAL
Age	Education	Marital Status	Persuasive	Weak	Arbitrary	
			% (N)	% (N)	% (N)	% (N)
17-21	Not HS grad.	Single	31 (58)	47 (51)	47 (38)	
17-21	Not HS grad.	Married	13 (23)	46 (13)	-- (6)	
17-21	HS grad.	Single	46 (78)	48 (44)	46 (54)	
17-21	HS grad.	Married	25 (12)	-- (9)	60 (10)	
22+	Not HS grad.	Single	18 (11)	-- (7)	-- (4)	
22+	Not HS grad.	Married	24 (33)	50 (12)	57 (14)	
22+	HS grad.	Single	35 (31)	54 (13)	60 (10)	
22+	HS grad.	Married	37 (30)	41 (17)	65 (31)	
17-21	Not HS grad.		26 (81)	47 (64)	45 (44)	
17-21	HS grad.		43 (90)	45 (53)	48 (64)	
22+	Not HS grad.		23 (44)	53 (19)	44 (18)	
22+	HS grad.		36 (61)	47 (30)	63 (41)	
17-21		Single	40 (136)	47 (95)	47 (92)	
17-21		Married	17 (35)	41 (22)	50 (16)	
22+		Single	31 (42)	55 (20)	43 (14)	
22+		Married	30 (63)	45 (29)	62 (45)	
	Not HS grad.	Single	29 (69)	48 (58)	43 (42)	
	Not HS grad.	Married	20 (56)	48 (25)	50 (20)	
	HS grad.	Single	43 (109)	49 (57)	48 (64)	
	HS grad.	Married	33 (42)	38 (26)	63 (41)	
17-21			35 (171)	46 (117)	47 (108)	42 (396)
22+			30 (105)	49 (49)	58 (59)	42 (213)
	Not HS grad.		25 (125)	48 (83)	45 (62)	37 (270)
	HS grad.		40 (151)	46 (83)	54 (105)	46 (339)
		Single	38 (178)	49 (115)	46 (106)	43 (399)
		Married	26 (98)	43 (51)	59 (61)	40 (210)
Total			33 (276)	47 (166)	51 (167)	42 (609)

HSG Comparisons

P < W (5-1-0)   L < H (5-2-1)
P < A (5-1-0)

Table E-16b

SHORT-TERM AWOL
(3 or more times in 16 weeks)

CHARACTERISTICS OF TRAINEES			LEADERSHIP CLIMATES			TOTAL
Age	Education	Marital Status	Persuasive	Weak	Arbitrary	
			% (N)	% (N)	% (N)	% (N)
17-21	Not HS grad.	Single	21 (58)	22 (51)	24 (38)	
17-21	Not HS grad.	Married	4 (23)	23 (13)	-- (6)	
17-21	HS grad.	Single	26 (78)	27 (44)	28 (54)	
17-21	HS grad.	Married	8 (12)	-- (9)	40 (10)	
22+	Not HS grad.	Single	9 (11)	-- (7)	-- (4)	
22+	Not HS grad.	Married	9 (33)	50 (12)	36 (14)	
22+	HS grad.	Single	23 (31)	31 (13)	30 (10)	
22+	HS grad.	Married	20 (30)	24 (17)	35 (31)	
17-21	Not HS grad.		16 (81)	22 (64)	23 (44)	
17-21	HS grad.		23 (90)	28 (53)	30 (64)	
22+	Not HS grad.		9 (44)	47 (19)	28 (18)	
22+	HS grad.		21 (61)	27 (30)	34 (41)	
17-21		Single	24 (136)	24 (95)	26 (92)	
17-21		Married	6 (35)	27 (22)	31 (16)	
22+		Single	19 (42)	35 (20)	21 (14)	
22+		Married	14 (63)	34 (29)	36 (45)	
	Not HS grad.	Single	19 (69)	24 (58)	21 (42)	
	Not HS grad.	Married	7 (56)	36 (25)	30 (20)	
	HS grad.	Single	25 (109)	28 (57)	28 (64)	
	HS grad.	Married	17 (42)	27 (26)	37 (41)	
17-21			20 (171)	25 (117)	27 (108)	23 (396)
22+			16 (105)	35 (49)	32 (59)	25 (213)
	Not HS grad.		14 (125)	28 (83)	24 (62)	21 (270)
	HS grad.		23 (151)	28 (83)	31 (105)	27 (339)
		Single	22 (178)	26 (115)	25 (106)	24 (399)
		Married	11 (98)	31 (51)	34 (61)	23 (210)
Total			18 (276)	28 (166)	29 (167)	24 (609)

HSG Comparisons
P < W (4-2-0)   L < H (5-2-1)
P < A (4-2-0)

Table E-17a

SICK CALL
(Never in 8 weeks)

CHARACTERISTICS OF TRAINEES			LEADERSHIP CLIMATES			TOTAL
Age	Education	Marital Status	Persuasive	Weak	Arbitrary	
			% (N)	% (N)	% (N)	% (N)
17-21	Not HS grad.	Single	50 (58)	42 (53)	71 (38)	
17-21	Not HS grad.	Married	67 (21)	21 (14)	-- (6)	
17-21	HS grad.	Single	45 (82)	43 (44)	59 (56)	
17-21	HS grad.	Married	58 (12)	-- (9)	60 (10)	
22+	Not HS grad.	Single	55 (11)	-- (8)	-- (4)	
22+	Not HS grad.	Married	45 (33)	42 (12)	54 (13)	
22+	HS grad.	Single	58 (31)	62 (13)	60 (10)	
22+	HS grad.	Married	48 (29)	47 (17)	61 (31)	
17-21	Not HS grad.		54 (79)	37 (67)	73 (44)	
17-21	HS grad.		47 (94)	41 (53)	59 (66)	
22+	Not HS grad.		48 (44)	40 (20)	59 (17)	
22+	HS grad.		53 (60)	53 (30)	61 (41)	
17-21		Single	47 (140)	42 (97)	64 (94)	
17-21		Married	64 (33)	26 (23)	69 (16)	
22+		Single	57 (42)	52 (21)	64 (14)	
22+		Married	47 (62)	45 (29)	59 (44)	
	Not HS grad.	Single	51 (69)	41 (61)	71 (42)	
	Not HS grad.	Married	54 (54)	31 (26)	63 (19)	
	HS grad.	Single	49 (113)	47 (57)	59 (66)	
	HS grad.	Married	51 (41)	42 (26)	61 (41)	
17-21			50 (173)	39 (120)	65 (110)	51 (403)
22+			51 (104)	48 (50)	60 (58)	53 (212)
	Not HS grad.		52 (123)	38 (87)	69 (61)	51 (271)
	HS grad.		49 (154)	46 (83)	60 (107)	52 (344)
		Single	49 (182)	44 (118)	64 (108)	52 (408)
		Married	53 (95)	37 (52)	62 (60)	51 (207)
Total			51 (277)	42 (170)	63 (168)	52 (615)

HSG Comparisons

P ≯ W (2-4-0)   W < A (12-0-0;2)
P < A (4-2-0)

Table E-17b

SICK CALL
(1 or 2 times in 8 weeks)

CHARACTERISTICS OF TRAINEES			LEADERSHIP CLIMATES			TOTAL
Age	Education	Marital Status	Persuasive	Weak	Arbitrary	
			% (N)	% (N)	% (N)	% (N)
17-21	Not HS grad.	Single	28 (58)	41 (53)	16 (38)	
17-21	Not HS grad.	Married	24 (21)	29 (14)	-- (6)	
17-21	HS grad.	Single	40 (82)	39 (44)	29 (56)	
17-21	HS grad.	Married	33 (12)	-- (9)	30 (10)	
22+	Not HS grad.	Single	18 (11)	-- (8)	-- (4)	
22+	Not HS grad.	Married	30 (33)	33 (12)	31 (13)	
22+	HS grad.	Single	36 (31)	23 (13)	40 (10)	
22+	HS grad.	Married	41 (29)	47 (17)	26 (31)	
17-21	Not HS grad.		27 (79)	39 (67)	14 (44)	
17-21	HS grad.		39 (94)	40 (53)	29 (66)	
22+	Not HS grad.		27 (44)	25 (20)	24 (17)	
22+	HS grad.		38 (60)	37 (30)	29 (41)	
17-21		Single	35 (140)	40 (97)	23 (94)	
17-21		Married	27 (33)	35 (23)	19 (16)	
22+		Single	31 (42)	19 (21)	29 (14)	
22+		Married	35 (62)	41 (29)	27 (44)	
	Not HS grad.	Single	26 (69)	38 (61)	14 (42)	
	Not HS grad.	Married	28 (54)	31 (26)	21 (19)	
	HS grad.	Single	39 (113)	35 (57)	30 (66)	
	HS grad.	Married	39 (41)	46 (26)	27 (41)	
17-21			34 (173)	39 (120)	23 (110)	32 (403)
22+			34 (104)	32 (50)	28 (58)	32 (212)
	Not HS grad.		27 (123)	36 (87)	16 (61)	27 (271)
	HS grad.		39 (154)	39 (83)	29 (107)	36 (344)
		Single	34 (182)	36 (118)	24 (108)	32 (408)
		Married	33 (95)	38 (52)	25 (60)	32 (207)
Total			34 (277)	37 (170)	24 (168)	32 (615)

HSG Comparisons
P > A (3-3-0)   L < H (6-1-1)
W > A (10-1-1;2)

Table E-17c

SICK CALL
(3 or more times in 8 weeks)

CHARACTERISTICS OF TRAINEES			LEADERSHIP CLIMATES			TOTAL
Age	Education	Marital Status	Persuasive	Weak	Arbitrary	
			% (N)	% (N)	% (N)	% (N)
17-21	Not HS grad.	Single	22 (58)	17 (53)	13 (38)	
17-21	Not HS grad.	Married	10 (21)	50 (14)	-- (6)	
17-21	HS grad.	Single	15 (82)	18 (44)	12 (56)	
17-21	HS grad.	Married	8 (12)	-- (9)	10 (10)	
22+	Not HS grad.	Single	27 (11)	-- (8)	-- (4)	
22+	Not HS grad.	Married	24 (33)	25 (12)	15 (13)	
22+	HS grad.	Single	6 (31)	15 (13)	00 (10)	
22+	HS grad.	Married	10 (29)	6 (17)	13 (31)	
17-21	Not HS grad.		19 (79)	24 (67)	14 (44)	
17-21	HS grad.		14 (94)	19 (53)	12 (66)	
22+	Not HS grad.		25 (44)	35 (20)	18 (17)	
22+	HS grad.		8 (60)	10 (30)	10 (41)	
17-21		Single	18 (140)	18 (97)	13 (94)	
17-21		Married	9 (33)	39 (23)	12 (16)	
22+		Single	12 (42)	29 (21)	7 (14)	
22+		Married	18 (62)	14 (29)	14 (44)	
	Not HS grad.	Single	23 (69)	21 (61)	14 (42)	
	Not HS grad.	Married	19 (54)	38 (26)	16 (19)	
	HS grad.	Single	12 (113)	18 (57)	11 (66)	
	HS grad.	Married	10 (41)	12 (26)	12 (41)	
17-21			16 (173)	22 (120)	13 (110)	17 (403)
22+			15 (104)	20 (50)	12 (58)	16 (212)
	Not HS grad.		21 (123)	26 (87)	15 (61)	21 (271)
	HS grad.		12 (154)	16 (83)	11 (107)	13 (344)
		Single	16 (182)	19 (118)	12 (108)	16 (408)
		Married	15 (95)	25 (52)	13 (60)	17 (207)
Total			16 (277)	21 (170)	12 (168)	17 (615)

HSG Comparisons

P ⪦ W (2-2-2) L > H (4-4-0)
W > A (9-3-0;2)

Appendix F

ADDITIONAL DATA ON MARITAL STATUS AND BEHAVIOR

Activity	Single	Single, going steady	Married, no children	Married, one or more children
	%	%	%	%
Sick call (times in 8 weeks):				
None	50	54	51	50
1-2	33	31	32	36
3 or more	17	15	17	14
Seeing one's wife or girl (1 or more times in 8 weeks)	59	68	67	71
AWOL (1 or more times in 16 weeks)	44	42	41	32
Eating between meals (21 or more times in 8 weeks)	73	75	70	75
Hobby (1 or more times in 16 weeks)	24	24	16	20
Drunkenness (1 or more times in 16 weeks)	35	30	23	35
Bull sessions (8 or more hours a week)	36	34	35	20
Chaplain (1 or more times in 16 weeks)	21	30	24	25
Chapel (8 or more times in 16 weeks)	39	49	43	45
Blowing one's top (8 or more times in 16 weeks)	32	32	26	29

ADDITIONAL DATA ON MARITAL STATUS AND BEHAVIOR
(CONT.)

Activity	Single	Single, going steady	Married no children	Married, one or more children
	%	%	%	%
Sports (1 or more hours a month)	45	49	39	42
Intercourse (times in 8 weeks):				
None	56	57	27	36
1-3	30	26	24	46
4 or more	14	17	49	18
Drinking (1 or more times in 8 weeks)	70	67	52	81
Fighting (1 or more times in 16 weeks)	25	27	14	29
Reading (4 or more hours a week)	31	30	19	25
Masturbation (1 or more times in 8 weeks)	25	20	8	9
Mass entertainment (8 or more times in 16 weeks)	60	52	42	37
Number of cases	(245)	(183)	(192)	(22)

Appendix G

PROBLEMS IN INTERPRETING THE CHANGE DATA

The data on changes in behavior from civilian life have been given much less consideration in this study than the data on behavior during basic training. From an analytical standpoint, the principal drawback to these change data is that they yield only the direction of the change from civilian life, not its magnitude. [1] Two trainees who went out drinking once during basic training might report that this was less than in a comparable period of civilian life, yet one may have been a heavy drinker and the other a virtual teetotaler.

Another source of difficulty is the necessity for the trainees to "think comparatively." On the average, about 10 per cent of the low-discrepancy trainees [2] did not answer each change question or else gave obviously impossible answers, such as claiming that they did not drink at all during basic training but that this was "more" than in civilian life. Many trainees apparently compared their civilian behavior with their training behavior, rather than vice-versa.

A third difficulty stems from inherent differences between military activities and the nearest point of comparison in civilian life. With what in his civilian experience should a trainee compare sick call? Some trainees might think of seeing their doctors (in the doctor's office?), but others might reject this as not being "the same" as going on sick call. And, even if all trainees did think of their doctors, it would be difficult to interpret this comparison, since the two activities differ in many ways— costs, availability, and so on. Primarily because of this lack of comparability, only thirteen activities are studied comparatively in Chapter VIII.

A final source of error in these comparative data is psychological:
the further people are asked to think back into the past, the less reliable
are their statements about how they behaved. Such distortions of mem-
ory undoubtedly did occur in our data, and they probably were not random.
However, as is evident in Chapter VIII, the consistency of the comparative material, both in itself and as it relates to the preceding analyses,
indicates that this source of error is not important enough to preclude a
meaningful analysis.

There is, of course, no reason to assume that trainees' memories are
faulty only with respect to their civilian behavior. To ask a man how
much time he spent in bull sessions sixteen weeks earlier is to invite
distortion. It would be possible to cut down this distortion considerably
by using the "panel" technique.[3] A three-wave panel--one questionnaire
at the start of basic training, the second a few weeks after, and the third
at the end--would enable one to separate the changes that take place immediately on entering the Army from those that require a period of weeks
or months to take effect. This would permit an empirical test of the
generally-held assumption that significant changes take place primarily
in the first few days or weeks.

NOTES TO APPENDIX G

1. See the behavior questionnaire in Appendix J.

2. The "low-discrepancy trainees" were the ones who were generally consistent in
filling out their leadership questionnaires and were therefore considered to be more
accurate in reporting their behavior (see Appendix B).

3. See the discussion of "panel studies" in Chapter IX.

Appendix H

HOMOGENEOUS SUBGROUP (HSG) TABLES OF NET CHANGES IN BEHAVIOR FROM CIVILIAN LIFE

These tables are numbered to correspond with the activities on the behavior questionnaire in Appendix J, except that certain questions have been omitted because the activities during basic training are not sufficiently comparable to those in civilian life. The construction of these tables is explained in Chapter VIII, the logic of HSG analysis in Chapter III, and the techniques of interpretation in Appendix C. Unlike the tables in Appendix E on behavior during basic training, these tables do not include the three-item tabulations (combinations of age, education, and marital status) because the number of cases for which "change" data are available is too small for computation of these percentages. All HSG comparisons are therefore based on combinations of two items.

The symbol (--) indicates that the percentage has not been computed because the base is less than 10. The same abbreviations that were explained in Appendix E are used here.

Table H-1

NET CHANGES FROM CIVILIAN LIFE: CHAPEL
(Percentage reporting "more" in basic training
minus percentage reporting "less")

CHARACTERISTICS OF TRAINEES			LEADERSHIP CLIMATES			TOTAL
Age	Education	Marital Status	Persuasive	Weak	Arbitrary	
			% (N)	% (N)	% (N)	% (N)
17-21	Not HS grad.		-43 (74)	-72 (49)	-43 (44)	
17-21	HS grad.		-33 (85)	-54 (48)	-36 (66)	
22+	Not HS grad.		-37 (33)	-29 (14)	-47 (17)	
22+	HS grad.		-29 (58)	-31 (26)	-26 (39)	
17-21		Single	-41 (131)	-65 (79)	-38 (94)	
17-21		Married	-21 (28)	-55 (18)	-44 (16)	
22+		Single	-46 (37)	-23 (17)	-62 (13)	
22+		Married	-22 (54)	-35 (23)	-23 (43)	
	Not HS grad.	Single	-51 (64)	-72 (46)	-47 (42)	
	Not HS grad.	Married	-25 (43)	-35 (17)	-37 (19)	
	HS grad.	Single	-36 (104)	-44 (50)	-37 (65)	
	HS grad.	Married	-18 (39)	-50 (24)	-25 (40)	
17-21			-37 (159)	-63 (97)	-39 (110)	-45 (366)
22+			-32 (91)	-30 (40)	-33 (56)	-32 (187)
	Not HS grad.		-41 (107)	-62 (63)	-45 (61)	-48 (231)
	HS grad.		-32 (143)	-46 (74)	-33 (105)	-35 (322)
		Single	-43 (168)	-58 (96)	-41 (107)	-46 (371)
		Married	-22 (82)	-44 (41)	-29 (59)	-30 (182)
Total			-36 (250)	-54 (137)	-37 (166)	-40 (553)

HSG Comparisons

P > W (9-1-2)   Y ⊀ O (8-1-3)
W < A (9-1-2)   L < H (10-1-1)
                       S < M (9-0-3)

Table H-2

NET CHANGES FROM CIVILIAN LIFE: CHAPLAIN
(Percentage reporting "more" in basic training
minus percentage reporting "less")

CHARACTERISTICS OF TRAINEES			LEADERSHIP CLIMATES			TOTAL
Age	Education	Marital Status	Persuasive	Weak	Arbitrary	
			% (N)	% (N)	% (N)	% (N)
17-21	Not HS grad.		-53 (49)	-61 (41)	-55 (37)	
17-21	HS grad.		-35 (69)	-50 (44)	-37 (62)	
22+	Not HS grad.		-64 (28)	- 9 (12)	-80 (15)	
22+	HS grad.		-39 (44)	-20 (25)	-37 (35)	
17-21		Single	-42 (96)	-57 (71)	-44 (85)	
17-21		Married	-46 (22)	-50 (14)	-36 (14)	
22+		Single	-49 (31)	-16 (18)	-28 (11)	
22+		Married	-49 (41)	-16 (19)	-56 (39)	
	Not HS grad.	Single	-57 (42)	-64 (39)	-57 (35)	
	Not HS grad.	Married	-57 (35)	- 7 (14)	-70 (17)	
	HS grad.	Single	-36 (85)	-36 (50)	-34 (61)	
	HS grad.	Married	-36 (28)	-47 (19)	-41 (36)	
17-21			-42 (118)	-56 (85)	-43 (99)	-46 (302)
22+			-49 (72)	-16 (37)	-50 (50)	-42 (159)
	Not HS grad.		-57 (77)	-49 (53)	-61 (52)	-57 (182)
	HS grad.		-36 (113)	-39 (69)	-36 (97)	-37 (279)
		Single	-43 (127)	-49 (89)	-43 (96)	-45 (312)
		Married	-47 (63)	-31 (33)	-51 (53)	-45 (149)
Total			-45 (190)	-43 (122)	-46 (149)	-45 (461)

HSG Comparisons

L < H (10-0-2)

Table H-3

NET CHANGES FROM CIVILIAN LIFE: MASS ENTERTAINMENT
(Percentage reporting "more" in basic training
minus percentage reporting "less")

CHARACTERISTICS OF TRAINEES			LEADERSHIP CLIMATES			TOTAL
Age	Education	Marital Status	Persuasive	Weak	Arbitrary	
			% (N)	% (N)	% (N)	% (N)
17-21	Not HS grad.		-65 (71)	-21 (57)	-27 (45)	
17-21	HS grad.		-50 (80)	-58 (50)	-49 (66)	
22+	Not HS grad.		-39 (36)	-53 (15)	-50 (16)	
22+	HS grad.		-56 (59)	-53 (30)	-65 (37)	
17-21		Single	-54 (122)	-39 (89)	-37 (95)	
17-21		Married	-69 (29)	-33 (18)	-56 (16)	
22+		Single	-46 (39)	-50 (20)	-38 (13)	
22+		Married	-52 (56)	-56 (25)	-68 (40)	
	Not HS grad.	Single	-51 (61)	-28 (54)	-26 (43)	
	Not HS grad.	Married	-63 (46)	-28 (18)	-50 (18)	
	HS grad.	Single	-53 (100)	-55 (55)	-45 (65)	
	HS grad.	Married	-51 (39)	-60 (25)	-71 (38)	
17-21			-57 (151)	-38 (107)	-40 (111)	-46 (369)
22+			-49 (95)	-53 (45)	-60 (53)	-53 (193)
	Not HS grad.		-56 (107)	-28 (72)	-33 (61)	-42 (240)
	HS grad.		-53 (139)	-56 (80)	-54 (103)	-54 (322)
		Single	-52 (161)	-41 (109)	-37 (108)	-45 (378)
		Married	-58 (85)	-47 (43)	-64 (56)	-57 (184)
Total			-54 (246)	-43 (152)	-46 (164)	-49 (562)

HSG Comparisons

P ≮ W (5-2-5)   Y ≯ O (7-1-4)
P ≮ A (7-1-4)   L > H (8-2-2)
                  S > M (9-2-1)

Table H-4

NET CHANGES FROM CIVILIAN LIFE: HOBBY
(Percentage reporting "more" in basic training
minus percentage reporting "less")

CHARACTERISTICS OF TRAINEES			LEADERSHIP CLIMATES			TOTAL
Age	Education	Marital Status	Persuasive	Weak	Arbitrary	
			% (N)	% (N)	% (N)	% (N)
17-21	Not HS grad.		-72 (43)	-61 (13)	-71 (31)	
17-21	HS grad.		-81 (57)	-51 (22)	-74 (51)	
22+	Not HS grad.		-72 (25)	-- (7)	-100 (14)	
22+	HS grad.		-77 (38)	-- (9)	-72 (32)	
17-21		Single	-77 (81)	-53 (32)	-76 (69)	
17-21		Married	-79 (19)	-- (3)	-62 (13)	
22+		Single	-84 (25)	-- (7)	-82 (11)	
22+		Married	-68 (38)	-- (9)	-80 (35)	
	Not HS grad.	Single	-68 (38)	-63 (16)	-77 (30)	
	Not HS grad.	Married	-76 (30)	-- (4)	-87 (15)	
	HS grad.	Single	-84 (68)	-53 (23)	-76 (50)	
	HS grad.	Married	-66 (27)	-- (8)	-69 (33)	
17-21			-77 (100)	-54 (35)	-73 (82)	-72 (217)
22+			-75 (63)	-69 (16)	-80 (46)	-76 (125)
	Not HS grad.		-72 (68)	-55 (20)	-80 (45)	-72 (133)
	HS grad.		-79 (95)	-62 (31)	-74 (83)	-75 (209)
		Single	-78 (106)	-57 (39)	-76 (80)	-73 (225)
		Married	-72 (57)	-67 (12)	-75 (48)	-73 (117)
Total			-76 (163)	-59 (51)	-76 (128)	-73 (342)

HSG Comparisons

P ◁ W (5-0-0)
W ▷ A (5-0-0)

Table H-5

NET CHANGES FROM CIVILIAN LIFE: SPORTS
(Percentage reporting "more" in basic training
minus percentage reporting "less")

CHARACTERISTICS OF TRAINEES			LEADERSHIP CLIMATES			TOTAL
Age	Education	Marital Status	Persuasive	Weak	Arbitrary	
			% (N)	% (N)	% (N)	% (N)
17-21	Not HS grad.		-70 (44)	-57 (16)	-73 (36)	
17-21	HS grad.		-73 (60)	-73 (26)	-65 (60)	
22+	Not HS grad.		-59 (27)	-- (9)	-56 (16)	
22+	HS grad.		-89 (37)	-54 (15)	-65 (34)	
17-21		Single	-72 (83)	-63 (35)	-67 (83)	
17-21		Married	-71 (21)	-- (7)	-69 (13)	
22+		Single	-79 (24)	-60 (10)	-59 (12)	
22+		Married	-75 (40)	-72 (14)	-63 (38)	
	Not HS grad.	Single	-65 (37)	-64 (17)	-67 (36)	
	Not HS grad.	Married	-68 (34)	-- (8)	-69 (16)	
	HS grad.	Single	-78 (70)	-60 (28)	-67 (59)	
	HS grad.	Married	-81 (27)	-77 (13)	-63 (35)	
17-21			-72 (104)	-66 (42)	-68 (96)	-69 (242)
22+			-76 (64)	-67 (24)	-62 (50)	-70 (138)
	Not HS grad.		-67 (71)	-68 (25)	-67 (52)	-67 (148)
	HS grad.		-79 (97)	-66 (41)	-65 (94)	-71 (232)
		Single	-73 (107)	-62 (45)	-67 (95)	-69 (247)
		Married	-74 (61)	-76 (21)	-65 (51)	-70 (133)
Total			-74 (168)	-67 (66)	-66 (146)	-70 (380)

HSG Comparisons

P < W (5-4-0)
P < A (7-5-0)

Table H-6

NET CHANGES FROM CIVILIAN LIFE: BULL SESSIONS
(Percentage reporting "more" in basic training
minus percentage reporting "less")

CHARACTERISTICS OF TRAINEES			LEADERSHIP CLIMATES			TOTAL
Age	Education	Marital Status	Persuasive	Weak	Arbitrary	
			% (N)	% (N)	% (N)	% (N)
17-21	Not HS grad.		-32 (38)	23 (13)	-23 (34)	
17-21	HS grad.		-15 (59)	14 (21)	0 (61)	
22+	Not HS grad.		-16 (25)	-- (9)	14 (14)	
22+	HS grad.		-18 (33)	0 (16)	3 (34)	
17-21		Single	-22 (78)	17 (29)	-14 (81)	
17-21		Married	-21 (19)	-- (5)	22 (14)	
22+		Single	-10 (20)	-- (9)	-19 (11)	
22+		Married	-21 (38)	13 (16)	14 (37)	
	Not HS grad.	Single	-29 (31)	14 (14)	-24 (33)	
	Not HS grad.	Married	-22 (32)	-- (8)	13 (15)	
	HS grad.	Single	-15 (67)	0 (24)	- 8 (59)	
	HS grad.	Married	-20 (25)	23 (13)	17 (36)	
17-21			-21 (97)	18 (34)	- 9 (95)	-10 (226)
22+			-17 (58)	- 4 (25)	6 (48)	- 6 (131)
	Not HS grad.		-26 (63)	10 (22)	-12 (48)	-15 (133)
	HS grad.		-17 (92)	8 (37)	1 (95)	- 5 (224)
		Single	-19 (98)	5 (38)	-14 (92)	-13 (228)
		Married	-21 (57)	14 (21)	16 (51)	- 1 (129)
Total			-20 (155)	8 (59)	- 4 (143)	- 9 (357)

HSG Comparisons

P < W (8-0-0)	L < H (6-2-1)
W > A (6-1-1)	S < M (6-1-2)
P < A (11-0-1)	

Table H-7

NET CHANGES FROM CIVILIAN LIFE: BLOWING ONE'S TOP
(Percentage reporting "more" in basic training
minus percentage reporting "less")

CHARACTERISTICS OF TRAINEES			LEADERSHIP CLIMATES			TOTAL
Age	Education	Marital Status	Persuasive	Weak	Arbitrary	
			% (N)	% (N)	% (N)	% (N)
17-21	Not HS grad.		3 (63)	21 (42)	-11 (38)	
17-21	HS grad.		48 (75)	35 (43)	39 (54)	
22+	Not HS grad.		31 (26)	8 (13)	27 (15)	
22+	HS grad.		36 (56)	21 (28)	27 (37)	
17-21		Single	26 (112)	26 (73)	15 (78)	
17-21		Married	35 (26)	42 (12)	36 (14)	
22+		Single	51 (35)	26 (19)	0 (13)	
22+		Married	21 (47)	9 (22)	36 (39)	
	Not HS grad.	Single	0 (52)	21 (43)	- 8 (38)	
	Not HS grad.	Married	27 (37)	8 (12)	20 (15)	
	HS grad.	Single	50 (95)	31 (49)	28 (53)	
	HS grad.	Married	25 (36)	27 (22)	42 (38)	
17-21			28 (138)	28 (85)	19 (92)	25 (315)
22+			34 (82)	17 (41)	27 (52)	28 (175)
	Not HS grad.		11 (89)	18 (55)	0 (53)	10 (197)
	HS grad.		43 (131)	30 (71)	34 (91)	37 (293)
		Single	32 (147)	26 (92)	13 (91)	25 (330)
		Married	26 (73)	21 (34)	36 (53)	28 (160)
Total			30 (220)	25 (126)	21 (144)	26 (490)

HSG Comparisons

P $\not>$ W (7-2-3)   L $<$ H (10-2-0)
P $>$ A (8-2-2)

Table H-8

NET CHANGES FROM CIVILIAN LIFE: FIGHTING
(Percentage reporting "more" in basic training
minus percentage reporting "less")

CHARACTERISTICS OF TRAINEES			LEADERSHIP CLIMATES			TOTAL
Age	Education	Marital Status	Persuasive	Weak	Arbitrary	
			% (N)	% (N)	% (N)	% (N)
17-21	Not HS grad.		-36 (54)	-33 (45)	-29 (35)	
17-21	HS grad.		8 (67)	-18 (43)	0 (53)	
22+	Not HS grad.		- 8 (27)	-36 (14)	31 (16)	
22+	HS grad.		14 (49)	- 4 (25)	- 9 (36)	
17-21		Single	-10 (96)	-24 (71)	-15 (76)	
17-21		Married	-16 (25)	-35 (17)	9 (12)	
22+		Single	16 (32)	-22 (18)	- 7 (13)	
22+		Married	0 (44)	- 9 (21)	8 (39)	
	Not HS grad.	Single	-32 (44)	-29 (44)	-29 (35)	
	Not HS grad.	Married	-19 (37)	-47 (15)	31 (16)	
	HS grad.	Single	11 (84)	-18 (45)	- 4 (54)	
	HS grad.	Married	10 (32)	- 4 (23)	- 2 (35)	
17-21			-11 (121)	-26 (88)	-11 (88)	-16 (297)
22+			6 (76)	-16 (39)	3 (52)	1 (167)
	Not HS grad.		-26 (81)	-34 (59)	- 9 (51)	-24 (191)
	HS grad.		11 (116)	-14 (68)	- 4 (89)	0 (273)
		Single	- 4 (128)	-24 (89)	-14 (89)	-12 (306)
		Married	- 5 (69)	-21 (38)	8 (51)	- 5 (158)
Total			- 4 (197)	-23 (127)	- 6 (140)	-10 (464)

HSG Comparisons

P > W (10-2-0)   Y < O (8-3-1)
W < A (9-2-1)   L < H (10-0-2)
                       S ≮ M (6-2-4)

Table H-10

NET CHANGES FROM CIVILIAN LIFE: DRINKING
(Percentage reporting "more" in basic training
minus percentage reporting "less")

CHARACTERISTICS OF TRAINEES			LEADERSHIP CLIMATES			TOTAL
Age	Education	Marital Status	Persuasive	Weak	Arbitrary	
			% (N)	% (N)	% (N)	% (N)
17-21	Not HS grad.		-23 (65)	- 5 (56)	-19 (41)	
17-21	HS grad.		- 6 (69)	- 2 (47)	-20 (55)	
22+	Not HS grad.		-17 (30)	-19 (16)	27 (15)	
22+	HS grad.		-32 (54)	-12 (25)	13 (38)	
17-21		Single	-12 (108)	0 (83)	-25 (83)	
17-21		Married	-23 (26)	-20 (20)	16 (13)	
22+		Single	-52 (33)	-11 (18)	- 7 (13)	
22+		Married	-10 (51)	-17 (23)	25 (40)	
	Not HS grad.	Single	-30 (54)	- 4 (52)	-16 (40)	
	Not HS grad.	Married	-10 (41)	-20 (20)	13 (16)	
	HS grad.	Single	-17 (87)	0 (49)	-28 (56)	
	HS grad.	Married	-20 (36)	-18 (23)	27 (37)	
17-21			-14 (134)	- 4 (103)	-20 (96)	-12 (333)
22+			-26 (84)	-15 (41)	17 (53)	-11 (178)
	Not HS grad.		-21 (95)	- 9 (72)	- 7 (56)	-14 (223)
	HS grad.		-17 (123)	- 5 (72)	- 6 (93)	-11 (288)
		Single	-22 (141)	- 2 (101)	-23 (96)	-16 (338)
		Married	-14 (77)	-18 (43)	23 (53)	- 4 (173)
Total			-18 (218)	- 7 (144)	- 7 (149)	-12 (511)

HSG Comparisons

P < W (7-3-2)   S ≮ M (6-1-5)
P < A (9-0-3)

Table H-11

NET CHANGES FROM CIVILIAN LIFE: DRUNKENNESS
(Percentage reporting "more" in basic training
minus percentage reporting "less")

CHARACTERISTICS OF TRAINEES			LEADERSHIP CLIMATES			TOTAL
Age	Education	Marital Status	Persuasive	Weak	Arbitrary	
			% (N)	% (N)	% (N)	% (N)
17-21	Not HS grad.		-26 (61)	-20 (50)	-20 (34)	
17-21	HS grad.		-18 (74)	2 (42)	-13 (54)	
22+	Not HS grad.		-14 (21)	- 7 (14)	22 (14)	
22+	HS grad.		-20 (45)	-25 (24)	23 (35)	
17-21		Single	-21 (109)	- 9 (74)	-22 (77)	
17-21		Married	-27 (26)	-11 (18)	27 (11)	
22+		Single	-29 (28)	-23 (17)	0 (10)	
22+		Married	-10 (38)	-14 (21)	28 (39)	
	Not HS grad.	Single	-34 (47)	-19 (47)	-26 (34)	
	Not HS grad.	Married	- 8 (35)	-11 (17)	36 (14)	
	HS grad.	Single	-15 (90)	- 5 (44)	-15 (53)	
	HS grad.	Married	-28 (29)	-14 (22)	26 (36)	
17-21			-22 (135)	-10 (92)	-16 (88)	-17 (315)
22+			-19 (66)	-18 (38)	22 (49)	- 5 (153)
	Not HS grad.		-23 (82)	-17 (64)	- 8 (48)	-17 (194)
	HS grad.		-18 (119)	- 7 (66)	1 (89)	-10 (274)
		Single	-22 (137)	-12 (91)	-19 (87)	-18 (315)
		Married	-17 (64)	-13 (39)	28 (50)	- 1 (153)
Total			-20 (201)	-12 (130)	- 2 (137)	-13 (468)

HSG Comparisons

P < W (9-1-2) Y ≮ O (6-3-3)
P < A (10-2-0) L ≮ H (6-2-4)
W ≮ A (7-1-4) S ≮ M (8-1-3)

Table H-13

NET CHANGES FROM CIVILIAN LIFE: READING
(Percentage reporting "more" in basic training
minus percentage reporting "less")

CHARACTERISTICS OF TRAINEES			LEADERSHIP CLIMATES			TOTAL
Age	Education	Marital Status	Persuasive	Weak	Arbitrary	
			% (N)	% (N)	% (N)	% (N)
17-21	Not HS grad.		-68 (38)	-57 (14)	-49 (33)	
17-21	HS grad.		-69 (64)	-64 (25)	-67 (57)	
22+	Not HS grad.		-54 (24)	-- (8)	-60 (15)	
22+	HS grad.		-84 (38)	-31 (16)	-75 (36)	
17-21		Single	-68 (83)	-58 (33)	-56 (79)	
17-21		Married	-74 (19)	-- (6)	-91 (11)	
22+		Single	-83 (24)	-70 (10)	-50 (12)	
22+		Married	-66 (38)	-36 (14)	-77 (39)	
	Not HS grad.	Single	-59 (32)	-60 (15)	-39 (33)	
	Not HS grad.	Married	-67 (30)	-- (7)	-80 (15)	
	HS grad.	Single	-76 (75)	-61 (28)	-64 (58)	
	HS grad.	Married	-70 (27)	-31 (13)	-80 (35)	
17-21			-69 (102)	-61 (39)	-60 (90)	-64 (231)
22+			-73 (62)	-50 (24)	-71 (51)	-68 (137)
	Not HS grad.		-63 (62)	-68 (22)	-52 (48)	-60 (132)
	HS grad.		-75 (102)	-51 (41)	-70 (93)	-69 (236)
		Single	-71 (107)	-60 (43)	-55 (91)	-63 (241)
		Married	-69 (57)	-50 (20)	-80 (50)	-70 (127)
Total			-70 (164)	-57 (63)	-64 (141)	-65 (368)

HSG Comparisons

P < W (8-1-0) Y ⊅ O (5-0-5)
P ≮ A (6-1-5) L > H (6-4-0)
W ⊅ A (3-3-3) S ⊅ M (6-0-4)

Table H-14

NET CHANGES FROM CIVILIAN LIFE: INTERCOURSE
(Percentage reporting "more" in basic training
minus percentage reporting "less")

CHARACTERISTICS OF TRAINEES			LEADERSHIP CLIMATES			TOTAL
Age	Education	Marital Status	Persuasive	Weak	Arbitrary	
			% (N)	% (N)	% (N)	% (N)
17-21	Not HS grad.		-71 (35)	-67 (15)	-58 (33)	
17-21	HS grad.		-41 (54)	-52 (25)	-62 (56)	
22+	Not HS grad.		-70 (20)	-- (7)	-100 (13)	
22+	HS grad.		-64 (36)	-33 (12)	-68 (37)	
17-21		Single	-49 (72)	-48 (33)	-59 (75)	
17-21		Married	-71 (17)	-- (7)	-72 (14)	
22+		Single	-50 (24)	-- (8)	-46 (11)	
22+		Married	-78 (32)	-55 (11)	-85 (39)	
	Not HS grad.	Single	-63 (30)	-67 (15)	-61 (31)	
	Not HS grad.	Married	-80 (25)	-- (7)	-87 (15)	
	HS grad.	Single	-42 (66)	-42 (26)	-55 (55)	
	HS grad.	Married	-71 (24)	-55 (11)	-79 (38)	
17-21			-53 (89)	-57 (40)	-61 (89)	-57 (218)
22+			-66 (56)	-58 (19(	-76 (50)	-69 (125)
	Not HS grad.		-71 (55)	-77 (22)	-70 (46)	-72 (123)
	HS grad.		-50 (90)	-46 (37)	-65 (93)	-55 (220)
		Single	-49 (96)	-51 (41)	-57 (86)	-53 (223)
		Married	-76 (49)	-72 (18)	-81 (53)	-77 (120)
Total			-58 (145)	-58 (59)	-66 (139)	-61 (343)

HSG Comparisons

P > A (8-3-1)   Y ⫸ O (5-2-2)
W > A (6-0-2)   L < H (9-0-1)
                 S > M (9-0-0)

Table H-15

NET CHANGES FROM CIVILIAN LIFE: MASTURBATION
(Percentage reporting "more" in basic training
minus percentage reporting "less")

CHARACTERISTICS OF TRAINEES			LEADERSHIP CLIMATES			TOTAL
Age	Education	Marital Status	Persuasive	Weak	Arbitrary	
			% (N)	% (N)	% (N)	% (N)
17-21	Not HS grad.		-46 (28)	-42 (14)	-39 (28)	
17-21	HS grad.		-25 (44)	-29 (24)	-29 (45)	
22+	Not HS grad.		6 (17)	-- (8)	-- (7)	
22+	HS grad.		-16 (31)	-23 (13)	-15 (34)	
17-21		Single	-29 (55)	-31 (32)	-37 (63)	
17-21		Married	-47 (17)	-- (6)	-10 (10)	
22+		Single	-11 (18)	-- (9)	-- (8)	
22+		Married	- 7 (30)	-16 (12)	-12 (33)	
	Not HS grad.	Single	-26 (23)	-36 (14)	-44 (25)	
	Not HS grad.	Married	-28 (22)	-- (8)	0 (10)	
	HS grad.	Single	-24 (50)	-33 (27)	-29 (46)	
	HS grad.	Married	-16 (25)	-10 (10)	-15 (33)	
17-21			-33 (72)	-34 (38)	-33 (73)	-34 (183)
22+			- 9 (48)	-29 (21)	-12 (41)	-14 (110)
	Not HS grad.		-27 (45)	-41 (22)	-31 (35)	-31 (102)
	HS grad.		-21 (75)	-27 (37)	-23 (79)	-23 (191)
		Single	-24 (73)	-35 (41)	-34 (71)	-30 (185)
		Married	-21 (57)	-28 (18)	-12 (43)	-18 (108)
Total			-23 (120)	-32 (59)	-25 (114)	-26 (293)

HSG Comparisons

P > W (5-2-1)   Y ⨤ O (6-1-0)
W ⨤ A (2-4-2)   L ⨤ H (5-2-2)
                       S < M (6-1-1)

Appendix I

A FACTOR-ANALYTIC STUDY OF NONDUTY BEHAVIOR

To make the explanation as simple as possible, this appendix has been divided into two main sections. The first part discusses some clusters of nonduty activities that have been identified by means of a factor analysis similar to, but not as precise as, the factor analysis of leadership discussed in Chapter II and Appendix A. The second part takes up the technical aspects of this factor analysis and some suggestions for further research.

PATTERNS OF NONDUTY BEHAVIOR

Most human beings spend their time in patterns or sequences of activities that generally "make sense," although the sense may not always be obvious to an onlooker. Occasionally, these patterns can be identified because the various activities have a common relationship to something else, either as cause or effect. Such, for example, is the case of the behavior found to characterize the married trainees or to occur frequently in the persuasive leadership climate. One pattern, which has been repeatedly noticed, includes the four "aggressive" activities of drinking, drunkenness, fighting, and blowing one's top. It often happens, however, that different kinds of behavior may cluster together without any clear relationship to an "external" variable. In such cases the search for

meaningful patterns may be based on the extent to which participation in
one activity is quantitatively associated with participation in others—that
is, a criterion of internal consistency.[1]

This was the logic behind the identification of the leadership factors
in Chapter II. The techniques of factor analysis merely served to trace
out the complicated networks of relationship and to construct three factors of perceived leadership underlying the fifteen specific questions
answered by the trainees. The success of the leadership analysis naturally suggests another factor analysis to identify meaningful configura-
tions in the trainees' nonduty behavior.

As we shall demonstrate, the factor-analytic approach yields valuable results here too, but not nearly to the same extent that it did for the
leadership data. The reasons for the less successful results of this behavior factor analysis are important to those who might wish to treat
similar data in this way: some of these reasons will be considered in
the second part of this appendix, but the disparities between the two analyses are so great as to warrant a word of explanation here.

The leadership analysis described the perceptions of an "average
trainee"; that is, the perceptions of the men in each company were averaged in order to arrive ultimately at group indices of leadership climate. These indices of leadership climate are truly aggregate properties, characterizing each group as a whole, rather than any one of the
individuals in it. The behavior factor analysis is concerned with what individual trainees actually do, not the "average trainee," nor the company as a whole. Consequently, the averaging technique has no place in
the factor analysis of behavior. Instead of correlating group averages
the task is to correlate individual frequencies.

This difference has important consequences (apart from the obvious
one that the focus of attention is on individuals, rather than groups). As
explained in Chapter II and in Appendix A, computing the correlations

from company averages eliminates most of the errors, misperceptions, and facetiousness, which occur more or less randomly from one trainee to another. Hence the correlations between averages are not attenuated by random errors: they reflect the common elements in the trainees' perceptions.

Since the behavior analysis is based on individual data, not on averages, the preceding condition does not hold, and the correlations are low. Thus the factor analysis to be discussed in the following pages is inherently less satisfactory than the leadership analysis. This is not to say, however, that it is without value. It confirms the existence of some clusters for which suggestive evidence was compiled previously; it isolates new and perhaps unexpected patterns of nonduty behavior; and it casts light on the meanings of these different forms of behavior to the trainees. The factors are tentative and uncertain, but they do indicate the types of findings that a more complete analysis might pursue further.[2]

Five factors of nonduty behavior

Five relatively clear factors of behavior emerge from the complicated web of correlations between the nineteen nonduty activities.[3] The interpretation of these factors depends on the activities that enter into each one and the relative importance of these activities. The relationships between the five factors and the nineteen activities are shown in Table I-1. Across the top of the table are listed the five factors in the order of their power as explanatory concepts (technically, according to the variation in behavior accounted for by each factor). The entries in the body of the table measure the relative importance of each item to the factor at the top of the column. For example, if we were to give a score on Aggressive Activity to each trainee, his frequency of drinking would count three times as much as his frequency of drunkenness.[4]

Aggressive Activity (Factor I).   Here is independent statistical confirmation of what has become increasingly clear in the preceding analyses—that drinking, drunkenness, fighting, and blowing one's top are closely related activities, which apparently embody some more basic tendency
toward violent release of tension.   This quality, which we have been call-
ing aggressiveness, is common to all four of these activities making
positive contributions to Factor I.   And this interpretation is supported
by the one item that is negatively related to the factor, engaging in a
hobby.   Men who have high scores on Aggressive Activity are less likely
to spend time at a hobby, and vice versa.   One might label this factor
"deviant behavior" were it not for the fact that, to some men at least,
these activities represent conformity to the norms of their own informal
groups.

Institutional Activity (Factor II).   Elements of this factor have appeared together in earlier analyses, but not as clearly and suggestively
as in this statistically derived factor.   Activities positively correlated
with it include: eating between meals (largely at the PX and the service
clubs); attendance at various forms of mass entertainment such as movies,
USO shows, and sporting events; and going to chapel.   These all involve
the use of facilities provided by the Army for soldiers' nonduty hours.

Further insight into the significance of Institutional Activity comes
from examining its correlations with the other four factors, as represented in Table I-2.   This factor has a correlation of -0.18 with Aggressive Activity (Factor I), indicating that there is a slight tendency for aggressiveness to be low when trainees make frequent use of Army leisure-
time facilities.   But this correlation is very small compared to the
correlation of -0.68 with Company-Area Activity (Factor IV).   (We shall
consider the meanings of this correlation later in this appendix; in order
to keep the discussion of the five factors as simple as possible, each
factor will be related to the lower-numbered factors only.)

Table I-1

DESCRIPTION OF FACTORIAL STRUCTURE OF BEHAVIOR*

FACTORS OF BEHAVIOR

	I Aggressive Activity	II Institutional Activity	III Sociosexual Activity	IV Company-Area Activity	V Dependent Activity
Drinking	.31		.03	-.04	
Drunkenness	.11				
Fighting	.04	-.09		.03	
Blowing one's top	.03				
Hobby	-.03				
Asking the Red Cross for help in getting a pass**		-.09		.12	
Eating between meals		.09		-.06	
Mass entertainment		.06			-.03
Seeing the Inspector General**		-.04		.05	.03
Chapel		.04			
Short-term AWOL		.03	.04		.04
Intercourse			.20		
Seeing one's wife or girl			.05		
Reading				.06	
Sports				.04	
Bull sessions				.04	
Chaplain					.12
Sick call					.05
Masturbation					.03

*For the complete wording of these questions, see the behavior questionnaire ("Personal Inventory") in Appendix J. Age, education, and marital status are not included in this table, although they were included in the original factorization, for reasons that are explained below.

**So few trainees went to the Red Cross or the Inspector General that correlations and percentages involving these activities are extremely unreliable. This is why they were omitted from the preceding analyses.

Table I-2

CORRELATIONS BETWEEN BEHAVIOR FACTORS*

		I	II	III	IV	V
I.	Aggressive Activity	----				
II.	Institutional Activity	-.18	----			
III.	Socio-sexual Activity	.05	.09	----		
IV.	Company-Area Activity	.34	-.68	-.06	----	
V.	Dependent Activity	-.12	-.15	-.22	.41	----

*The reasons for using correlated (oblique) factors rather than uncorrelated (orthogonal) factors are discussed in Appendix A.

Socio-sexual Activity (Factor III). Socio-sexual Activity is largely the expression of a single form of behavior, sexual intercourse. In Table I-1 the importance of intercourse to this factor is four times as great as that of "seeing one's wife or girl" and five times as great as that of short-term AWOL, the only other activities that make appreciable contributions.[5]

Conspicuously absent from this factor is masturbation. Since all sexual outlets leading to orgasm are more or less functional equivalents, one might have expected masturbation to be negatively correlated with Socio-sexual Activity. But its correlation with intercourse, the most important component of this factor, is -0.01, or essentially zero: men who have sexual intercourse frequently are neither more nor less likely to masturbate than are those who seldom have intercourse.

A man's pattern of Socio-sexual Activity is less affected by his patterns of behavior in other areas of life than is true for any of the other four factors. In Table I-2 the correlation of this factor with each of the other factors is virtually zero, except for the moderate negative correlation of -0.22 with Dependent Activity (Factor V). Thus, neither aggressiveness nor utilization of recreational facilities affects a trainee's sexual behavior one way or the other.

Company-Area Activity (Factor IV). At first glance this factor involves such a heterogeneous combination of behavior that no one interpretation seems to fit. Going to the Red Cross or the Inspector General, reading, fighting, and engaging in sports or bull sessions do not have any evident common theme. However, the picture becomes clearer when the Red Cross and I.G. visits are removed; so few trainees engage in these activities that their positions in the factorial structure of behavior are not at all certain.

The remaining forms of behavior positively correlated with this factor are reading, engaging in sports, participating in bull sessions, and fighting. Generally speaking, these are activities that are started and carried on through the trainees' own initiative and make little or no use of Army facilities. In fact, all of these positively correlated activities can be undertaken without leaving the company area. In contrast, to engage in the negatively correlated activities—drinking and eating between meals—a trainee must usually leave the company area or even the post. The interpretation of this factor as Company-area Activity is supported by its large negative correlation, −0.68, with Institutional Activity (Factor II). The man who spends his leisure-time in and around the company area is less likely to make use of official leisure-time facilities.

Dependent Activity (Factor V). "Dependent activity" suggests a tendency to rely on other people or agencies to soften the impact of basic training and a corresponding avoidance of Army recreational facilities. Of the four positively correlated activities in this factor, three (seeing the chaplain, going on sick call, and short-term AWOL) are ways of seeking solace or redress of grievances through institutionalized channels or else of escaping temporarily from the unpleasant training situation. [6]

This tendency toward withdrawal is even more noticeable in the pattern of correlations with other factors in Table I-2. Dependent Activity has small negative correlations with Aggressive Activity, Institutional Activity, and Socio-sexual Activity. Only with Company-Area Activity does it have a moderately high positive correlation, 0.41. Men who try to get out of duty or who seek emotional support through official channels are likely to avoid recreational activities that take them outside the company area. Their off-duty movements are limited to the narrow world of the company area and to the comforting presence of the chaplain; when they do leave the company area, they are likely to go AWOL— apparently in order to get away from the post entirely for a few hours. Whether there is a cause-and-effect relationship here in either direction, or whether Dependent Activity and Company-Area Activity both stem from some more fundamental variables, such as type of personality, cannot be determined from our data.

Procedures of factor analysis

The correlation between the frequencies with which trainees engaged in the different activities are presented in Table I-3. Because of certain changes that were made to facilitate computation,[7] these correlations are probably somewhat lower than the "true" correlations that would be obtained from the original data. These changes consisted of supplying missing data (taking omitted response as having been at the mean frequency for that activity among all trainees who answered the question) and coding the higher frequencies of behavior in such a way that equal intervals between the code values used in computation correspond to successively larger ranges of activity. The effect of these procedures was to lower the average correlation to some degree, but probably not to change the essential nature of the factor analysis significantly.

Three questions that appear in the questionnaire in Appendix J were dropped from the factor analysis for various reasons, and one question was added (question 23 in Table I-3). The trainees were instructed to put an "X" at the top of their questionnaire if they seriously objected to answering questions on their leisure-time behavior. Contrary to our expectations, there were no meaningful and important correlations between this question and the various factors of behavior.

A more important addition to the nonduty activities was the set of individual characteristics—age, education, and marital status. These are not, of course, forms of behavior, but they have significant effects in predisposing trainees to many kinds of behavior, as demonstrated in Chapters VI through VIII. By including them in the factor analysis it was possible to utilize their high correlations with many activities to raise the communalities—the proportion of the variance of each activity explained by the factors.

At the same time, it seems desirable that they should not intrude on the process of interpretation, for behavior and background are two fundamentally different kinds of variables.[8] It may well be that the link between these two sets of variables is personality. The different activities are to some extent manifestations of personality, and the individual characteristics, particularly education, are correlates of personality. One has only to cite the differences in child-rearing practices between the middle class and the lower class to see why education, which is an important component of social-class position, is related to personality.

Six factors were extracted by Thurstone's "complete centroid method."[9] However, the sixth factor is a "residual" factor that virtually defies interpretation. Furthermore, its high correlation with Factor II, 0.83, indicates that it does not represent an additional dimension of behavior.

The matrix in Table I-4 was rotated to oblique simple structure

Table I-3

BEHAVIORAL INTERCORRELATIONS*

	1	2	3	4	5	6	7	8	9	10	11	12	13	14	15	16	17	18	19	20	21	22	23
1 Education	--																						
2 Age	07	--																					
3 Marital status	15	45	--																				
4 Chapel	07	02	02	--																			
5 Chaplain	08	08	06	05	--																		
6 Mass entertainment	08	18	15	11	09	--																	
7 Hobby	01	10	03	05	22	05	--																
8 Sports	07	02	02	09	05	13	24	--															
9 Bull sessions	22	02	09	10	00	25	03	28	--														
10 Blowing one's top	01	09	08	00	06	07	04	07	06	--													
11 Fighting	05	00	00	09	03	04	09	07	12	28	--												
12 Eating between meals	03	01	08	08	02	06	05	01	11	14	21	--											
13 Drinking	01	14	23	03	02	12	07	07	09	24	22	05	--										
14 Drunkenness	09	02	03	06	06	02	04	06	04	16	09	02	44	--									
15 Seeing one's wife or girl	16	16	04	08	04	02	02	02	16	00	15	06	12	09	05	--							
16 Reading	06	11	15	01	00	15	04	27	17	10	02	02	10	02	02	--							
17 Intercourse	03	22	32	00	01	06	03	12	13	04	04	06	08	22	35	05	--						
18 Masturbation	01	08	12	02	06	02	01	02	08	08	04	03	01	00	02	10	01	--					
19 Short-term AWOL	15	01	07	06	09	09	00	05	23	01	05	01	22	21	20	08	30	04	--				
20 Sick call	03	04	04	01	12	06	10	05	04	14	16	06	09	12	05	06	13	11	--				
21 Seeing the I. G.	03	01	02	01	02	17	05	01	02	09	01	21	03	02	08	06	04	03	00	16	--		
22 Asking Red Cross help	07	01	08	04	13	07	03	06	09	13	17	06	06	03	09	06	10	02	02	13	--		
23 Attitude	02	10	14	04	06	01	08	04	10	07	09	17	07	01	01	02	06	09	00	06	04	02	--

*See questionnaire in Appendix J for complete wording of questions. Decimal points have been omitted; negative signs are indicated by underscoring.

using the procedures set forth by Cattell.[10] The rotational matrix is shown in Table I-5 and the final matrix of <u>reference vectors</u> in Table I-6. The correlations between the <u>factors</u> were shown in Table I-2. The decision to seek oblique simple structure rather than orthogonal simple structure rested on the assumption that the additional labor would result in a more realistic depiction of the "structure" of nonduty behavior; independence of factors apparently makes for mathematical simplicity, but it does not necessarily lead to the most illuminating factorial representation of behavior.

Table I-4

UNROTATED MATRIX OF CORRELATIONS OF
BEHAVIOR ITEMS WITH REFERENCE VECTORS

		R_1	R_2	R_3	R_4	R_5	R_6	h^2
1	Education	18	-15	21	13	-14	-14	15
2	Age	-22	22	36	27	05	21	35
3	Marital status	-32	30	34	21	24	34	53
4	Chapel	15	-10	09	11	-07	05	06
5	Chaplain	23	04	17	-24	-25	-05	21
6	Mass entertainment	26	-36	-14	17	12	05	26
7	Hobby	11	-04	19	-18	-14	24	16
8	Sports	37	-22	34	-06	25	18	40
9	Bull sessions	36	-27	24	19	22	-18	38
10	Blowing one's top	43	15	-24	-10	12	29	37
11	Fighting	14	43	-22	-17	14	08	31
12	Eating between meals	10	-26	-03	20	-19	18	19
13	Drinking	51	20	-37	19	17	-18	53
14	Drunkenness	28	30	-19	26	16	-04	30
15	Seeing one's wife or girl	29	21	21	21	-11	24	29
16	Reading	25	-21	05	-19	30	-04	24
17	Intercourse	17	39	34	36	08	05	44
18	Masturbation	19	03	04	-21	-03	-08	09
19	Short-term AWOL	38	16	13	31	-16	-20	35
20	Sick call	24	23	04	-19	-12	10	17
21	Seeing the I. G.	-06	20	24	-15	04	-25	19
22	Asking Red Cross help	06	20	16	-26	25	-14	22
23	Attitude	12	10	-12	-19	-15	04	10

Table I-5

TRANSFORMATION MATRIX*

	R'_1	R'_2	R'_3	R'_4	R'_5	R'_6
R_1	15	01	-03	-46	-03	40
R_2	20	-55	65	35	-30	15
R_3	-57	26	52	-48	-05	-04
R_4	44	42	55	21	-03	-30
R_5	-11	-02	-03	-61	69	08
R_6	-63	-68	07	-16	66	85

*Entries are direction cosines of angles between unrotated reference vectors in Table I-4 and final reference vector system in Table I-6.

Table I-6

FINAL REFERENCE-VECTOR MATRIX*

		R'_1	R'_2	R'_3	R'_4	R'_5	R'_6
1	Education	04	29	07	-10	-16	13
2	Age	-21	-06	50	00	09	03
3	Marital status	-33	-23	51	-07	29	15
4	Chapel	-02	09	04	-09	00	05
5	Chaplain	-10	-04	-02	-06	-23	10
6	Mass entertainment	08	20	-22	-22	22	06
7	Hobby	-31	-16	-01	-15	07	28
8	Sports	-35	06	-01	-60	33	29
9	Bull sessions	04	41	02	-44	09	-10
10	Blowing one's top	-01	-38	-08	-17	23	49
11	Fighting	09	-42	07	06	03	26
12	Eating between meals	-02	10	-06	01	06	08
13	Drinking	51	00	01	-02	-06	05
14	Drunkenness	33	08	22	03	-01	07
15	Seeing one's wife or girl	-08	-13	37	-09	-01	27
16	Reading	-12	07	-23	-43	24	11
17	Intercourse	03	-01	62	-09	-06	05
18	Masturbation	-03	-04	-09	-11	-08	07
19	Short-term AWOL	29	22	32	01	-32	-10
20	Sick call	-07	-26	07	-03	-09	26
21	Seeing the I. G.	-02	06	16	-03	-20	-17
22	Asking Red Cross help	-10	-09	05	-22	02	03
23	Attitude	01	-19	-10	08	-10	15

*This is the original set of reference vectors in Table I-4 rotated to oblique simple structure.

Table I-7

<u>ENTRIES OMITTED FROM TABLE I-1</u>

FACTORS OF BEHAVIOR

	II Institutional activity	III Socio-sexual activity	V Dependent activity
High school graduate	.03		
Married		.19	−.09
22 or older		.12	

NOTES TO APPENDIX I

1. We are not concerned here with a priori typologies, such as the distinction between "deviant" and "nondeviant" behavior, but rather with the sets of activities that are actually observed to cluster together. The classification of behavior as deviant or nondeviant would be a valuable addition to the present study, but it presupposes data that we do not have--the norms of each trainee. It might be thought that this classification could be based on certain "generally accepted" social norms; but what is accepted in one group-- e.g., social scientists--might be rejected in another--e.g., Army trainees. Even among trainees it is unlikely that all groups have the same norms. Data on individual norms could be used to identify those trainees who deviate from their own standards or from the informal social norms of their companies or smaller groups.

2. Many of the problems faced in this analysis were also encountered in Sewell's recent study of child-training practices, notably the low level of the correlations. William H. Sewell, Paul H. Mussen, and Chester W. Harris, "Relationships among child-training practices," American Sociological Review, 20, 1955, 137-148. It is not hard to suggest why behavior correlations are lower than those between attitudes or aptitudes, which are more usual subjects for factor analysis. There is no limit, at least in theory, to the number of different aptitudes, attitudes, or other similar psychological entities that a given individual can hold at any one time--a person can be both liberal and conservative at the same time on different issues. But the number of different activities that a trainee can engage in is limited by the time at his disposal. If he goes to the movies, he cannot read at the same time; if he sees his wife or girl, he cannot be simultaneously complaining to the Inspector General. Hence correlations between different forms of behavior that compete with each other for time cannot, of necessity, be as high as those between attitudes or aptitudes, large numbers of which can exist simultaneously in the same person.

3. Strictly speaking, five factors do not account for all or even most of the variation in trainees' behavior, but these five are the only ones that have a distinctive character.

4. It might seem that drunkenness and fighting should count for more than drinking, since they are obviously more "aggressive" than is drinking by itself. However, the figures in this table take into account not only the direct relationship between the factor and each component item, but also the indirect relationship that comes about through the interrelationship of the component items with each other. In other words, the high contribution of drinking to Aggressive Activity is due in large part to the fact that drinking is correlated with each of the other components of this factor.

5. Since the most useful technique for removing facetious or otherwise defective responses was developed after the factorization had been completed, the location of intercourse and masturbation in the factorial structure of behavior is probably more subject to error than is the case for the other activities.

6. Seeing the Inspector General has been excluded from the analysis for the reasons previously cited; note, however, that its position in this factorial structure makes sense.

7. The computations for this study were made before the widespread availability of factor-analytic programs for electronic computers. What formerly took weeks or months now requires several minutes on machines like the IBM 741.

8. Age, education, and marital status were omitted from Table I-1; for completeness, the relations between the factors and these three characteristics are shown in Table I-7. With the exception of Socio-sexual Activity, Factor III, these characteristics do not contribute importantly to the behavior factors.

9. Thurstone, op. cit., p. 161.   10. Op. cit., Chap. 13.

Appendix J

QUESTIONNAIRES

MHCS QUESTIONNAIRE
[Leadership]

This questionnaire is a part of a study which is being made to help men who are just beginning basic training. You men who have just about completed your training can give us valuable help by answering the questions below.

Read the instructions and the questions carefully, and take time to think about your answers if necessary. You will note that we do not ask you to identify yourself, so above all try to give us really honest answers.

INSTRUCTIONS:

This questionnaire is something like a rating sheet. You will be asked to rate your CO, your Executive Officer, your platoon officer, your first sergeant, your field first sergeant, and your platoon sergeant.

Fifteen statements are listed below which describe certain qualities which are sometimes found in training cadre. Read these statements carefully. Next to these statements are six columns with the name of one of your cadremen in each column. After reading the statement we would like you to rate each of the men listed in the columns in the following way:

Place the number 1 under the name of the man or men which the statement describes the MOST.

Place the number 2 under the name of the man or men which the statement describes LESS.

Place the number 3 under the name of the man or men which the statement describes the LEAST OR NOT AT ALL.

It might well be that all of the men should be rated high or rated low in certain questions so that you may want to place, say a 1 in every column or a 3 in every column. This is quite all right to do.

Let's look at an example. Here is a sample question.

Statement	CO	Exec. Off.	Pltn. Off.	1st Sgt.	Field 1/Sgt.	Pltn. Sgt.
In some units the men in charge find time to tell jokes during ten minute breaks in the field. Place the No. 1 in the column under the name or names of those men who do this <u>most</u> of the time; the No. 2 under the name or names of the men who do this <u>less</u> of the time; and the No. 3 under the name or names of the men who do this <u>least</u> of the time or not at all.	1	3	1	2	1	1

You will note that by the way the question is answered we can tell that the CO, the Platoon Officer, the field first sergeant and the platoon sergeant tell jokes during breaks most of the time, while the first sergeant tells stories less of the time and that the executive officer who hasn't got much of a sense of humor hardly ever tells stories.

Do you get the idea?

Before beginning the questions there is one more thing to discuss. In some units key personnel are missing. So if you have no executive officer or field first sergeant or any other of the men listed in the columns draw a circle around the name of the man at the top of the column and leave the column empty when you answer the questions. Now it is likely that you have had more than one platoon sergeant, field 1st sergeant, or other cadremen in your unit during the cycle. If this is the case we would like you to rate each of the men who filled cadre positions for more than two weeks in the following way.

Place the rating of the first cadreman you had in your training cycle near the top of the column in each question section. Place the rating for the second cadreman who filled the same position directly below the first rating, the rating for the third man, if there was one, directly below that, and so on. Let's look at an example.

Suppose you had 3 different field first sergeants in your training cycle, 2 CO's and 2 platoon leaders. Your answers to the same sample question given before might look something like this.

Statement	CO	Exec. Off.	Pltn. Off.	1st Sgt.	Field 1/Sgt.	Pltn. Sgt.
In some units the men in charge find time to tell jokes during ten minute breaks in the field. Place the No. 1 in the column under the name or names of those men who do this most of the time; the No. 2 under the name or names of the men who do this less of the time; and the No. 3 under the name or names of the men who do this least of the time or not at all.	2 1	3	1	2	1 3 2	1 1

Note that there is one number for each man who had occupied these positions during your cycle.

Statement	CO	Exec. Off.	Pltn. Off.	1st Sgt.	Field 1/Sgt.	Pltn. Sgt.
1. The six men listed on the right side of this paper are all important in the life of a trainee. Place the No. 1 in the column under the name or names of the men who had the MOST influence on your life as a trainee; the No. 2 in the column under the name or names of the men who had LESS influence and the No. 3 in the column under the name or names of the men who had the LEAST influence or NONE AT ALL.						
2. In some companies there are men in charge who command real and genuine respect from the trainees. Use No. 1 for those men who are outstanding in this respect MOST of the time; No. 2 for those men who are outstanding LESS of the time; and No. 3 for those men who are outstanding LEAST of the time or not at all.						

Statement	CO	Exec. Off.	Pltn. Off.	1st Sgt.	Field 1/Sgt.	Pltn. Sgt.
3. In some companies some of the men in charge are "suckers" for "sob stories." Use No. 1 for those men in your outfit who are MOST like this; No. 2 for those men who are LESS like this; and No. 3 for those men who are LEAST like this or not at all.						
4. In some companies some of the men in charge are "good joes" one minute and mean as HELL the next minute. Use No. 1 for those men who are MOST like this; No. 2 for those men who are LESS like this; and No. 3 for those men who are LEAST like this or not at all.						
5. In some companies some of the men in charge are able to create in the trainee a real fight- ing spirit against the enemy. Use No. 1 for those men in your outfit who are MOST able to create this; No. 2 for those men who are LESS able to do this; and No. 3 for those men who are LEAST able to do this or not at all.						
6. In some companies some of the men in charge act in such a way so that the trainees are afraid of them. Use No. 1 for those men in your unit who made you MOST afraid; No. 2 for those men who made you LESS afraid; and No. 3 for those men who made you LEAST afraid or not at all.						

Statement	CO	Exec. Off.	Pltn. Off.	1st Sgt.	Field 1/Sgt.	Pltn. Sgt.
7. In some companies the trainees cannot depend on some of the men in charge to keep their promises. Use No. 1 for those men in your unit who broke the MOST promises; No. 2 for those men who broke LESS promises; and No. 3 for those men who broke the LEAST promises or none at all.						
8. In some companies there are men in charge whose ability and knowledge of soldiering create a feeling of great confidence in the trainees. Use No. 1 for those men in your unit who are this way MOST of the time; No. 2 for those men who are like this LESS of the time; and No. 3 for those men who are like this LEAST of the time or not at all.						
9. In some companies some of the men in charge let the trainees know when they feel that an order from higher authority is unfair or silly. Use No. 1 for those men in your unit who do this MOST of the time; No. 2 for those men who do this LESS of the time; and No. 3 for those men who do this LEAST of the time or not at all.						
10. In some companies some of the men in charge have shown a real interest in the trainees but have strictly avoided "babying" them. Use No. 1 for those men who are MOST like this; No. 2 for those men who are LESS like this; and No. 3 for those men who are LEAST like this or not at all like this.						

Statement	CO	Exec. Off.	Pltn. Off.	1st Sgt.	Field 1/Sgt.	Pltn. Sgt.
11. In some companies some of the men in charge treat the trainees "like dirt." Use No. 1 for those men who treated the trainees like this MOST of the time; No. 2 for those men who treated the trainees like this LESS of the time and No. 3 for those who did this LEAST of the time or not at all.						
12. In some companies some of the men in charge give more breaks to their favorite trainees than to others. Use No. 1 for those men in your unit who are MOST like this; No. 2 for those men who are LESS like this; and No. 3 for those men who are LEAST like this or not at all.						
13. In some units some of the men in charge seem never to let an opportunity go by to punish the trainees in some way for each and every little thing they may do that is wrong. Use No. 1 for those men who do this MOST of the time; No. 2 for those men who do this LESS of the time; and No. 3 for those men who do this LEAST of the time or not at all.						
14. In some companies some of the men in charge make special efforts to get their men off the dirty details ordered by higher authority. Use No. 1 for those who go to bat for the trainee in this manner MOST of the time; No. 2 for those who do this LESS of the time; and No. 3 for those men who do this LEAST of the time or not at all.						

Statement	CO	Exec. Off.	Pltn. Off.	1st Sgt.	Field 1/Sgt.	Pltn. Sgt.
15. If you were ordered into combat and you could choose the men who would be your leaders, use the No. 1 for those men in your unit you would like MOST to lead you; No. 2 for those men whom you would like LESS to lead you; and the No. 3 for those men whom you would like LEAST to lead you if at all.						

How many Company Commanders have you had during your training cycle?

How many Executive Officers have you had during your training cycle? _____

How many Platoon Officers have you had during your training cycle? _____

How many First Sergeants have you had during your training cycle? _____

How many Field First Sgts have you had during your training cycle? _____

How many Platoon Sgts have you had during your training cycle? _____

PERSONAL INVENTORY

[Behavior Questionnaire]

I.   A.   Age_____.

      B.   Highest grade of school completed_____.

      C.   State from which inducted or enlisted _____.

(Check or answer the following)

      E.   Married_____ Single_____ Divorced_____ Going steady_____
          Number of children_____.

II.   Before you is a list of questions. Read each one carefully and place
your answer in the column labeled "NUMBER." There are three other
columns, labeled "MORE," "LESS," "SAME." If it is more than in
civilian life, place a check mark in the column labeled "MORE," next
to the corresponding number of the statement. If it is less than in
civilian life, place a check mark in the column labeled "LESS." If it
is about the same as in civilian life, place a check mark in the column labeled "SAME." Use an average four month period of time in
determining the answers to questions concerning civilian life.

QUESTION	NUMBER	MORE	LESS	SAME
1. How many times did you attend chapel or church since the start of your basic training, both on and off Post?				
2. How many times did you visit your chaplain (minister, priest, rabbi) since the start of your basic training, both on and off Post?				
3. How many times during basic training did you go to the movies, USO shows or sporting events, both on and off duty?				
4. If you have a hobby, how many times during basic training were you able to spend at it, both on and off Post?				

QUESTION	NUMBER	MORE	LESS	SAME
5. How many hours per month did you spend taking part in sports that were not a part of your training since you started basic, both on and off Post?				
6. How many hours per week do you think you spent in taking part in bull sessions since the start of your basic training, both on and off duty?				
7. How many times during your basic training did you blow your top, both on and off duty?				
8. How many fights have you had since the start of your basic training, both on and off duty?				
9. How many times per week did you visit the PX Service Clubs, restaurants or tap rooms in the Fort Dix area only for food after meal times (do not include eating at restaurants while on furlough or weekend pass)?				
10. How many times a month did you go out "drinking" while you were in basic?				
11. How many times during your basic training were you really drunk?				
12. How many times per week were you able to see your wife or a girl friend during your basic training (both on and off Post)?				
13. How many hours a week did you spend reading books, magazines, etc., both on and off Post?				
14. How many times did you have intercourse during your basic training?				

QUESTION	NUMBER	MORE	LESS	SAME
15. During your basic training, how many times a month have you masturbated (both on and off Post)?				
16. How many times during your basic training have you gone AWOL for periods of less than 24 hours (this includes breaking restriction within the company area)?				
17. How many times per month did you actually go on sick call during your basic training?				
18. What is the average number of cigarettes you smoked each day during your basic training, both on and off the Post?				

III. Before you is a list of questions. Read each one carefully and answer them to the best of your ability.

   1. How many times have you been to see the IG_____?

   2. How many times during your basic training did you go to the Red Cross for help in getting a pass_____?

   3. How many times per month did you ask to go on sick call during basic training_____?

   4. Have you ever had intercourse_____?